'NO MIDDLE PATH'

Owen O'Shea, from Milltown, Co. Kerry, is a historian and author of several books on history and politics in his native county. A former press officer with the Labour Party, and a former print and broadcast journalist, O'Shea currently works as Media, Communications and Customer Relations Officer with Kerry County Council. He is an Irish Research Council-funded PhD student at University College Dublin, researching electioneering and politics in Kerry in the decade after the Civil War.

Other works by this author

Ballymacandy: The Story of a Kerry Ambush
(Merrion Press, 2021)

'Party organisation, political engagement and electioneering in Kerry, 1927–1966' in *Kerry: History and Society*, edited by Maurice J. Bric (Geography Publications, 2020)

A Century of Politics in the Kingdom: A County Kerry Compendium, with Gordon Revington (Merrion Press, 2018)

Kerry 1916: Histories and Legacies of the Easter Rising – A Centenary Record, edited with Bridget McAuliffe and Mary McAuliffe (Irish Historical Publications, 2016)

Heirs to the Kingdom: Kerry's Political Dynasties
(O'Brien Press, 2011)

'NO MIDDLE PATH'
THE CIVIL WAR IN KERRY

OWEN O'SHEA

MERRION
PRESS

First published hardback in 2022 by
Merrion Press
10 George's Street
Newbridge
Co. Kildare
Ireland
www.merrionpress.ie

This paperback edition first published in 2023

978 1 78537 453 1 (Paper)
978 1 78537 434 0 (Ebook)

A CIP catalogue record for this book is available from the British Library.

Typeset in Sabon LT Std 11/17 pt

Cover design: edit+ www.stuartcoughlan.com

Front cover: Injured soldier being helped by the Red Cross, courtesy of the National Library of Ireland. Colourised version courtesy of John Breslin, taken from *Old Ireland in Colour 2*.
Back cover: Free State soldiers in Kerry, *c.* 1922, J.J. Greene Album, courtesy of the National Library of Ireland.

Merrion Press is a member of Publishing Ireland.

CONTENTS

'One fella called us Irish bastards and he was an Irishman himself'

The tremor throughout his body, wracked by old age, was evident to everyone watching, even though only his face was visible on the television screen. Eighty-year-old Stephen Fuller stared into the distance as he spoke, looking beyond rather than into the camera, unaccustomed as the Kerry farmer was to being interviewed for television. It was 1980 and Fuller, the only survivor of the most notorious and cataclysmic event of the Civil War in his native county, was recounting the shocking brutality of what had occurred in March 1923, when he and eight other Irish Republican Army (IRA) prisoners were strapped to a mine and blown up by members of the newly established National Army (commonly referred to as the Free State Army) of the independent Irish state. Remarkably, the historian and BBC presenter Robert Kee had convinced the IRA veteran – whose name was forever synonymous with the depths of the visceral violence in Kerry in 1923 – to talk about one of the darkest days in Ireland's most bitter and divisive of conflicts. Kee's award-winning, thirteen-episode *Ireland: A Television History*, which was broadcast on BBC television in 1981 (and later on RTÉ), was presented as a sweeping televisual survey of 1,000 years of Irish history and was partly an attempt to provide UK viewers with some context for the spiral of violence in Northern Ireland in the 1970s and 1980s in what had come to be known as 'The Troubles'.[1] As the first ever televisual history of Ireland, it was, Kee claimed, a series designed to 'ungarble the past', documenting Ireland's history from the time of Brian Boru right up to 1980.[2]

Ahead of the documentary series, the BBC had placed a notice in Irish newspapers stating that 'they would very much like to hear from survivors or eyewitnesses, on either side, of the Easter Rising in 1916, the subsequent Anglo-Irish War, and the Civil War between the pro-Treaty and anti-Treaty forces'.[3] It was an ambitious and bold call. Many of those who had participated in the events of the Rising, the War of Independence and the Civil War were dead, or had emigrated with the tens of thousands of others who could not sustain a living in the new Irish state. Others still had taken an informal omertà or vow of silence, deliberately deciding never to speak publicly, and in many cases privately, about the brutality and misery of the war against the Crown Forces and, particularly, the Civil War which followed, or the toll those conflicts had taken on them and their families.

Among those who had, for decades, resolutely refused to talk about what they had been through was Stephen Fuller. Born on a farm at Fahavane, Kilflynn, on Christmas Day in 1900, like many of his fellow Irishmen he had been motivated to take up arms against the Crown Forces during the War of Independence. He joined G Company of the 2nd Battalion of the Kerry IRA under the command of George O'Shea and, during the so-called Tan War, was involved in numerous engagements with the Royal Irish Constabulary (RIC), the Auxiliaries and the Black and Tans.[4] When Britain and representatives of the Irish Republic agreed a treaty to end that conflict at the end of 1921, Fuller, like the majority of the Kerry IRA, was aghast. Appalled at provisions in the Anglo-Irish Treaty, which required the swearing of an oath of allegiance to the British Crown by members of the Irish parliament and failed to grant full separation from the British Empire or to secure the Republic for which he and his comrades had fought, Fuller opposed the Treaty. Along with thousands of members of the IRA and the women's organisation, Cumann na mBan, across Kerry, he took up arms against the newly established Free State government and, with many others, bore the brunt of some of the worst brutality meted out by the Kerry Command of the new Free State Army in County Kerry in late 1922 and early 1923.

Remarkably, despite his notoriety as the only man to survive the explosion of a mine at Ballyseedy Cross in the early hours of 7 March 1923, Fuller had never before spoken publicly about the incident, even during his career in public life, when he sat as a member of Dáil Éireann in the late 1930s and early 1940s.[5] Many of the veterans of Ireland's revolution who went on to have a career in politics often hailed their IRA pedigrees from the election platforms; their contribution to the achievement of an independent Ireland or, in many cases, their endeavours to oppose it and achieve a true republic, were relayed to audiences on the campaign trail. Even when Fuller stood for election to the Dáil, however, he pointedly refused to make a political play of his role in the Civil War or what he had endured at the hands of the army who operated in the name of the government of President W.T. Cosgrave. He could have used his treatment as an anti-Treaty prisoner in the spring of 1923 to shore up the vote for his candidacy and his political party, Fianna Fáil, but he pointedly chose not to do so.

Almost sixty years after the explosion from which he miraculously escaped, and with the frankness and honesty that the approach of the end of life can sometimes bring, Stephen Fuller answered Robert Kee's appeal for participants for his documentary series. There appeared to be a willingness to speak: Fuller told *The Kerryman* that he was surprised that it had taken a British broadcaster to approach him for an interview and that RTÉ television had made no such approach.[6] The BBC producer John Ranelagh was quoted as considering the interview 'a major coup, particularly as we got it so clearly. He [Fuller] was delightful, marvellous and remarkably accurate.'[7] The excerpt from the interview with Fuller was broadcast during the tenth episode of *Ireland: A Television History*, which aired on the BBC on Tuesday, 3 February 1981. As he spoke – softly but firmly and despite a tremulous voice – Fuller's description of the removal of prisoners from Tralee Gaol in retaliation for the deaths of five Free State Army officers at Knocknagoshel in north Kerry just hours previously, lacked nothing in terms of detail or impact:

> He [a Free State soldier] gave us a cigarette and he said: 'That's the last cigarette ye'll ever again smoke.' He said: 'We're going to blow ye up with a mine' … Anyone didn't say anything. We were removed out into the yard, then marched into a lorry and made to lie flat down in the lorry and taken out to Ballyseedy.
>
> We arrived out anyway. The language was abusive language; it wasn't too good. One fella called us Irish bastards and he was an Irishman himself.
>
> One of our lads asked to be left say his prayers. He said, 'No prayers.' He said, 'Our fellas [those killed at Knocknagoshel] didn't get any time for prayers,' and he said, 'Maybe some of ye might go to Heaven … ye might meet our fellas there.'
>
> They tied us then, our hands behind our back and left about a foot between the hands and the next fellow. They tied

us in a circle then around the mine and they tied our legs then and the knees as well with a rope.

And then they threw off our caps and they said we could be praying away now as long as we like. So the next fellow to me said his prayers and I said mine too. But I still kept watching where they went, like. It was that that saved me afterwards.

He said goodbye then, and I said goodbye, and the next fellow picked it up and he said, 'Goodbye, goodbye lads' and up it went ... and I went up with it, of course.[8]

Fuller escaped, despite being blown into the air, but eight of his fellow prisoners – Timothy Tuomey, George O'Shea, Patrick Hartnett, Patrick Buckley, John Daly, John O'Connor, James Walsh and Michael O'Connell were either killed instantly or died within minutes. Fuller managed to a crawl to a nearby house; weeks later, the fragments of gravel and shrapnel were still being picked from his body.[9] The barbarity of what had occurred at Ballyseedy in the spring of 1923 – which still overshadows the equally shocking events of the previous and subsequent days in other parts of Kerry – ensured that 'Ballyseedy' would become a catchcry of Civil War politics in Kerry and Ireland for generations.

+++

Robert Kee's presence in Kerry while he was recording his documentary series became known around Kilflynn and throughout the county. Fuller would, it was noted, 'for the first time, in public, describe Ballyseedy'.[10] Perhaps matters had progressed to a stage where combatants were now comfortable enough to speak publicly about the Civil War, 'sitting in suburban sitting rooms in their cardigans, calmly retelling the events of nearly sixty years before'.[11]

When a reporter with *The Kerryman*, Peter Levy, learned of Kee's venture, he also managed to persuade Fuller to speak to him about the massacre at Ballyseedy. Levy noted that 'by necessity, television interviews are short', so he asked Fuller to elaborate some more and to throw 'some new light on Ballyseedy'.[12] To coincide with the broadcast of *Ireland: A Television History*, *The Kerryman* published Levy's interview with Fuller, much of which replicated his comments to the BBC. The emergence of these interviews reopened old wounds and prompted a flurry of commentary and correspondence in *The Kerryman*, with letter-writers insisting on and disputing the 'true facts' of the events.[13]

When speaking to *The Kerryman*, Stephen Fuller also recounted an episode during the interrogation of anti-Treaty prisoners by the Kerry Command officers in Tralee: 'One fellow had a hammer and he kept tapping my shoulder with it, but an officer told him to stop, saying that I was a good fellow in the Tan time.'[14] This brief but evocative comment on the conflicting approaches of his interrogators betrayed not only the intimidatory and sinister treatment of prisoners as the Civil War plumbed new depths of violence and depravity, but also pointed to the torment and predicament of men who had once stood side by side against a common enemy and who now were now turning on each other in a fratricidal war. Fuller had, in his own mind and in those of his comrades, been a 'good fellow in the Tan time'. He joined the Kilflynn Volunteers of the IRA when he was just seventeen years old and was involved in numerous attacks against the forces of the Crown.[15] Among those in the Kilflynn Company with him was his neighbour from Fahavane, John Brosnan. When the split came after the signing of the Treaty, the Kilflynn IRA, like many other units, divided, with Fuller opposing and Brosnan supporting the accord. In an unfortunate symmetry, Brosnan joined the Free State Army in August 1922 at Ballymullen Barracks in Tralee, the same barracks in which his friend and neighbour was tortured and abused before being tethered to a mine at Ballyseedy Cross.[16] In microcosm, the rupture within the Kilflynn IRA, which left two neighbours from rural north Kerry on either side of the political divide, represents the chasm that the Civil War in Kerry created, a rift which would cause great bitterness and antagonism for years to come.

CHAPTER 1

'The bones of the dead Republicans will rattle in your ears'

Fionán Lynch rose from his seat, cleared his throat and began to speak. It was Tuesday, 20 December 1921, but thoughts of Christmas were far from Lynch's mind. Though only the second Teachta Dála (TD) to contribute to the debate that morning, Lynch was following dozens of his colleagues who had spent several days agonising and baring their souls over a treaty that had been negotiated in London just weeks previously, one which would lead to the bitter sundering of Dáil Éireann and the people of Ireland. As Lynch rose, he surveyed those gathered around him in the University College Dublin council chambers at Earlsfort Terrace in Dublin's city centre, where the country's elected representatives had gathered to debate the Anglo-Irish Treaty.[1] The thirty-two-year-old, a native of Kilmackerin near Waterville in south Kerry, recognised the faces of the other TDs with whom he had the privilege of representing the Kerry constituency in Ireland's self-declared independent parliament. Seated across the chamber were Austin Stack from Tralee, James Crowley of Listowel, and Piaras Béaslaí, whose family came from

Aghadoe near Killarney. Along with Lynch, they had been elected as the four MPs for Kerry in December 1918, in a general election in which Sinn Féin swept through the constituencies on a popular wave of support to assert their demands for an Irish Republic. Weeks later, the four became members of the new parliament, Dáil Éireann. Lynch, Stack, Crowley and Béaslaí had been re-elected to the Dáil, without opposition, in May 1921, just two months before the War of Independence concluded, along with new TDs and fellow IRA leaders Paddy Cahill from Tralee and Thomas O'Donoghue of Renard.

Between them, the six Dáil representatives from Kerry who were present for the debates on the Treaty in the winter of 1921–22 had a shared traumatic experience of the turmoil, hardship, misery and bloodshed that had brought the British Empire to the negotiating table. During the Easter Rising, Lynch had fought in the Four Courts and served time in several jails in England. He was on hunger strike in Mountjoy Prison in September 1917 when Thomas Ashe from Kinard in west Kerry died after being forcibly fed by prison authorities.[2] In October 1919, after Lynch was released from jail, he was involved in helping Stack and Béaslaí to escape from Strangeways Prison in England. Lynch had joined the General Headquarters (GHQ) staff of the IRA during the War of Independence, and in early 1920 became assistant director of organisation. Now, however, as the fissures began to emerge over the Treaty hammered out by the British and Irish political leaders, the unity of purpose and friendships between Kerry's TDs during the war against the Crown Forces were being sorely tested, and the men began to drift apart, politically and personally, with lethal consequences.

Fionán Lynch knew intimately the details and content of the document he was about to address in front of his peers. He had been in London just a few weeks earlier as one of the secretaries to the so-called plenipotentiaries, the men sent by Ireland's republican government to negotiate the terms of a treaty with the British government. Though his role as part of the delegation has been described as 'minimal' – he was chosen to satisfy de Valera's ambition to have a fluent Irish-speaker included – Lynch was responsible for sourcing accommodation for the negotiating team and no doubt kept apace of developments.[3] By the time he came to speak in the Dáil, a few days before Christmas 1921, Lynch's views on the Treaty had clarified and been reinforced, and he stood implacably in favour of what had been agreed. The *Irish Independent* described his demeanour as he spoke in the Dáil on 20 December: 'Fionán Lynch, with fire flashing from his eyes, and with a grim look on his ruddy countenance, and speaking with a clear, ringing voice, held the floor for 18 minutes. "The bones of the dead have been rattled indecently in the face of this Assembly," he declared.'[4]

Lynch told the Dáil that he stood fully behind the Treaty for four main reasons:

> ... because it gives us an army, because it gives us evacuation, because it gives us control over the finances of the country, and lastly, and greatest of all to me, because it gives us control over our education ... I know what the people want, I know that I can speak for my own people – for the people of South Kerry, where I was bred and born ... I will have none of the compromise that drives this country again into a welter of blood.[5]

As Lynch spoke, there was an interruption from the gallery, which was packed full of members of the public who wanted to witness history unfolding before their eyes. 'No!' shouted a woman. The interjection is recorded in the official transcript of the debates, but the identity of the woman does not appear. The interrupter was

Lady Albinia Brodrick, one of Lynch's constituents from south Kerry.[6] She would come to epitomise republican opposition to the Treaty in her home county, but her personal and political life point to the complexities of politics at the time and the diverse profile and pedigree of those lined up on either side of the Treaty debate.

Albinia Brodrick was not your standard Irish republican.[7] A daughter of the 8th Viscount Midleton, Brodrick was born in London in 1861 and, as a member of the British aristocracy, regularly attended lavish balls and concerts at Buckingham Palace. Her father had a large estate in County Cork and during visits to Ireland she became politicised; she was particularly revolted by social conditions and poverty in rural areas. She also became devoted to the Irish language and a Sinn Féin supporter. Much to the chagrin of her family, which was staunchly unionist, she decried the occupation of Ireland as 'the bastard product of a conquest miscalled civilising'.[8] A qualified nurse, Brodrick moved to south Kerry, where she set up an agricultural co-operative and developed plans for a hospital for the poor near Caherdaniel. Ironically, during the 1918 general election, she had campaigned for Fionán Lynch as the Sinn Féin candidate in South Kerry, and in 1920 she was elected to Kerry County Council for Sinn Féin, becoming the first woman ever elected to that local authority. She became a vocal opponent of the Anglo-Irish Treaty, often sparring verbally with opponents over the issue within the various local statutory bodies of which she was a member.[9] Her political stance put her at odds with her family and her brother, John Brodrick, the Earl of Midleton, who was embarrassed by her republican outpourings. In a further political twist, he had been part of the Irish Unionist Alliance, which had lobbied the British government for unionist representation in negotiations on the Treaty. That a British aristocrat nurse was now one of the most outspoken republican opponents of the Treaty was indicative not only of the deepening divisions in Kerry and around Ireland, but also of the nuances and subtleties in Irish political allegiances at this time.

As he was heckled, Lynch, clearly aware of who his opponent was and with similarly mutual disdain, responded to Brodrick's jibe: 'Yes, a minority of one against [the Treaty], an Englishwoman. Well, if I am interrupted from the body of the Hall, I will reply, I say that that person should be removed from the Hall, a person who interferes with a speaker in this assembly, and I ask the chair to protect me.'[10]

It would not be the last occasion on which Lynch and the Right Honourable Lady Albinia Brodrick would exchange invective over the future direction of their country.

+++

Apart from Fionán Lynch, just two other Kerry TDs spoke during the Dáil debate on the Treaty, one on either side of the divide. Piaras Béaslaí was another veteran of the Easter Rising and had used his role as a journalist, including as editor of the Irish Volunteers' newspaper, *An t-Óglach*, to advance the republican cause.[11] Béaslaí, who would leave politics during the Civil War to join the Free State Army, was firmly in the pro-Treaty camp. He has been credited with coining the term 'Irregulars', which was used to describe those opposed to the Treaty.[12] He told fellow deputies that the choice for him was quite simple:

> What we are asked is, to choose between this Treaty on the one hand, and, on the other hand, bloodshed, political and social chaos and the frustration of all our hopes of national regeneration ... We can make our own Constitution, control our own finances, have our own schools and colleges, our own

courts, our own flag, our own coinage and stamps, our own police, aye, and last but not least, our own army ...[13]

It was left to Austin Stack to be the only Kerry TD to vocalise the anti-Treaty sentiment in his native county. Stack, the Minister for Home Affairs in the Provisional Government, was the most senior figure in preparations for the Easter Rising in Kerry, and he had been briefed privately by Patrick Pearse on the plans for rebellion.[14] As Minister for Home Affairs from November 1919 – Stack was the first Kerry TD to hold a cabinet post in an Irish government – he presided over the establishment and administration of the Dáil courts, which were set up to supplant the British legal system in Ireland. Stack had travelled to London with Éamon de Valera in July 1921 for the opening of talks with British Prime Minister David Lloyd George, and his views on the Treaty hadn't changed since he saw the first proposals put forward by the so-called 'Welsh Wizard'. One of the British civil servants involved in the negotiations on the Treaty, Thomas Jones, claimed that Stack was the most uncompromising of all the republicans he dealt with.[15]

In the words of his biographer, J. Anthony Gaughan, Stack considered the Treaty to be 'a disaster'.[16] Like many of his colleagues, he was incensed when he discovered that the document had been signed without reference to the cabinet for consideration.[17] Reflecting his close personal and political relationship with the head of that government, Éamon de Valera, Stack had the honour of speaking immediately after the President of the Irish Republic in the Treaty debate on 19 December 1921. Recent research by Mícheál Ó Fathartaigh and Liam Weeks, in which they conducted a detailed analysis of all contributions on the Treaty, suggests that Stack offered many more positives about the settlement than may have been portrayed subsequently,[18] but he ultimately decried the Treaty as 'a rotten document'

and said he could not countenance any agreement which required
TDs to swear an oath of allegiance to the British Crown. His father,
William Moore Stack, a member of the Fenians in the 1860s, would
have rejected it, he believed:

> I was nurtured in the traditions of Fenianism. My father wore
> England's uniform as a comrade of Charles Kickham and
> O'Donovan Rossa when as a '67 man he was sentenced to
> ten years for being a rebel, but he wore it minus the oath of
> allegiance. If I, as I hope I will, try to continue to fight for
> Ireland's liberty, even if this rotten document be accepted, I will
> fight minus the oath of allegiance and to wipe out the oath of
> allegiance if I can do it ... has any man here the hardihood to
> stand up and say that it was for this our fathers have suffered,
> that it was for this our comrades have died on the field and in
> the barrack yard[?][19]

The days at hand, he added, would be 'the most fateful days in Irish
history'.

The Dáil adjourned for Christmas and would resume its delib-
erations on 3 January 1922. But while some TDs may have availed
of the respite the few days' break offered, Stack lost no opportunity
to maintain political pressure against the Treaty in his native county.
On St Stephen's Day he reviewed a parade of IRA companies in
Tralee.[20] The IRA needed to be ready to mobilise again if the anti-
Treaty cause was lost on the floor of parliament.

+++

On New Year's Day, Major Markham Richard Leeson Marshall
of Callinafercy, Milltown, a former officer in the Royal Munster

Fusiliers, made the daily entry to his diary, noting that 95 per cent of the country was 'willing' to support the Treaty while 'extremists are fighting it'.[21] While the members of Dáil Éireann continued to consider and debate the terms of the Treaty during Christmas and the New Year period of 1921–22, supporters and party activists mobilised on both sides of the divide in Kerry. Public meetings were held in several parts of the county, which called on TDs to ratify the agreement. A New Year's Day meeting held in Killarney declared the 'unbounded gratitude' of the people of Killarney for those who had won for Ireland the 'freedom from alien control [for] which she [Ireland] has fought for centuries' and demanded that the Treaty be ratified as it was 'the best which under the circumstances could be wrung from England'.[22] A meeting of farmers in Tralee called on all of the Kerry TDs to be 'unanimous in ratifying the peace terms as signed by the Irish plenipotentiaries', while in Listowel the parish priest presided over a public meeting that made a similar appeal to the county's representatives.[23] Public meetings held in Cahersiveen and Foilmore on the same day resolved that there was 'no alternative to the Treaty but Chaos and Disunion' and a resolution was passed in favour of the agreement 'by large majorities'.[24] In a report published two days after Christmas, the *Evening Echo* noted that the people of east Kerry were behind the plenipotentiaries and what had been agreed in London:

> KERRY AND RATIFICATION
> Killarney, Monday – The people of East Kerry view with profound regret the sharp conflict of opinion amongst the Teachtaí [TDs] as to the merits or otherwise of the Treaty of Peace. They think, notwithstanding the defeats urged by its opponents, the Treaty in effect gives real and substantial freedom, that with the army of occupation gone and England's

stranglehold of our chances released, the way to the most complete and absolute freedom will be entirely in our own hands. For these reasons and moreover, for the reasons urged that there is no national alternative, they desire to see the treaty ratified.[25]

The reportage of the meeting was indicative of the strong pro-Treaty stance which would be adopted and maintained by the Kerry press in the build-up to and during the Civil War. But there were also appeals for unity and consensus, seeking to offset the very clear cleavages that were becoming more and more apparent. In a letter to the *Irish Independent*, the chairman of Killarney Urban District Council pleaded that 'unity between Irishmen is to-day more necessary than peace with England. Every effort should be made to bridge the gap between our leaders.'[26] The editor of the *Kerry People*, Maurice Ryle, reminded readers that 'the history of Ireland is strewn with the wreckage of division. Let us take due heed of the warning lights of the past' and said he hoped for an end to acrimony in politics.[27]

There were plenty willing to give voice to anti-Treatyism too. When some of Kerry's deputies departed the county by train for Dublin to continue the debate on the Treaty ahead of the final Dáil vote on 7 January 1922, they were met with demonstrations. Anti-Treaty campaigners, including members of Cumann na mBan and Fianna Éireann (the youth wing of the IRA), gathered at the railway station in Tralee as Fionán Lynch and Paddy Cahill – by now bitterly divided over the Treaty – boarded the train. According to the *Kerry People*, there was:

A remarkable demonstration ... A large number of demon-strators composed of Fianna boys in uniform, members of Cumann na mBan and several young men bearing flags, appeared on the platform all bearing printed placards. The inscriptions on the placards were:

'Young Ireland is as at heart Republican – no partition'

'No partition but unity in Ireland'

'The bones of the dead Republicans will rattle in your ears, Mr Lynch'

As the train steamed out of the platform, cheers were called for the Republic and heartily responded to.[28]

Lynch felt compelled to write to *The Cork Examiner*, which also reported on the demonstration, insisting that it consisted of nothing more than 'eight men, four boys and two women'.[29]

When the Dáil finally voted on 7 January, sixty-four members approved of the agreement, while fifty-seven were against. Kerry's six deputies divided evenly on the matter. Without contributing to the debate, Thomas O'Donoghue and Paddy Cahill joined Austin Stack in voting against the Treaty. With Fionán Lynch and Piaras Béaslaí on the pro-Treaty side was James Crowley from Listowel, who had also remained silent during the debate. Significantly, for the future of the country as well as his native county, Austin Stack left the Dáil chamber with de Valera following the debate. After voting on the Treaty, he told TDs that he was 'ready to commit suicide the moment Mr. de Valera let us down'.[30] Through his actions and words, Stack would cement his reputation and position as the leading political voice in anti-Treatyism in Kerry.

+++

The divisions within the IRA in Kerry came swiftly and ran deep. At the beginning of 1922, the Kerry IRA was organisationally stronger than it had been at any time since the end of the War of Independence and was 'strongly predisposed to resist political compromise'.[31] The fissures had begun to show many months earlier, despite efforts by the chief of staff of the IRA, Richard Mulcahy, during a tour of brigades around the country, to persuade doubters to back the Treaty. John Joe Rice of Kenmare was among those who attended a meeting with Mulcahy in Mallow, where the chief of staff was 'trying to patch up the difference between the two sections of the army'. Rice was suspicious, however, that Mulcahy only had one agenda and that headquarters 'had agreed to accept less than the Republic'.[32] Rice would go on to become Officer Commanding (O/C) of the anti-Treaty Kerry No. 2 Brigade during the Civil War. He was one of many Kerry IRA figures at the centre of the national split in the organisation.

'The 9th of April 1922 was the day the split started,' recalled Dan Mulvihill.[33] The Castlemaine man was referring to the decision of the reconvened IRA convention – which, though banned by the government, had first met on 26 March – in Dublin to elect an army executive under a new chief of staff, Liam Lynch. The meeting, which Mulvihill attended, reiterated its rejection of the Treaty and formally repudiated any links to Dáil Éireann and the Provisional Govern-ment.[34] It was also attended by other Kerry representatives, inclu-ding Tadhg Brosnan, Tom Daly, Tom McEllistrim, Denis Daly, John Joe Rice and Humphrey Murphy. Four days later, the IRA executive took over the Four Courts and demanded an end to the Provisional Government and the suspension of any planned elections.

Divisions among the rank and file reflected the ruptures at the top. Tadhg Kennedy of Annascaul, a close ally of Michael Collins, immediately realised that the agreement 'would not be acceptable to the vast majority of the IRA in Kerry'.[35] For Jeremiah Murphy of Headford, the Treaty was unpalatable for one simple reason: 'the agreement presented nothing more than a poor bargain to an uncompromising patriot.'[36] All three Kerry IRA brigades came out against the Treaty,[37] but there were more complicated divisions within some of the individual IRA companies in the county. About half of the 3rd Battalion of Kerry No. 1 Brigade in the north Kerry area joined the Free State Army.[38] The IRA in the Listowel district was 45 per cent pro-Treaty, 40 per cent anti-Treaty and the rest 'neutral'.[39] 'In the Split,' Tom O'Connor of Milltown recalled, 'the active men in the Tan War [in Kerry] remained staunch' to the Republic and opposed the Treaty, although some of the IRA members in Killorglin and Glencar 'went Free State' and supported the accord.[40] Within the Kilflynn Company, its captain, George O'Shea, found himself in the minority, with most members backing the Treaty.[41] In west Kerry, the Annascaul Company was supportive of the Treaty 'bar 2 or 3', and of eighty-four members of the Lispole Company, it was just '4 or 6', but a lot of them 'were lackadaisical' according to Gregory Ashe.[42] Where members did turn 'Free State', only a few of them, John Joe Rice suggested dismissively, 'were of any importance'.[43]

The IRA split in Kerry had as much to do with internal power struggles and hostility towards headquarters in Dublin as it had with the terms of the Anglo-Irish Treaty. The decision to suspend Paddy Cahill – who voted against the Treaty – as O/C of the Kerry No. 1 Brigade a few months before the War of Independence had ended, had soured relations with GHQ.[44] There was a perception that the Kerry brigades were underperforming against the Crown Forces, despite much evidence to the contrary. To add to this, as Tom Doyle describes, 'local pride was hurt' when Dublin tried to reorganise the No. 2 Brigade area.[45] The settling of old scores within the rank and file also amplified divisions, and affairs of state were often relegated beneath pride and personal antagonisms.[46] The net result of those tensions and disputes was that when the Civil War broke out, there would be a 'no-holds-barred' approach to armed incursions into Kerry from those representing the pro-Treaty regime.[47]

Within Sinn Féin in Kerry, too, there were significant cleavages. In Waterville, for example, the local Sinn Féin cumann split twenty-eight votes to eight in favour of the Treaty and on whether to back a declaration of support for local TD, Fionán Lynch, 'in standing for the ratification of the Treaty'.[48] Lynch also gained the support of the South Kerry Comhairle Ceantair, which warned of 'the chaos which may be likely to follow a serious split in the ranks of the Sinn Féin party'.[49] And while the Sinn Féin branch in Sneem backed the Treaty, those in the Rathass Thomas Ashe Cumann in Tralee 're-affirmed their allegiance to the Irish Republic'.[50] West Kerry branches had a greater anti-Treaty majority – in Cloghane there was just 'one dissident', while Castlegregory, Dingle, Ballydavid, Lispole and Ballyferriter were unanimous in selecting anti-Treaty delegates to attend the Sinn Féin Ard-Fheis in Dublin.[51] Insofar as reports and records exist, Cumann na mBan branches in Kerry were more universally opposed: Rathmore members insisted they could not support the Articles of Agreement contained in the Treaty, while the Cahersiveen branch was 'for the Republic'.[52]

It has been estimated that some 1,000 IRA members in Kerry would take the fight to the new Free State regime during 1922–23.[53] The Kerry anti-Treaty IRA was divided between three brigades: Kerry No. 1 in Tralee, north Kerry and the Dingle Peninsula, and Killorglin; Kerry No. 2 including Killarney, Castleisland, Kenmare and the surrounding areas; and Kerry No. 3, which covered Cahersiveen and most of the Iveragh Peninsula. The brigades were armed with Thompson and Lewis machine guns, revolvers, grenades, explosives and ammunition.[54]

The army of the new government, which would take the fight to the IRA, would be led by men such as Paddy O'Daly.[55] The Dublin native was a member of Michael Collins's special intelligence unit and group of assassins known as 'The Squad' during the War of Independence, and he was a hardened military tactician. On 1 February 1922 he led the very first uniformed contingent of forty-six officers of the new Free State Army in a march through the centre of Dublin to their new headquarters at Beggar's Bush. As they marched past City Hall, their salute was taken by Michael Collins and Arthur Griffith. At Beggar's Bush, following an address by Chief of Staff Eoin O'Duffy, the Irish flag was raised and the national anthem played.[56] O'Daly ordered his men to fall out. Within a year, he would become the most feared and most loathed army officer in Kerry.

CHAPTER 2

'They will have to wade through Irish blood'

K ate Breen waited patiently for the arrival of 'The Chief' on a chilly March afternoon. Éamon de Valera was on a countrywide tour to campaign against the Treaty, and Breen, a Sinn Féin member of Killarney Urban District Council, was one of those who would rally the crowd ahead of the keynote address in Killarney the day after St Patrick's Day 1922. An estimated 4,000 people had been gathering from three o'clock in the afternoon at the Market Field to hear from de Valera. Many shops and businesses closed early so that workers could attend the meeting.[1] From a staunchly republican family, Breen had risen through the ranks of Cumann na mBan, spent time in jail during the War of Independence and was elected to the urban council in January 1920.[2] When the executive of Cumann na mBan had assembled to take a position on the Treaty, she spoke strongly against it.[3] In preparation for de Valera's visit to Kerry, and as views hardened, one branch of Cumann na mBan had pledged that 'in the coming struggles for our country's freedom, we are sure our old dear "Kingdom" will maintain its proud record for pure and unsullied patriotism'.[4]

Kate Breen was one of just a handful of women in politics in Kerry at the time. Among her ten brothers numbered Fr Joseph (Joe) Breen, one of the few anti-Treaty Catholic clerics at the time. Addressing the crowd, Kate said that Killarney Cumann na mBan had discussed the Treaty and 'they had only two votes for Griffith and Collins' in support of the agreement. The pair were dismissed as 'decent, respectable girls who innocently believed it was Michael Collins alone won the war'.[5] The men and women of Killarney were proud to welcome the president of the Irish Republic to republican Kerry, she said, and to pledge him their allegiance.[6] As de Valera arrived, he was greeted by marching bands, men on horseback and dozens of torchbearers.[7]

De Valera's declaration at the Killarney meeting that republicans aspiring to achieve freedom would have to 'march over the dead bodies of their own brothers' and 'wade through Irish blood' has gone down in Irish history as either outrageously careless and provocative, or as a reasoned assessment of the political realities.[8] In his diary, Major Leeson Marshall of Callinafercy recorded that as de Valera spoke, thousands listened 'as he preaches civil war'.[9] Fergal Keane contends that de Valera was speaking in a flame-soaked building and he knew it, even if, as Ryle Dwyer contended, he was not personally threatening civil war but warning of its inevitability if the people backed the Treaty at the polls.[10] Either way, his speech infused the rhetoric in the weeks before the Civil War with a new venom. When de Valera's opposite number, Michael Collins, arrived in Kerry a few weeks later, the mood had darkened further and the atmosphere offered a portent of the extent of hostility towards the Free State government in the county.

Ahead of the pro-Treaty rallies that were due to be addressed by Collins in Killarney and Tralee on 22 and 23 April, local IRA leaders John Joe Rice and Humphrey Murphy insisted that they not go ahead.[11] Posters erected around Killarney declared that the pro-Treaty events should not proceed because 'the Free State Army is entering this county in a provocative manner with armoured cars and lorries' and that Collins was coming to smash the IRA and break up the Irish Republic. Civilians were advised to 'keep off the streets'.[12] Collins arrived with General Seán MacEoin, Kevin O'Higgins, Fionán Lynch – now Minister for Education in the new Free State government – and an armed guard. As they left Killarney railway station, they were confronted by an armed man. Among those present was Hannah Mary Moynihan from Rathmore, whose husband, Patrick, was in the Free State Army. As the armed man approached Collins, Hannah Mary 'threw back the die-hard officer when he put the gun to Mr Collins' face'.[13]

The Collins party managed to proceed to the centre of town. The platform that was meant to be used for the speeches had been burned to the ground by the anti-Treaty IRA, and attempts were made to prevent Collins and his party from leaving the home of Dr William O'Sullivan on New Street, but the meeting went ahead at the Franciscan friary. In Tralee, the following day, shots were fired on the perimeter of Collins's meeting on Denny Street, which was attended by some 4,000 people.[14] Notices had been published in the town condemning the 'invaders' led by Collins, but the anti-Treatyites under Humphrey Murphy committed to remaining in Ballymullen Barracks – which had been taken over by the IRA from the British Army the previous month – and allowing the meeting to proceed.[15] Despite the protests and the simmering violence, the pro-Treaty press insisted that the meetings had been 'an unqualified success'.[16] Adversaries Humphrey Murphy and General Seán MacEoin even shook hands at Collins's insistence, after the pair had a row. The gesture, Ryle Dwyer notes, showed that the shared personal bonds – MacEoin and Murphy had been brethren in the Irish Republican Brotherhood – remained strong, although they would not be enough to avert war.[17]

+++

If the voters of Kerry had been looking for a means to express their opinion of the Anglo-Irish Treaty through the ballot box, they were to be sorely disappointed. A general election was scheduled to take place in June 1922. Whatever about offering voters the chance to elect a new Dáil, it would also provide an opportunity for an unofficial referendum on the Anglo-Irish Treaty and allow public sentiment on it to be gauged. Preparations for a poll had been underway in Kerry on both sides of the divide in the weeks before the election, with meetings convened to co-ordinate the campaigns. In Kenmare, for example, a 'Free State Election Committee' was formed and delegates to select Dáil candidates were agreed.[18] Nationally, maintaining a semblance of unity was the objective: candidates for the June 1922 election who supported and opposed the Anglo-Irish Treaty would be presented on agreed candidate panels in an attempt to give representation to both sides of the Treaty divide and ensure the new Dáil would replicate the old one, both in terms of parties and personnel.[19] Following the election, it was envisaged, a coalition of both wings of the party would be formed and thereby offer political stability to the new state. The discussions which led to this agreement had included Kerrymen such as Humphrey Murphy, Tadhg Kennedy and TDs Tom McEllistrim and Paddy Cahill. Murphy and Kennedy were with Cathal Brugha and others when the agreement was signed at the Clarence Hotel in Dublin.[20] The pact – the election became known as the 'Pact Election' – was indicative that, even at such a late stage, there was political will on both sides to attempt to avert a military engagement over the Treaty.

But the election in Kerry failed to deliver any meaningful result and it did not offer any insights into popular support for or opposition to the Treaty. That is because in Kerry – like many other constituencies – there was no real election. For the poll of 16 June 1922, each of the eight sitting TDs for Kerry–Limerick West was nominated without opposition. It was open to other parties to nominate candidates, but there were no other contenders in Kerry. The Farmers' Party held a selection convention and picked three candidates, but they withdrew their nominations a few days later 'in the interests of national unity', while Labour put forward no nominees.[21] Lady Edith Gordon of Caragh Lake suggested that some parties were too intimidated to get involved: 'In Kerry, where bullets are generally considered a more efficacious method than votes for deciding political issues, there were no elections, nobody feeling sufficiently optimistic to oppose the Republican candidates.'[22] Nationally, pro-Treaty Sinn Féin secured fifty-eight Dáil seats, with thirty-six being won by its anti-Treaty wing, a result offering a popular endorsement of the Treaty despite the unusual circumstances in which the poll was held. The result was widely dismissed by republicans in Kerry: Jeremiah Murphy of the Rathmore IRA called the whole thing 'a farce'.[23]

+++

Two weeks after the 'Pact Election', the Civil War erupted in Kerry. Since April, anti-Treaty forces under Rory O'Connor and Liam Mellows had been occupying the Four Courts in Dublin. They demanded the complete withdrawal of British military forces from Ireland, an end to recruitment to the new Free State Army and the disbandment of the new police force, the Civic Guard. While the government initially decided against military action, that all changed following the assassination in London on 22 June of Field Marshal Sir Henry Wilson.[24] The British government increased demands on Michael Collins and his colleagues to move against the Four Courts garrison, insisting that London would act if Dublin did not. The order to react finally came on 28 June and artillery shells rained down on the Four Courts, marking the commencement of a conflagration whose flames spread swiftly across the country. Among those involved in the assault on the Four Courts was Rathmore native James Dempsey, who would later serve in Kerry as a member of the army's Dublin Guard.[25]

Reports of the events in Dublin in the final days of June 1922 reached Kerry amid confusion and rumour. 'A number of wild rumours were afloat today regarding the position in Dublin,' recorded the local newspaper, which noted that the 'wires, both telegraphic and telephonic, with Dublin are cut and therefore no news can come through'.[26] Many years after the events of 1922, it was clear that the circumstances of the taking over of the Four Courts and the absence of any clear military strategy behind it still rankled with many republicans. Kerry IRA leader Dan Mulvihill insisted that the forces assembled in the Four Courts 'were asked if they wanted help. Rory O'Connor said NO! They could deal with the situation themselves. We were in a position to throw ten thousand riflemen around the area. We had at least ten thousand rifles in 1st Southern [Division].'[27] A Free State Army officer, Niall Harrington, who was born in Tralee, noted a widely accepted view that the Four Courts occupation had been a largely symbolic act: 'There was no cohesion, no communication in any military sense, no prepared knowledge of who was there and how mobilisation could be affected. It was a total failure in every sense, regardless of whatever might be said about noble sacrifice.'[28]

Within forty-eight hours of the assault on the Four Courts, on the morning of Friday 30 June, the opening shots of the Civil War in Kerry were fired. Tensions had been building in Listowel for weeks. Along with Skibbereen in Cork and Adare in Limerick, the north Kerry town had been identified as a location to establish a Free State Army garrison.[29] Both the republicans, under Humphrey Murphy and including members of Kerry No. 1 and No. 2 brigades, and

Free State forces, under Thomas Kennelly, ratcheted up their presence in the town. From the beginning of May, Listowel had been a 'busy military area', with the republicans taking charge of the police barracks, as well as a number of houses and shops, while Free State soldiers occupied the workhouse with 250 fully armed men.[30] Republicans were equipped with 280 rifles and half a dozen Lewis guns.[31] Civilians were afraid to leave their homes as there were fears of 'a clash' at any moment.[32] The *Kerry People* recorded the ferocity of the engagement on the early morning of 30 June:

> At 8.30 on Friday morning hostilities broke out between the Republican and Free State troops in Listowel ... All the points and positions of vantage were taken up in different parts of the town by the contending forces, but the battle raged more fiercely in Market St, where the engagement between those of the Free State garrisoned in the large corner-house drapery establishment of Mr TJ Walsh, and those of the Republican army in the opposite hardware corner-house of Mr J Scanlon, was held almost incessantly for some hours.[33]

The battle claimed the life of the first victim of the Civil War in Kerry: Private Ned Sheehy, an egg-packer before he joined the National Army and described as 'a boy of something over 20 years, a magnificent type of young manhood' and the son of a local insurance agent Edward Sheehy, was shot dead.[34] By five o'clock in the evening, the Free State garrison had surrendered unconditionally, and some fifty men detained by the republicans were transported to Tralee. By nightfall, the largest town in north Kerry was firmly in the hands of republicans; Skibbereen fell to the anti-Treatyites four days later. In further evidence of the confused and complex politics of the early days of the conflict, some fifty of the 250 Free State soldiers in Listowel switched sides and abandoned the army to join the anti-Treatyites under Humphrey Murphy. It was, Niall Harrington noted somewhat pithily, 'that kind of war, especially in the early days'.[35]

+++

Despite the ferocity of the fighting and the loss of life in Listowel, there were signs in the hours and days that followed that both sides still recognised the need to avoid further conflict if possible. A statement from the Kerry No. 1 Brigade on the outbreak of violence insisted that there was nothing to be gained from a continuation of the conflict. In a significant display of magnanimity, a joint statement signed by the commanding officers of both forces in Listowel insisted that further bloodshed was avoidable:

> We, the officers of the opposing forces in the Kerry No. 1 Brigade area have decided that Ireland's interest cannot be decided by civil war. When comrades who have fought together have shot one another down, neither the Republic nor Free State will benefit. We differed conscientiously since the signing of the Treaty as to whether the Treaty should be worked or the Republic upheld. Unfortunately, the dreaded spectre of civil war is now in our midst. Developments in the last few days have all the more emphasised the necessity for unity. As patriotic Irishmen, we have decided to unite in the face of the common enemy. We hope that this will be a headline for every other county in Ireland. – Signed, H. Murphy, T.J. Kennelly.[36]

Two days later, there was further evidence that not everyone on the two sides of the growing rupture was fully committed to violence. Private Ned Sheehy's funeral, local journalists noted, was attended

by several republican soldiers.[37] In what *The Cork Examiner* called
a 'pathetic feature' of the funeral, the Free State Army members
present, having been relieved of their guns by their opponents, were
provided with rifles to fire shots over Sheehy's grave.[38] Whatever
their divisions, this respectful gesture of the victors in the battle for
Listowel offered some hope that a further descent into war could
be avoided. It was, as Fergal Keane suggested, 'a last moment of
brotherhood in north Kerry, the final shared gesture of the dying
revolution'.[39]

There were efforts, too, in the wider community to attain and
retain peace. The Kerry Farmers' Union called a public meeting at
the end of July, to which Humphrey Murphy was invited. Farmers
insisted that 'in the interests of all classes, the deplorable war pro-
ceeding should be at once ended and peace restored'.[40] This position
was in keeping with the approach of Kerry farmers' representatives
since the Treaty had been signed. Weeks after the decision at Down-
ing Street, farm leaders in the county had called for its endorsement,
despite its 'many faults'.[41] At the meeting, Murphy was reminded
that farmers had stepped back from contesting the general election
in Kerry on the assurance that a coalition would be formed. When
Murphy attempted to explain the anti-Treaty position, he was heckled and some of those attending the meeting withdrew. Murphy,
however, left his audience in no doubt as to where the IRA now
stood. In stark contrast to the position he adopted in his joint statement with Thomas Kennelly after the battle in Listowel, and in a
reflection, perhaps, of the febrile and confused thinking within the
IRA at the time, Murphy's approach was combative:

> I am as certain as that I am standing here that they [the
> Provisional Government] are going to fail, as the B & Ts [Black
> and Tans] failed, because the war did not start properly until it

comes into Cork and Kerry. We will defend every town to the last, and you know what the result will be. You will have towns in ruins, and Ireland in ruins, and famine finishing what has escaped the bullets ... we will stop at nothing in that defensive fight ...[42]

If Murphy's aim had been to bring farmers round to the republican side, talk of famine among those representing an already depressed sector was hardly the best strategy. Beyond that, however, it pointed to a deterioration in the political discourse at a critical juncture. The battle was far from over.

In the days after the fall of Listowel to republicans, many of the anti-Treaty IRA in Kerry went to Limerick to defend the 'mythical defence line' between Limerick and Waterford that bordered what became known as the 'Munster Republic'.[43] A few short weeks later, on 31 July, a boat set sail from Dublin bound for the Kerry coast as part of a military manoeuvre that would irrevocably change the course of the war, with immediate and long-lasting consequences for County Kerry.

CHAPTER 3

'For God's sake, don't shoot an unarmed man'

Johnny Sheehan squinted, convinced he could see the outline of something on the horizon. A resident of the coastal village of Fenit, he was shepherding a flock of goslings to a field known locally as 'The Pound' when a ship at sea caught his eye. It was after nine o'clock on the morning of Wednesday, 2 August 1922. Ships were nothing unusual along the coastline at Fenit, which overlooked Tralee Bay. It was a busy spot for local fishermen, as well as for commercial activity. Coal, timber, flour, grain and salt were among the many commodities landed there and boats from distant lands in South America, Russia and many other parts of Europe regularly docked in the busy harbour.[1] But this vessel looked a bit out of place. Sheehan had worked in Ramsgate in Kent during the First World War and recognised a boat bearing military personnel when he saw one.[2] As the vessel came closer, he thought he could see uniformed men on deck. Sheehan ran to alert the local coastguard station, which had been commandeered by republican forces, and he ran through the village to tell his neighbours of the imminent landing. A short distance away, a local pilot, John Fitzgerald from Tawlaght, asked his sons to row him out to the ship in his canoe. Near

Samphire Island, Fitzgerald boarded the vessel, querying what lay under the tarpaulins on deck. Within minutes he was in the custody of men in uniform and was 'peremptorily ordered to take the ship to anchorage at the pier'.[3]

As the ship approached the Kerry coastline, a young officer, Corporal Niall C. Harrington, was nudged from his sleep by Colonel David Neligan, one of his commanding officers. Major General Paddy O'Daly wanted to see him. O'Daly was in charge of the 450 Free State Army troops on board the *Lady Wicklow*, which had left Dublin the previous night. As well as members of the army's Dublin Guard, the ship also carried an eighteen-pounder gun, other weapons and ammunition, and an armoured car named the 'Ex-Mutineer', which had been seized during the battle for the Four Courts. The plan for seaborne landings in Cork and Kerry had been devised to accelerate the Free State Army response on the so-called 'Munster Republic'. It had proven difficult to penetrate a notional land border between Limerick and Waterford, southwest of which anti-Treaty forces were in the ascendancy. O'Daly, along with other senior army figures like Neligan, James Dempsey and James McGuinness, had been selected by Michael Collins to crush the 'Irregulars' in Kerry. The Dublin Guard were, Gearóid Ó Tuathaigh claimed, 'the crack core element, comprised of the Dublin Active Service Unit and of Collins's hit squad. You could not get a more determined, a more ruthless group sent in to confront the anti-Treatyites in Kerry.'[4]

But the Dublin Guard was in unfamiliar territory and Corporal Harrington had that very essential currency in warfare: local knowledge. Harrington had been reared in Tralee. His father, Timothy Harrington, had been an Irish Parliamentary Party MP from 1880 to 1910, and after his death, Niall and his brother moved to Tralee to live with an uncle, Dan. Dan Harrington had published the influential *Kerry Sentinel* newspaper for many years. Niall went to school

in Tralee and joined Fianna Éireann with young men like Jerry
Myles and Percy Hanafin, whose names would become synonymous
with the War of Independence in Tralee.[5] After a period working in
Roscommon, where he was active in the Tan War, Harrington joined
the Free State Army in Dublin as a member of the Dublin Guard.
Now, O'Daly wanted his advice before the troops made landfall at
Fenit pier. In his valuable account of the Fenit landing, Harrington
recorded how dependent the operation was on his own knowledge
of the Tralee area:

> [O'Daly] was alone and seated looking over a large map spread
> on a sea desk ... I was soon talking away with him without
> a thought for his notable fighting record. I was surprised to
> learn from him that I was the only person on board with a
> knowledge of Fenit and Tralee. He questioned me and, using
> the map, told me to point out the routes we should take from
> Fenit to Tralee, the capture of which was our objective.

It was an objective which was to be achieved with great speed.[6]

The arrival of Free State troops on the coast was not entirely
unexpected by the local IRA. They had placed a mine on Fenit pier
that was connected by a wire to the republican post at the coastguard station, which was manned by about twenty members of the
1st and 7th battalions of the Kerry No. 1 Brigade. If and when there
was a landing of troops, the mine could be detonated with devastating consequences for those on the pier. But locals were aware of
the placement of the mine and were acutely fearful of the impact of
the destruction of the pier on commercial activity and local liveli-
hoods. In the early hours of 27 July, just days before the landing and
unknown to the republicans, the wire was cut by Denis McCarthy,
the local schoolmaster.[7] Niall Harrington later described the act as

'totally apolitical, dictated by a bread and butter issue', namely the survival of critical infrastructure.[8] Decisively, the nearby republican post was blissfully unaware of the sabotage.

Within minutes of disembarking, the coastguard station, police station and railway station were in the hands of Free State soldiers, who then began a rapid advance towards Tralee. Though some of the anti-Treaty forces engaged with the soldiers at Fenit, their attempt to alert brigade headquarters at Ballymullen was delayed as the telephone exchange operator in Fenit had abandoned her duties and begun to pray the rosary.[9] The first that local civilian Timothy Egan knew of the landing of the Free State forces was when uniformed men approached him as he was digging potatoes in a field known locally as 'An Móinéir' (The Meadow). They asked him for horses and ploughing equipment, and commandeered his father's horse, Dolly, and the chains of a plough. Dolly was taken to the pier to pull the cart bearing the army field gun to Tralee.[10] The advance on the capital of Kerry was underway.

+++

Hanna O'Connor left her work at J.M. Kelliher and Sons at Rock Street in Tralee 'without permission' when a messenger arrived with news that the Free State Army had landed at Fenit. With members of Cumann na mBan from Rock Street, Strand Street and Boherbee, she mobilised at the Grand Hotel under Lizanne O'Brien. An improvised first aid centre was established, with the benefit of 'field dressing' and other medical supplies which the women had been preparing for weeks in anticipation of an attack on Tralee.[11] The hotel was not just a treatment centre for anti-Treatyites caught up in the fighting that began when the army arrived in the town, however. Along with Dr Maurice Quinlan and Fr Ayres of the Dominican priory, O'Connor and her comrades also looked after wounded Free State soldiers, one of whom 'died almost immediately'.[12]

When word of the landing finally reached Ballymullen, IRA leaders John Joe Sheehy and Mick McGlynn decided to set fire to the barracks there to prevent the Dublin Guard acquiring a military headquarters. In the haste of setting the blaze, it was forgotten that three injured IRA men were still in the building, and they had to be rescued. In the end, the fire only partially damaged the barracks. Other senior republicans, meanwhile, were scrambling to respond. Brigade O/C Humphrey Murphy was at his home at Ballybeg, Currow, and Paddy Paul Fitzgerald of the 9th Battalion was at home on Spa Road, Tralee, while many of the defensive positions in place around Tralee were unmanned.[13]

As the Free State Army advanced from Fenit, it came under heavy fire from a high outcrop known as Sammy's Rock near The Spa, provoking an exchange in which Private Edward Byrne and IRA Volunteer John O'Sullivan were killed. By about 1.30 p.m., O'Daly and his men had entered Tralee, and there followed heavy fighting in the Rock Street and Pembroke Street areas. The railway gates at Pembroke Street had been locked and chained by members of A Company of the republican forces, but the gates were smashed open amid heavy fighting. The IRA's Jim O'Shea recounted firing from a nearby property: 'I saw the Staters advance in extended formation along the railway line and we blazed away at them.'[14] Dozens of shops and homes were damaged, windows smashed, and cars and bicycles stolen during the fighting.[15] Six members of the Dublin Guard were killed in the exchanges, but the army had advanced to the town centre within a short time. By evening, O'Daly had established his headquarters at Ballymullen Barracks, the former British Army base on the eastern side of Tralee recently abandoned by the republicans. The Free State Army sustained a number of casualties on 2 and

3 August, including Corporal William D. Carson, Corporal Michael Farrell, Sergeant Patrick Gillespie, Privates James O'Connor, Patrick O'Reilly, Thomas Larkin, John Kenny and father of three Private Patrick Quinn.[16] A medic with the army, Private Patrick Harding, died in Tralee of a bullet wound to the head.[17] In paying tribute to the dead men, General Eoin O'Duffy declared that they 'gave their lives for Ireland, and, like their comrades who fell in 1916 and since, to carry out the will of the Irish people'.[18] The battle for Tralee was over, but the 'war in Kerry was only beginning'.[19]

+++

The landing at Fenit and the rapid taking of Tralee by the Free State forces represented not only a massive military blow to their opponents, but also had a psychological impact. If the IRA could not hold the largest town in Kerry for even a day, as Ryle Dwyer noted, 'this was just another indication that they could never win the Civil War'.[20] In a dispatch to Humphrey Murphy shortly after Tralee was lost, local commander Paddy Cahill predicted, presciently, the Free State Army's next move: 'Tarbert is more probable for [a] drive on Listowel, and then link up with Limerick.'[21] At 3 a.m. on 3 August, 240 troops from the army's First Western Division under Colonel Michael Hogan, a native of Galway and brother of Minister for Agriculture Paddy Hogan, came ashore at Tarbert, having crossed the mouth of the River Shannon from County Clare. They soon regained control of Listowel, which had been held by republicans since the end of June and had effectively been isolated since the war began.[22] By nightfall on 3 August, Hogan's forces had linked up with O'Daly's in Tralee and the larger urban centres in north Kerry were under the control of the Free State Army. The capture of many of the other principal towns in the county would follow quickly.

Within three weeks, Castleisland, Farranfore, Killarney, Kenmare, Rathmore, Cahersiveen and Killorglin would be in the hands of that army.

The landings of almost 1,000 Free State soldiers at Fenit and Tarbert on 2–3 August and at Kenmare on 11 August had happened with significant speed, little resistance and relatively few casualties. By the third week of August, it appeared that 'Republican resistance in Kerry had evaporated and that the war would soon be over.'[23] But within days of the landing at Fenit, Kerry IRA units who had been engaged in fighting in west Limerick had returned to the county in large numbers. For many Kerry republicans 'defence of the kingdom of Kerry took precedence' over defending the front line.[24] While Tom McEllistrim of Ballymacelligott later stated that he 'knew the war was over when we left Limerick',[25] this pessimistic conclusion was premature. What anti-Treatyites had lost in their control of urban centres, they made up for in rural areas. The republicans operating from rural bases, as Niall Harrington noted, 'proved to be formidable foes', and the remainder of the war in Kerry was typified by a guerrilla warfare based largely in the countryside, which the Free State Army struggled to control and suppress.[26] The Free State Army, Gavin Foster adds, may have secured the sizeable towns in the county, but the situation in rural areas was more complicated:

> Although south-west Kerry – the Third Brigade area – was also considered staunchly republican territory it saw relatively low IRA activity once Free State forces landed in Cahersiveen and took over vacated British garrisons. Mid- and north Kerry had more varied experiences and political geographies. Tralee became a major Free State garrison yet the local population was considered heavily republican whereas Listowel had many strong farmers and shopkeepers who supported the Treaty ...

yet republican columns operated in the area throughout the Civil War.[27]

+++

The weekend of 9 and 10 September was an important one for republicans in Kerry as they regained control of two important coastal towns: Tarbert and Kenmare. The Tarbert initiative saw anti-Treaty forces pour petrol into the army headquarters, and Captain Brian O'Grady and his men were forced to 'use every pot, pan and container they could find' to collect the fuel and prevent the building from going up in flames, before they were finally subdued.[28] Early on the morning of 9 September, about seventy republicans under John Joe Rice entered Kenmare (Rice's home town) from the west and quickly subdued the Free State forces at locations including the library, the workhouse and the National Bank, taking control of the town by early afternoon. Some 125 Free State soldiers were taken prison by the republicans, but because there was nowhere to detain them, they were released, the IRA taking some solace from the enormous haul of arms they secured.[29] Among those seriously injured in the fighting was Matthew Daly, a Free State Army officer from Gneeveguilla who was shot through the lung – the bullet remained in his body a year later.[30] Militarily, the loss of Tarbert and Kenmare to the anti-Treaty forces was a major setback for the Kerry Command, although the army would reclaim Kenmare in December 1922. While the Tarbert incident passed without any fatalities, the assault in Kenmare by anti-Treaty forces led to deaths which would forever be synonymous with the conflict in Kerry.

As the republican assault on Kenmare began, at about 7 a.m. a group of republicans including Con Looney and Dan Healy burst into the bakery owned by the O'Connor-Scarteen family at

5 Main Street. Brigadier General Tom and Captain John O'Connor-Scarteen, both members of the Free State Army, were asleep in their beds upstairs. The sentries keeping an eye out for republicans had earlier been sent home. It was a premeditated attack: it was later claimed that the local IRA had 'cast lots' to decide who would carry out the murders.[31] What followed remains a matter of controversy. John was shot in the bedroom and Tom at the bottom of the stairs. The latter reportedly pleaded with the republicans: 'For God's sake, don't shoot an unarmed man.'[32] Republicans disputed whether the pair were unarmed and insisted they were reaching for their weapons when they were killed.[33]

The shooting of the Scarteen brothers resonated beyond Kenmare and beyond the confines of the Civil War. Notwithstanding the 'exceptional circumstances' of the conflict in Kerry at the time, a report on the deaths noted that the killings 'caused very strong feeling throughout Kerry'.[34] Many republicans were horrified: Tom McEllistrim visited the family home to express his condolences, and republicans chose to vacate the town temporarily while the funerals took place.[35] In a similar act of magnanimity in the midst of the bloodshed, Deborah O'Connor-Scarteen's first reaction on hearing of her son's deaths was to ask the priest to say Mass for 'the souls of the people who killed her boys'.[36]

The incident also highlighted the complexities of the tensions and rivalries within the Kerry IRA before and during the Civil War. Tom O'Connor-Scarteen and John Joe Rice had fallen out during the War of Independence – for reasons varying from a dispute over a motorbike seized from a British officer to rivalry over promotions in the Kerry No. 2 Brigade – and the divisions prompted the Scarteen brothers to join the new army.[37] Having heard Michael Collins speak in Killarney in April 1922, Tom and John returned to Kenmare to enlist. But the bitterness and divisions from the War of Independence remained, and as the Civil War dragged on, some republicans saw an opportunity to settle old scores. Fionán Lynch later described the murder of the Scarteen brothers as 'the saddest day in my life'.[38] Politically, the death of the Scarteens would remain to the fore in the history and politics of the county for decades, with two of their brothers, a nephew and a grand-nephew all serving in either local or national politics as representatives of Fine Gael.

+++

Despite this descent into a more violent fratricide in September 1922, there were attempts to end to the war in Kerry. Informal talks that month about a ceasefire were attended by Paddy O'Daly and David Neligan of the Kerry Command, and Johnny O'Connor and Tom McEllistrim of the IRA, at the home of Cecil Peet, a neighbour of McEllistrim's in Ballymacelligott. Peet was described in official documents as 'a gentleman who goes a bit of the road with everybody' and who had 'curried favour with both parties during the Civil War'.[39] He was known to have the ear of Paddy O'Daly but was also friendly with anti-Treatyites like McEllistrim. Peet had brought word to McEllistrim that O'Daly was 'very anxious' to discuss a 'non-aggression pact in that part of Kerry'.[40] Although there were agreements in principle not to carry arms, both sides brought weapons to Peet's home. The talks were inconclusive: McEllistrim asked O'Daly if it was safe to remain in Ballymacelligott, to which the latter replied, 'Oh yes, for a few days,' but, as Johnny O'Connor later recalled, the army 'were in to the village in two hours'.[41] O'Connor admitted that 'we were sorry that we had agreed to meet them'.[42] A similar meeting was held in east Kerry around the same time. At Kilcummin post office, Mrs Sullivan made tea while the Free State Army represented by David Neligan, Jim McGuinness and Stanley Bishop, and the republican delegation of Humphrey Murphy, John Joe Rice and Tom McEllistrim discussed the terms of a ceasefire.

The meetings at Ballymacelligott and Kilcummin yielded no cessation in the conflict. John Joe Rice was sceptical of the 'peace feelers' put out by the Kerry Command, whom he believed were only interested in insisting that the republicans accept the Treaty.[43] Events elsewhere in the autumn of 1922 would offer further evidence that there was little hope of reconciliation and peace.

CHAPTER 4

His toddler child 'walking in his blood'

As the boat approached the shore of Innisfallen, the largest island on Killarney's Lough Leane, Robert Roberts's oars sliced through the still waters with ease. An experienced boatman from Clovers Lane in Killarney, Roberts knew the lake well, particularly the short crossing from Ross Castle to Innisfallen, where St Finian had established a monastery in the seventh century. His passengers on that sunny Friday afternoon in August 1922 were two medical orderlies with the Free State Army, who were enjoying a day's leave. Eighteen-year-old Cecil Fitzgerald and twenty-year-old John O'Meara, both from Galway, had joined the army just a few months previously and had recently been posted to Kerry with the First Western Division and assigned to its medical corps. The stillness of the waters around the island of Innisfallen offered some short respite from the war, which was taking hold in Kerry. Robert Roberts slowed his oars and steered his boat towards the shoreline. As Fitzgerald and O'Meara stepped onto the sand, the deafening sound of the first gunshot reverberated across the lake. Two concealed snipers on the island fired upon the two orderlies and 'they reeled back dead'.[1]

Roberts was wounded, but he managed to push away from the shore and row at pace back to the pier at Ross Castle.[2] The Free State Army garrison at the Great Southern Hotel in the town was alerted and troops were transported to Innisfallen to search for the assailants, who were never found or brought to justice. 'Big crowds assembled' to see the remains brought back to the Killarney, reported the *Saturday Herald*, and as the coffins were removed to the church, 'the whole town turned out for the cortege'.[3] The report added that although the victims were off duty, they were wearing Red Cross armbands when they were killed. The murders were condemned at Mass in Killarney for their brutality and viciousness, and the Bishop of Kerry, Charles O'Sullivan, published a condemnation of the deaths: 'No language can be strong enough to denounce this atrocious crime. Even the infidel Turk respects the Red Cross. To add to the infamy of this revolting crime, the assassins, we are informed, sacrilegiously made use of the sacred ruin in Innisfallen, known as the Oratory, to effect their murderous decisions.'[4]

Cecil Fitzgerald, the younger of the two men killed, was the eldest of nine children. A neighbour visited his mother bearing a newspaper with 'the account of his death in it', the first she learned of her son's killing.[5] As her husband was a retired RIC officer in receipt of a pension, Mrs Fitzgerald was denied any compensation for the death of her son because of the family's means. On the first anniversary of the two men's deaths, the local branch of the pro-Treaty women's organisation, Cumann na Saoirse, arranged Mass for the deceased at the Franciscan friary.[6]

The killing of Privates Fitzgerald and O'Meara not only shocked the people of Killarney, but also highlighted the very young age of many of those who died in Kerry during the Civil War. Corporal David Carson of University Avenue in Belfast was just twenty when he was killed in Tralee as the Dublin Guard arrived from Fenit. He died of a gunshot wound in the abdomen at Tralee Infirmary.[7] Also twenty, Private John Joseph Young of North James's Street, Dublin, was shot through the lung in an ambush at The Bower in Rathmore in October 1922 and died ten days later.[8] Many of those killed were only teenagers. Private James Byrne was eighteen years old when he died in an ambush in Duagh, also in October 1922.[9] Michael J. Ryle, a member of Fianna Éireann, was the same age when he was killed after he was spotted by a Free State Army convoy on the outskirts of Tralee a few days after the army gained control of the town.[10] He had been 'hiding in the tall August grass in the meadow overlooking the [Castleisland] road but this did not afford him adequate cover when he was spotted by the soldiers. Fire was opened on his position by an armoured car and he was shot in the head. He died instantly at the scene.'[11] James O'Connor was nineteen when he was killed by machine-gun fire near Ardfert in February 1923.[12] Eighteen-year-old Michael Sinnott from The Spa died near a dugout in the same month, while twenty-year-old Tadhg Keating was killed near Ballin-skelligs in March.[13] Eugene Fitzgerald from Tralee was just twenty when he was thrown from a lorry and shot in January 1923.[14]

One of the most shocking deaths was that of a seventeen-year-old boy from Castleisland. Bertie Murphy, a member of Fianna Éireann, was killed in controversial circumstances at the hands of Colonel David Neligan at the Free State Army headquarters in the Great Southern Hotel, Killarney. The improvised barracks would become renowned as a place where beatings and torture took place: a young man whose brother was an IRA captain was taken there and 'mercilessly beaten to get him to reveal information'. He was then 'thrown down a coal chute and left as dead'.[15] On 27 September, an army convoy was ambushed at Brennan's Glen on the Tralee road and two officers, Daniel Hannon and John Martin, were killed. Bertie Murphy had been in one of the vehicles, where he was being used by the army as a hostage in an attempt to prevent attacks by anti-Treaty forces.[16] When the convoy returned to the Great Southern, Neligan demanded to know why the soldiers had not taken any prisoners. He then proceeded to take out his anger over what had happened on Murphy, who was beaten on the steps of the hotel and then shot. He lived 'until the priest came', but died soon after.[17] Another prisoner in the hotel at the time, Con O'Leary from Glenflesk, was brought down from his cell to identify the dead man; so extensive were Murphy's facial injuries that O'Leary was unable to identify the remains.[18] Newspapers wrongly reported that he had been wounded during the engagement at Brennan's Glen and had 'succumbed to his injuries' on returning to Killarney.[19] At Murphy's inquest, Major General Paddy O'Daly reminded those present that deaths like Murphy's were the fault of reckless IRA leaders who refused to accept the authority of the people.[20] 'It is the women and children', he said, 'that are suffering, and for all the suffering that is being endured those leaders are to blame.'[21]

+++

The death of Bertie Murphy coincided with a critical turning point in the Civil War in Kerry. Just hours before he was killed in Killarney, republicans launched what would be their last major military offensive against the Free State Army in the county.[22] Buoyed by their success in securing Kenmare at the beginning of September, republicans turned their sights on Killorglin, which was held by about eighty members of the Free State Army's First Western Division under the command of Captain Donal Lehane. For several weeks, there had been intermittent fighting and sniping in and around the town.[23] Anti-Treaty forces under John Joe Rice and David Robinson, a former British Army officer, launched an assault on the town at about 6 a.m. on 27 September. Civilians knew what was coming: the republicans had issued a warning that an attack was imminent and advised residents to flee.

Hanna Dodd, a widow, lived adjacent to the army barracks, which was occupied by Free State soldiers and was at the epicentre of the fighting. The previous night, republican sappers had tunnelled under Upper Bridge Street and entered Mrs Dodd's home. In an attempt to access the barracks, they blew a hole in the wall between Mrs Dodd's house and the army headquarters, and they 'tried to fire from there into the barracks'. They also detonated explosives in an attempt to demolish the wall, which resulted in Mrs Dodd's house being set on fire. The bill for the damage done and loss of property came to £1,277.[24] Another property near the barracks was badly damaged: Denis O'Sullivan's shop was 'heavily damaged by bombs and rifle fire' during the combat.[25]

The toll on civilians is indicative of the dangers, as well as the financial implications, which non-combatants faced when such engagements occurred. As the fighting took place, James Guerin of Lower Bridge Street was walking along the main street when, 'without any warning whatever', he was fired upon and wounded in the thigh by bullets from a machine gun or a Lewis gun, and a 'large portion of the muscles of the leg were entirely torn away'.[26] Guerin 'fell against the door of an empty house and lay in the hallway pouring out blood for many hours with no one attending him'.[27] Compensation claims for damage were later submitted to the courts from twenty-five different applicants from Killorglin, all relating to 27 September 1922, when fighting in the town was at its most intense, including:

James J. Stephens: Ford motor car taken at Castleconway
Denis Clifford: One pig killed by bullets penetrating the sty at Mill Road

Elizabeth O'Neill: Damage to premises and goods stolen at
    Upper Bridge Street

Alice M. Sweeney: Cooking implements and personal effects
    damaged at courthouse

John O'Sullivan: Goods and cash taken at Iveragh Road

William Purcell: Windows of National Bank broken and rugs
    and blankets stolen

John V. Evans: Pony wounded and outhouses damaged at
    Dromavally

Jeffrey Morris: Damage to hotel and barrels of stouts seized
    from pier at Ballykissane[28]

One resident told *The Irish Times* that 'the plight of Killorglin people was appalling. Many people could not cook any food, and milk and bread could not be obtained.'[29] The reporter added that the town 'presents a battered appearance with smashed windows and bullet-scarred walls. The internal destruction in many of the houses from which the Irregulars were delivering their heaviest attacks is considerable.' Major Leeson Marshall of nearby Callinafercy House penned a first-hand survey of the destruction: 'Not a pane of glass left in town … Inhabitants suffered cruelly, not known when death would come, bullets through their rooms, no milk for children, little food except potatoes … Women and children looking pale, haggard & jumpy …'[30]

As the fighting continued, parish priest Fr James Nolan cycled to Tralee to summon army reinforcements, which arrived the following day. Those reinforcements, under General W.R. English-Murphy and Colonel Michael Hogan, with the support of an armoured car called *Danny Boy*, ensured that many republican posts were abandoned and the fighting came to an end. Over the course of thirty hours of combat, there were two fatalities among the anti-Treaty forces. Con

Looney of Kenmare, who had been involved in the deaths of the O'Connor-Scarteen brothers in his home town, and Patrick Murphy of Dooks died during the fighting, while a third IRA man, Jer 'Romey' Keating from Cahersiveen, later died of his injuries. The Free State Army commander, Donal Lehane, was shot dead as he ran along Langford Street, and an army scout, Denis O'Connor, was also fatally wounded.[31]

Killorglin was undoubtedly a turning point in the war in Kerry.[32] Whereas successes for republicans at Kenmare and Tarbert represented the 'high-water mark' of the anti-Treaty campaign, those advances were negated by the failure to capture Killorglin at the end of September.[33]

The immediate aftermath of the fighting in Killorglin involved yet another controversial treatment of a prisoner, when ten republicans were being removed to jail in Tralee. It was claimed that one of them, Jack Galvin, had admitted to the killing of Captain James Burke in Castlemaine a few weeks earlier and that his arm was broken during a beating when he was captured.[34] As a convoy taking the prisoners, which was led by Colonel Michael Hogan, a friend of Burke's, was passing through Ballyseedy, it was forced to stop on the road to remove trees blocking its path. Hogan had developed a brutal reputation and had been accused by IRA man Johnny 'Machine Gun' Connor of having a strategy to 'polish off the prisoners as if they were attempting to escape'.[35] It was also claimed that he was 'worshipped by his men'. As the debris was cleared from the road, Galvin remained under Hogan's watch and, while out of sight of most of the rest of the group, the prisoner was 'riddled with bullets, his head partly blown off' and his body dumped in a ditch.[36] Local Cumann na mBan member Annie Mary Sugrue recovered Galvin's body, which she said was 'in a terrible condition'. Her intervention prompted an unnamed Free State colonel to abuse and ill-treat her

as she returned to her home.[37] In protest at the refusal of Hogan to
pursue a full investigation into Galvin's death, another army officer,
Brigadier Éamon Horan – who would contest an election on behalf
of Clann Éireann in Kerry in 1927 – resigned from the army.[38] The
Galvin murder was an ominous portent of the type of extrajudicial
murder that would come to typify the war in Kerry over the following months.

Wednesday, 27 September 1922 was important not only because
of the battle raging in Killorglin and the murder of Bertie Murphy
at the Great Southern Hotel, but also because, ironically, it was the
date on which new legislation was passed by Dáil Éireann, designed,
in part, to prevent the type of ad hoc killings suffered by Murphy
by defining offences for which execution was acceptable. The Public Safety Bill provided wide-ranging powers of imprisonment and
execution for offences including possession of ammunition or a
weapon, and arson and looting, as well as involvement in attacks on
Free State forces. For Bertie Murphy and others, the legislation came
too late, and even though, as Tom Doyle notes, it would be several
months before the powers contained in the legislation were used in
Kerry, the killings, ad hoc and otherwise, continued apace.[39]

As winter approached, the tit-for-tat warfare claimed several
lives. It has been contended that there was 'no coordinated republican campaign at this point' in the war in October and November 1922, and that individual units operated independently of each
other.[40] Ambushes, sniping and sweeps of rural areas continued. During October and November, the Free State command lost a number
of soldiers, including John Browne and Jason Byrne near Duagh, Privates Gilchrist and Kiely near Abbeydorney, John Corcoran at Law-
lor's Cross near Killarney, and Sgt John O'Callaghan, who was shot
in the chest by an unidentified republican sentry while he walked
with his girlfriend in Cahersiveen. Among the republican casualties

were Michael Ahern, who was killed at Pallas, Beaufort; William O'Riordan from Glenbeigh, who died near Killorglin; Mickey Joe Flynn of Tralee, who was killed near Derrymore; and Mick 'Cud' O'Sullivan, who was killed in his native Headford. Patrick Lynch of The Glen in Ballinskelligs was shot outside his home by Free State soldiers, who then carried his remains back into his home, his toddler child 'walking in his blood'; he had temporarily returned home from being on the run to 'plough the fields of his small farm'.[41] A shootout during an army sweep of Annagh and Curraheen, west of Tralee, on 20 October resulted in one fatality each for the two sides, both of whom were Kerry men. Billy Myles from Moyderwell, Tralee, was shot dead close to where he and members of the IRA had been hiding in a dugout. Private Daniel Nagle from Henn Street, Killarney, was injured in the crossfire and died of his injuries four days later.[42]

There were, however, some moments of mercy amid all of the fratricide. Colonel James Dempsey of the Free State Army, a native of Rathmore who had been injured during the Easter Rising and involved in the assault on the Four Courts that started the Civil War, was badly wounded in the eye while involved in a search for republicans near the Gap of Dunloe on 28 November.[43] He was taken prisoner by republicans including John Kevins of Beaufort and subsequently treated by Dr Ned Carey and Lily O'Sullivan, a nurse with Cumann na mBan. Kevins released Dempsey from his custody and the colonel was later transferred to hospital in Dublin.

Several months later, Kevins himself was apprehended at Carnahone, Beaufort, and shot, but not killed, by a group of soldiers that included Colonel Michael 'Stanley' Bishop. Bishop and his men retired to a nearby hotel run by Lily O'Sullivan, the nurse who had treated Dempsey in November 1922. She pleaded with Bishop to allow her to treat the wounded man, but he refused. The following morning, as the wounded Kevins was being taken to Killarney, he was thrown from a mail cart and bayoneted to death. A soldier, who was drunk, refused to allow his mother to see the remains.[44]

+++

As 1922 drew to a close, there was a series of attacks on Protestant families, homes and businesses, as well as places of worship, which point to a sectarian underbelly to the conflict in Kerry. The Presbyterian church in Tralee was damaged in October by 'unknown persons', while the Methodist church in Killarney sustained damage on several occasions between March and September 1922.[45] Meanwhile, the secretary of the vestry of the parish of Tralee, Dr A.A. Hargrave, detailed the damage done to the Church of Ireland churches in Tralee and Fenit, as well as a break-in and damage at the parochial school in Tralee. The rectory in Ardfert was broken into an extraordinary nine times in August and September 1922.[46] A Methodist school at Edward Street in Tralee was damaged and set ablaze on 8 September.[47] Despite the widespread damage to properties – Catholic churches were sometimes, but less frequently, attacked too – it is difficult to conclude that these incidents were motivated by anything other than religious or sectarian impulses.

Senior Protestants in the county had set a respectful tone in March 1922 in response to the brutal murder of six Catholics at the home of the McMahon family in Belfast as sectarian tensions escalated in Northern Ireland. It was time, wrote one Protestant landowner, Major Leeson Marshall of Callinafercy, Milltown, for 'public opinion of all creeds' to protest against the 'blood lust which is ruining Ireland'.[48] A series of letters to the *Kerry People* newspaper from Protestant families decried the 'Belfast barbarities' and committed to supporting a relief fund for Catholics in the city.[49] Such magnanimity was not always universally well received, however. One of those who joined Tralee Protestants in their condemnation, a Mr Smith of Greenville, sustained injury when stones were thrown through the windows of his residence the day after the condemnatory statement was issued.[50]

During the Civil War, the IRA exploited the legal and policing vacuum, particularly as the Crown Forces departed Ireland, and there were sectarian undertones to many attacks on Protestant businesses and homes. Thomas Earls FitzGerald cites a number of intimidatory attacks on Protestants, including trespassing and vandalism at the home of Margaret Duncan from Kenmare, who was subject to repeated attacks on her home.[51] He also highlights a series of attacks on the Blennerhassett family of Ballyseedy, which occurred during the War of Independence and continued throughout 1922–23. A number of Protestant families in the Tralee area had been ordered 'to leave the country' in the summer of 1922.[52] A report by the Kerry Command, which was sent to General Mulcahy, described how, on 21 December, near Beaufort: 'Armed men went to the house of Thos. [Thomas] Blennerhassett and ordered him and his brother Wm. [William] to open the door. They refused. The raiders gained entrance through a back window, sprinkled furniture etc., with paraffin oil, and set the house on fire. All the occupants escaped through an upper window. The house was completely destroyed.'[53]

In May 1922 Fr Alexander O'Sullivan of Milltown complained to the Minister for Home Affairs, Eamon Duggan, about the 'harrying, plundering and hourly danger to the life of a protestant farmer of this parish' and subsequent eviction of the Stephens family from their 70-acre farm:

> The occupation of his [Stephens's] house, which took place without resistance on his part about two weeks ago was

immediately reported to the I.R.A. and I.R.P. [Irish Republican Police] at Killorglin, who did nothing. In a few days, the invaders drove out Stephens' stock and installed their own cattle. This was reported to the same I.R.A. and I.R.P. who again did nothing.[54]

According to further correspondence, another Protestant farmer, the priest wrote, was evicted and another had a pregnant mare shot dead. 'Active partisans', he wrote, 'have been entrusted locally with police duties, to the terror of the disarmed population ... The common people are heartily sick of being fooled and being policed by criminals.'[55] In the same week, near Killorglin, 'a crowd of 50 or 60' evicted a farmer from his land and shots were fired into his house.[56] As with other incidents of this nature, however, it has been argued that it owed its origins to the Land War rather than any particularly sectarian motives.[57] In March 1922, for example, Arthur Blennerhassett was 'kidnapped till he signed away 80 acres of demesne' to local farm labourers.[58] The Wade family abandoned their rectory in Aghadoe 'after a year's persecution [and] eight raids'.[59] FitzGerald argues that the IRA simultaneously turned a blind eye and sometimes encouraged these sort of attacks and intimidation of Protestants.[60]

Terence Dooley identifies nine big houses that were burned in Kerry in the period between January 1922 and April 1923. This compares to twenty-nine in Tipperary and nineteen in Cork.[61] The delineation of political and sectarian motives was not always clearly apparent in these attacks. Large houses were often targeted, as John Knightly details, for arms and ammunition that could be used in combat.[62] Lands were also used by anti-Treaty forces for training and target practice, with the owners left with little choice but to turn a blind eye. When Derreen, the home of Lord Lansdowne, was burned near Killarney in 1922, it was noted that 'the offenders were Republicans and Free Staters in about equal proportion', suggesting that the motive was agrarian as well as political.[63] The destruction was enormous: 'The house is absolutely destroyed, doors all smashed, every particle of furniture taken … they got at the cellars and the men were all half drunk, fighting and revolver shots going off … there is nothing left of Derreen and its surroundings.'[64]

Norah Evaleen Hood of Dromore Castle near Kenmare, whose grandfather had been a proselytising Church of Ireland minister, was terrorised and subjected to litany of attacks on her property, which are catalogued in the compensation applications submitted to the Department of Finance:

> Boats and nets taken away and a fisherman's watch house damaged by Irregular forces, October 1922; fishery damaged at Maulcallee and Dromore by Irregular forces on 29 May 1922; damage done to Dromore Castle and Demesne by Irregular forces in the months of July, August and September 1922; cattle and farming implements taken at Dromore by Irregular forces on 5 October 1922; trees cut down at Dromore by Irregular forces and others from 13 to 17 April 1922; trees cut down and taken away at Maulcallee, by Irregular forces in October and November 1922.[65]

Aghadoe House, a residence of Lord Headley near Killarney, was firebombed in October 1922 in a bid to prevent the building being taken over by Free State forces, while the home of the Heard family at Rossdohan Island in Kenmare Bay was ransacked and burned.[66] Similarly, the homes of the Crosbie family at Ardfert Abbey and Derryquin Castle, home of Colonel Warden near Kenmare, were targeted to prevent their use by the army as military bases. In this sense, Tom Doyle is correct to conclude that it was the suitability of such properties as army barracks rather than their associations with the Protestant landowning class that made them the subject of attack.[67] Moreover, the acquisition of land and agrarian troubles, which John Knightly suggests as the reason for repeated attacks on Ardfert Abbey, were often the motive for such attacks.[68] In the case of Derryquin, the owner was 'despised locally because of evictions in the 1890s'.[69] As such, it can be concluded that there was no co-ordinated strategy among anti-Treaty forces in Kerry to destroy big houses or dislodge loyalists and Protestants for sectarian reasons, but a proclivity for deliberately attacking Protestants and members of the Anglo-Irish community would remain a feature of the war in Kerry for its duration.

CHAPTER 5

'On the alert for the swag and for anarchy'

Patrick Griffin urged his horse onwards towards Caragh Lake as he made his way home from the school where he taught on the afternoon of 29 September 1922.[1] His wife and children were beside him on the trap and noticed masked men ahead of them on the road. Griffin brought his horse and trap to a halt. At gunpoint, the family was ordered off the trap and the party of men made off with it and the horse, leaving Griffin and his family standing on the roadside. Without transport to travel the four miles from his home to school each day, Griffin was forced to hire a car at his own expense. The bill for car hire for fifty-eight days came to £29. Two months later, the horse was returned. It had 'two bad legs' and was 'sick, swollen and diseased'. The trap had been smashed and its harness, rugs and cushions were missing. The motive for the attack was assumed to be robbery, a phenomenon that came to represent the increased lawlessness across Kerry as the Civil War intensified.

Patrick Griffin's encounters with republicans were far from over, however. Five months after the theft of his horse and cart, a 'large body of armed men' turned up at his home 'to arrest me'. But Griffin was not at home. Shots were fired through the windows and three bicycles and an overcoat were stolen before the raiders ran off. The following day, the men turned up at his school and dragged Griffin away. He was 'taken through the mountains in dreadful weather at [the] dead of night and kept a prisoner for five weeks ... I was brutally treated, half-starved and often threatened with [a] revolver and rifle.' It soon became apparent that Griffin's detention had more to do with money than politics. A hostage situation quickly developed. While being detained in an isolated rural area:

> I was one day taken out by masked and armed men and blindfolded as if for execution and was brought into an outhouse about ¼ mile off and asked whether I was willing to pay £100 to save me from execution. My answer was 'No!' ... I got a letter from the Irregular leader directing me to write home to my wife and get her to pay £50 to secure my release. I declined to write such a letter.[2]

Griffin's captors eventually gave up. Instead of suffering the fate of many who were detained in this way during the Civil War, the prisoner was stripped of his overcoat, boots and trousers and returned to his home. He was warned 'there was more in store'. Griffin reported the matter to Major General Paddy O'Daly, and the family was later awarded £63 in compensation for loss and damage to property. Patrick Griffin's health 'suffered considerably' following the ordeal, and several months later his wife and children were 'suffering from the effects of shock and nervousness'.[3]

The case of Patrick Griffin highlights the disruption, lawlessness, intimidation and criminal behaviour that often prevailed in Kerry in 1922–23. 'It is doubtful', suggested one memoir from the period, 'that there was ever quite so discreditable a silence as that with which crime and outrage were met in 1922. People were so terrified that they would submit to any loss or personal humiliation in order to save their lives.'[4] Another noted that there was 'brigandage everywhere' and many 'nasty things' happening locally.[5] Ordinary crime was, as Tom Doyle has rightly concluded, probably under-reported and not the focus of many newspaper reports because of the prevailing political and military crisis, which dominated report-age.[6] In a letter to *The Times* of London in the summer of 1923, the playwright George Bernard Shaw told its readers that Ireland was 'probably the safest country in the world for visitors' and that 'Cork and Kerry are much safer in respect of both person and property than the administrative County of London.'[7] What evidence Shaw used to make his deduction is unclear, but his views were certainly in the minority and at significant variance with the reality, even though the war had ended by this time. In the same month as Shaw made his claim, *The Liberator*, the tri-weekly Tralee edition of *The Kerry-man* reported that there were claims of £1.7m for malicious injuries in Kerry alone.[8]

When new public safety legislation was brought before the Dáil in December 1923, Kerry was cited as one of a handful of counties where the conditions were unsatisfactory and which made it neces-sary, under the new law, 'to vest in the Executive the power of arrest-ing and detaining known blackguards against whom there is no evidence in connection with a specific offence'.[9] A shopkeeper from west Kerry, who wrote to the Ministry of Home Affairs, bemoaned the lack of law and order in the Dingle area and condemned the 'thrifters' and idle anti-Treatyites who were 'on the alert for the swag and for anarchy'. William Long of Ballyferriter reminded his addressee that he was of the same political creed and had the 'plea-sure of recording a No. 2 vote' for Cumann na nGaedheal at the recent general election. He summarised the lack of civil order in the locality and the pressures that placed on small businesses:

> One word please in regard to west Kerry scoundrelism. Owing to the long term since we had any law or court of law in this outlandish district, assignments for debt-evading and pensions-getting is the game of the day here. It is now some four years since a County Court was held in Dingle. Hence we shopkeepers (Free Staters) have suffered severely as we can't round up devil-may-cares of Anarchists and [de] Valeraite [sic] customers ... Hoping you provide a remedy and that very soon and get these scoundrels netted.[10]

Apart from army officers and the newly established Civic Guard, which was charged with upholding law and order, others connected with the administration of justice were vulnerable to intimidation and violence. Just a few days after he was appointed state solicitor for Kerry, at the beginning of March 1923, the home of Terence Liston was broken into, sprinkled with petrol and set ablaze.[11] When the intruders were asked whose orders they were acting on, the response was: 'Well, not Dick Mulcahy's order, anyway.'[12] Ten days later, the home of Diarmaid Crean in Annascaul was bombed after he had taken up the position of district court registrar.[13] The infrastructure underpinning the administration of justice was significantly depleted after the Civil War and made the holding of court sittings more difficult, as State Solicitor Liston informed the Department of Home Affairs in August 1923: 'Continuance of present arrangement as to holding of courts undesirable but courthouse in Listowel and Kenmare destroyed and difficulties exist in the way of acquiring or using any other building in these two places.'[14]

+++

Extensive evidence of the mayhem, crime and lawlessness that affected normal civilian life in the county is contained in records in the National Archives. In May 1923 legislation was introduced to provide for compensation claims for damage to property which occurred between the Truce of 11 July 1921 and up to 20 March 1923.[15] The scheme, which allowed for claims to be made for damage to or theft of actual property, as opposed to any loss suffered by an individual, was administered by the county courts on behalf of the State. The 1,203 applications held in Department of Finance files in the National Archives from civilians and property owners in Kerry reveal a litany of theft, looting, arson, damage and other forms of intimidation and disruption. A short sample list of the compensation claims not only illustrates the diversity of damage inflicted by the war on a wide range of civilians and businesses, but also speaks loudly of the enormous destruction and turmoil which the conflict caused to individuals and their families:

> Daniel Daly, Kilsarcon, Scartaglin: Hay set on fire at Glendeagh, on 4 April 1922[16]
>
> Micheal O'Neill, merchant, Cahersiveen: Foodstuffs/provisions taken by IRA on various dates from May 1921 to 6 September 1922
>
> James Keating, Church Lane, Killarney: Motor boat commandeered at Cromane by IRA from 4 to 7 September 1922
>
> John Buckley, Caherlehillan, Kells: One heifer taken away at Garrydine by armed men on 4 December 1922
>
> Maurice J. O'Callaghan, Spa, Tralee: Trees cut and fence damaged in order to block the public road at Ballymakegogue, by armed men on 3 August 1922
>
> Michael O'Sullivan, Ballyhar: Two cattle killed and destroyed

at Lisheenacanina by unknown persons on 5 September 1922

Patrick O'Sullivan, Cloushmore, Dingle: One heifer killed by a motor car driven by Irregular forces at Cloushmore on 11 December 1922

Denis Barton, Clogherbrien, Tralee: Lands damaged and crops destroyed due to flooding caused by destruction of a bridge at Clogherbrien, Tralee, by Irregular forces on 2 August 1922

Thomas MacNally, Castlegregory: Cart damaged and a quantity of fish destroyed due to horse falling on stones put there to obstruct National Troops at Stradbally on 14 October 1922

Rev Alexander O'Sullivan, Milltown: One boat burned and destroyed at Rathpoge, Milltown by Irregular forces on 29 September 1922

John T. O'Sullivan, Gurranearagh, Cahersiveen: Five ricks of turf destroyed at Dirreen on 22 January 1923

John T. Huggard, hotelier, Waterville: Shop goods and bedding taken, apartments and dinners forcibly demanded at Waterville by Irregular forces in April and May 1922

In November 1923 Tralee Court was told there were 2,225 claims for compensation under the Damage to Property Act, 1923.[17] There was a further £533,000 in malicious damages claims, including £450,000 for damage to property and the remainder relating to personal injury claims.[18]

Shopkeepers were particularly vulnerable: the compensation claims from Kerry include over eighty separate claims for damage to shops that were looted and burned or damaged by combatants and non-combatants. The more that anti-Treaty combatants were forced into hiding and into remote areas, the more difficult it was for them to acquire food and supplies. The problem of supplying food to hungry men was not easily solved, Jeremiah Murphy wrote, and 'one method was to commandeer supplies from those who seemed antagonistic to or unsympathetic to our cause. This created more bad feeling but we had to eat.'[19] In August 1922 'breakfasts, dinners and teas' were 'commandeered' from Margaret Dwyer of Killorglin, while John Mansfield, a victualler in Waterville, was relieved of 'meat, vegetables and boots' during various raids in the early months of that year.[20] Alcohol and tobacco were much in demand: the Imperial Tobacco Company of Bristol, England, would submit compensation claims for almost a dozen seizures of tobacco products at various locations in the county during 1922 and 1923.[21]

In some cases, armed raiders cleared premises of everything on their shelves. On the night of 23 September 1922, a group of republicans arrived on three carts, entered the shop of James W. Murphy in Milltown and seized almost all the 'goods and chattels' on the property to the value of £1,515.[22] In seeking compensation, Murphy was required to list dozens of items which were seized including: '2 carcasses mutton; 12 tins biscuits; 3 dozen tinned fruit; 1 bucket dripping; 1 chest ointment; 6 dozen postcards; 8 bottles Bovril; 2 hams 20lb; 40 packets oatmeal; 8lbs tobacco; 5 dozen saucepans; 20 dozen boot polish; 20 bottles Jeyes fluid …' The IRA also attempted to coerce Murphy and his father to buy flour looted from a creamery in Fybough, but he refused. Separately, a quantity of flour was stolen from Murphy as he travelled through Castlemaine. On suspicion that he may have provided information to the Free State Army, his shop was again looted, and Murphy, a father of eight children, was kidnapped by anti-Treatyites and held 'in the mountains' for five weeks, at a time when they were said to have had 'complete control of the district'.

Murphy's neighbour and fellow shopkeeper, Samuel Lombard, also experienced looting in his shop. He listed items worth £39, which were stolen from his shop 'under duress'.[23] Lombard's work as a manager of local creameries was hampered by the theft of his bicycle. Elsewhere, Daniel Donoghue, a shopkeeper from Caragh Lake, who was described as an 'active supporter of the National Army [and] had recruited for it', was kidnapped and his shop looted.[24] Shops were not the only target. The Innisfallen Hotel in Killarney was damaged several times between April and July 1922 and the nearby Railway Hotel was burned down by republicans in August 1922 after it was looted. Among the looters was Margaret Rice-O'Sullivan, who was prosecuted for the theft of 'six copper-topped card tables and five occasional plush-topped chairs', which she contended were the property of 'the Irish Republican Army'.[25] In many cases, shops and businesses which had been looted 'closed down'.[26]

Supplying, or being suspected of supplying, foodstuffs and other items to either side of the conflict brought with it inherent dangers. In the early hours of 3 March 1922, a shop run by Mary Agnes Sheehy and Church Street in Listowel was set ablaze, as was the adjacent house and 'five tons of hay'. Sheehy's sin was that she was 'a supporter of the Government' and her shop supplied goods to the Free State Army. She told her local TD, James Crowley, that her premises were attacked because of 'my backing of the Treaty'. It was noted in official documents that several notices had been posted around Listowel 'threatening those who supplied the troops with goods'. Sheehy was awarded £50 in compensation, but six years later she was still in the process of rebuilding the premises and her solicitor appealed for further financial support from the Department of Finance.[27]

The targeting of livestock and farm animals was common as a means of disrupting farming activity and spreading terror. The compensation files for Kerry include fifty-seven cases of the theft, injury or killing of horses, donkeys or ponies, as well as thirty-seven incidents of the theft or killing of sheep: thirty sheep were stolen by republicans from the farm of Patrick Taylor in Glencar in December 1922.[28] The seizure of cattle was a more frequent occurrence. When several of Canon Carmody's bullocks were seized by the IRA in Rathmore, the cattle of a local man, Jeremiah Reen, were also seized and 'driven away to Killarney to be heard of no more'.[29] Two of Martin Fitzgerald's cattle were killed in Tralee and 'a threatening note was left on the cow house door'.[30] In a similar vein, the words 'Up De Valera' and 'Traitors Beware' were daubed on the livestock of Michael O'Connell on Valentia Island.[31] Arrests and prosecutions for such offences were rare. An unusual example was the jailing of men who had driven cattle off the land of Thomas Knightly of Lachtacallow, Castlemaine.[32]

Damage to farmland, gates and fences, as well as the burning of hay, haysheds and ricks of turf, was also frequent throughout the Civil War, with 'land dispute' usually provided as the reason in the compensation claim files. 'Old claims' were often at their root.[33] Cattle-driving prosecutions appear in newspaper reports in 1923 and 1924 and forced District Justice Richard Johnson to remind those responsible that claims to land should be settled in the courts: the State would not be 'bull-dozed by anybody' taking the law into their own hands.[34] The theft of animals was borne out in the claims submitted to local courts. Among the cases heard by Cahersiveen court in September 1924 were claims including:

Daniel Mangan, Coomdeveen, claimed £15 for sheep
   taken
Mary Casey, Tulligealane, claimed £75 for cattle taken
Michael Keating, Coumduff, claimed £10 for cattle
   taken

> Wm. Granfield, Cappanwee, claimed £8 for heifer
> taken[35]

Disputes over land were often at the root of such attacks. Many tenant farmers who had been evicted from their holdings during the Great Famine and the Land War of the late nineteenth century exploited the political and legal vacuum to reclaim land they considered to be rightfully theirs and to seek revenge against landlords and their agents. In many cases, the instigators were not identified by their politics and referred to merely as 'armed men'. The home and lands belonging to the Marquis of Lansdowne in Kenmare were occupied in September 1922.[36] James Butler of Waterville House was 'dispossessed of lands' in April 1922, and later had his boathouse and fish farm destroyed.[37] Attempts were made to seize the land of Arthur and Robert Gentleman in Lixnaw, as well as the farm of land agent Marshall Hill in Listowel, while, in Ballybunion, the property of land agent Hugh Bracken was burned down.[38]

In other cases, local jealousies and enmities prevailed and intimidation of neighbours, inevitably influenced by the political divisions, was the modus operandi. William Moore's bullock was found with its throat cut at Kilmorna during a dispute with 'landless men in the district'.[39] In Lauragh, on the Beara Peninsula, the meadow of Patrick Leary was destroyed when horses were 'driven into it' and his potatoes, sheep and cattle were stolen.[40] Labourers were warned by 'landless men' that they would be in danger if they worked for Michael Buckley on his farm near Listowel.[41] In further evidence of the difficulty in policing the county and apprehending criminals, the thieves were sometimes brazen: when cattle and goods were stolen from Lord Ventry's estate near Dingle, receipts which were signed by the O/C of 'Keel and Castle[Gregory] Active Service Unit', James O'Sullivan, were left behind.[42]

The settling of old scores also extended to those who had served in the disbanded RIC, and the lawlessness which prevailed often facilitated attacks on former officers and their properties. John Lynch from New Street, Killarney, had been an RIC sergeant: during two break-ins at his home in June 1922, furniture and personal belongings were stolen.[43] Republicans also raided the home of Jeremiah Dennehy in Headford, and goods belonging to Denis Sheehan of Kells were seized in transit.[44] Elsewhere, John Kennelly, a fisherman from Ballylongford, had his canoe burned by armed raiders on the day of the first engagements of the war in Kerry. He had been engaged to transport an RIC sergeant across the mouth of the River Shannon from Kerry to Clare.[45] Former RIC barracks and accommodation in Kenmare, Ballybunion, Tralee, Killarney, Cahersiveen and Dingle were attacked or burned in the weeks after the conflict began and as republicans rid the county of the remaining vestiges of the former police force, while also denying their use by the new police force and the army as suitable military headquarters.[46]

+++

Civilians who overtly pinned their political allegiances to the mast often did so at great personal risk, as well as creating a risk to their property. Intimidation remained a modus operandi for both sides in the conflict. Many civilians were clever enough not to antagonise the combatants. 'The people were sound,' claimed John Joe Rice, O/C of the Kerry No. 2 Brigade. 'I could ride on horseback around the area. Even people who had F/S [Free State] leanings would help us.'[47] But others did not shirk from overtly supporting one side or the other, and if a clear political allegiance was known, it brought inherent dangers. Patrick Palmer, a teacher from Sneem and later a Fine Gael TD for Kerry South, who was active in Cumann na nGaedheal, was twice raided by armed men who stole bicycles and clothing.[48] The home of Timothy Devane of Rathanny, Tralee, who was described as a 'supporter of the National Army', often hosted dances, even at the height of the Civil War.[49] In a letter to Cumann na nGaedheal TD Fionán Lynch, Devane claimed that republicans were 'jealous of any other one's liberty in attending [the dances]'.[50] Armed men arrived to Devane's door late one night, warning that the dances 'should be stopped'. But when some of his friends joined the Free State Army, the threats from the anti-Treaty IRA became actions:

> ... one night a porter-ball was held in my house and those friends of mine in the National Army attended. This enraged the 'runaways' and it poisoned their minds against me, and not long after (1st Feb [1923]) at 2.30 a.m. I was called from my bed by some neighbours that my hayshed was on fire, but when I got up it was almost completely gutted out, together with 35 tons of hay, Mowing machine, Pony's car and rail, calf, 16 rails of turf, 4 tons of turnips, timber for horse's car, 3 ash trees, spades, shovels, rakers, meal sacks, ladder, ropes, and all furnishing utensils, to the total amount of £425 (without being insured).[51]

Soldiers of the Free State Army and their families were also frequently the subject of threat and intimidation. The Department of Defence received a report that while he served in the army, the cattle of Lieutenant Patrick Moynihan of Maghauntourig, Gneeveguilla, were 'stolen from his lands at Rathmore'.[52] Army headquarters claimed that when he enlisted, he 'received unwelcome attention from the anti-Government Forces and a few weeks after his marriage was compelled to leave the district ... He found it hazardous to visit his home.'[53] In correspondence with the department, Moynihan's widow, Hannah Mary, described the family's ordeal when he left to join the army:

> Our shop was completely wrecked, windows broken & 6 cattle taken. Then my first baby was born & still the house was watched as they expected the father to come to see his son. At last after 6 weeks quite unexpectedly one night he paid a visit after walking from Millstreet which is about 8 miles from here he came thro [sic] fields & was drenched with rain ... We both felt this very much and I know it was the cause of his early death ...[54]

The father of Private Patrick O'Sullivan of Rathbeg, Rathmore, 'incurred the hostility of the Executive Forces [anti-Treaty IRA] and was brutally treated on several occasions', according to a garda report from 1926. Following Patrick's discharge from the army, his father continued to have 'a rough time with Irregular supporters'.[55] The Horan family of Ballinclemesig, Ballyheigue, also endured intimidation. William Horan had been part of an IRA flying column in 1918–19, but he enlisted with the Free State Army at Ballymullen Barracks in 1922 and was headquartered in Castleisland. His family 'were strictly boycotted and suffered terrible persecution by the Irregulars'.[56] Horan emigrated to the United States and lived at ten different addresses in New Jersey, where he and his wife, Jane, raised four children. The intimidation endured by Horan and his fellow soldiers was neither an evident concern nor a priority for the army leadership in Kerry, however. As the end of 1922 approached, it was the political and military pressure being brought to bear to crush the anti-Treatyites that dominated the thinking within the upper ranks of the Kerry Command.

CHAPTER 6

'Then you can mark off Kerry as finished'

William Richard English-Murphy composed himself as he sat at his desk in Ballymullen Barracks on the outskirts of Tralee. Evening was approaching and the army garrison was relatively quiet. It was a few weeks before Christmas 1922 and the thirty-two-year-old was preparing another of the seemingly never-ending flurry of weekly intelligence dispatches to army headquarters. The Wexford native was major general of the Free State Army force in Kerry and was no stranger to warfare. Having joined the British Army in Belfast in 1915, he was wounded at the Battle of Loos and fought at the Battle of the Somme. He was second in command to Eoin O'Duffy at the Battle of Kilmallock in the last week of July and the first week of August 1922, before his appointment as major general in Kerry. Since the arrival of the Dublin Guard in the county on board the *Lady Wicklow* at the start of August, however, English-Murphy felt a little bit undermined by the brash and assertive Dublin Guard leader Paddy O'Daly, who had come to Kerry on a mission to crush the anti-Treaty forces in the county. Even though English-Murphy was nominally in command of the army in Kerry, it was O'Daly who did the day-to-day heavy lifting. But despite feeling less than certain of his position as head of the Kerry Command, English-Murphy felt confident as he penned his pre-Christmas dispatch to army headquarters. He had many positive things to say from the army's perspective. The army in Kerry was emboldened by the provisions of the recently passed emergency legislation – which allowed for the execution of anyone found guilty of possession of arms or explosives and for aiding and abetting attacks on the Free State Army – that were coming into being.

English-Murphy believed that the republicans were on the back foot. Kenmare had just been recaptured in a closely co-ordinated three-pronged attack on the town involving the Kerry Command and the First Western Division, which met with little resistance, and he was of the firm opinion that he and his colleagues were gaining the upper hand across the county:

> The Irregular organisation here is well-nigh broken up. Several of the best men have ceased to act. T. [Thomas] McEllistrim is living at home and not very active … There is quarrelling in the tents of H. [Humphrey] Murphy's gang. [John Joe] Rice we nearly had last week – only for a bog we did not know the tracks of. The capture of Kenmare will dispose of their last rallying ground. North and Mid Kerry are marvellously quiet. I understand [Austin] Stack wrote from Dublin saying Kerry is not active enough. It won't be active either … Then you can mark off Kerry as finished.[1]

Just a few weeks later, Major General English-Murphy buttressed an appeal for additional resources with a table of figures which detailed the casualty toll between 2 August, when the Dublin Guard arrived at Fenit, and the beginning of December 1922:

	Killed	Wounded	Prisoners	Deserters
Irregulars	79	119	704	–
Army	52	117	Nil	7

He added that between those killed, wounded and jailed on the anti-Treaty side, there were '902 Irregulars disposed of'.[2]

The reality of the military situation in many of parts of Kerry was somewhat different and suggests that English-Murphy's assessment of the situation was excessively optimistic and designed to impress his superiors in Dublin. Republicans continued to prevail in rural Kerry, and the army continually struggled to apprehend IRA leaders who had the shelter and protection of the countryside and its residents. As John Joe Rice recalled, 'the Free State had to stick to the roads and we could move across [the] country as we wished'.[3] Army reports from the spring of 1923 betray not only the difficulties presented by trying to fight off republicans in remote rural areas, but also a deep frustration amongst the army rank and file:

> It will never be possible to clear the mountainous districts of Kerry except by very cooperative movement between [army] posts. This country is so difficult and extensive that it affords excellent cover and easy retreat for the Irregulars ...[4]
>
> The rural areas southwards from the points Headford, Killarney, Killorglin, Sneem are their 'happy hunting grounds' being mountainous and extensive, and affording easy retreat from danger and facilities for concealment in 'dug outs.'[5]

The dugout was a critical feature of the war for republicans, a phenomenon which had stood the IRA in good stead against the Auxiliaries and the Black and Tans. They were built anywhere that offered good cover and protection from the enemy; as John Joe Rice recalled, 'in bushes and caves, in the hills and in the mountains, in gables and banks and in places where there were no roads'.[6] Some of the less luxurious ones, as Dwyer has noted, were built under reeks of turf, and in one case, under a pile of manure.[7] Hay sheds and barns were particularly sought after, offering warmth and comfort during the colder winter months.[8] Improvisation was essential: one dugout in Castlegregory used the sail of a boat for shelter.[9] The occupants of dugouts and other hideouts often only returned to their homes out of necessity, such as 'for a change of clothes'.[10] Jeremiah Sullivan from Glenbeigh would return home from a dugout in some rural part of mid-Kerry 'for about a day and be away again'.[11]

Many of the dugouts that had been used during the War of Independence had to be scrapped, however, because the Free State forces, many of whom had been in the Kerry IRA before the split, knew where they were. As Martin Moore has pointed out, 'their haunts and habits were known to former comrades'.[12] Moreover, arms dumps had to be kept separate from dugouts to prevent both men and arms being simultaneously captured, but this meant that unarmed or poorly armed men in a rural hideout had no recourse to additional weaponry if surrounded by a superior Free State Army force.[13] Willie O'Leary from Lixnaw, who was a TD for Kerry between 1927 and 1932, recalled that:

When the Civil War broke out, all the dugouts and dumps we had constructed, we had to scrap them. A certain number of people joined the army which meant we had to shift that stuff further away. Where we had it stored, they had a knowledge of the places ... We had to start all over again and build fresh ones.[14]

Another key aspect of the war against the Dublin Guard and the other divisions of the Free State Army in Kerry was the gathering and use of intelligence. Cumann na mBan performed an essential role in observing the movements of soldiers, relaying information to the IRA and carrying messages between isolated outposts. 'I had to do very hard work,' stated Sally Sheehy of Boherbee, Tralee, 'not suitable to a woman at all. Walking and cycling long distances against time.'[15] Other members showed great ingenuity in covert communications. The account of her activities compiled by Mary Cremin from Carhoobeg, Beaufort, describes in detail the 'signals' that were used to warn the IRA men who were located in the mountains. Cremin would move the white cow which her family owned to the 'peaceful field' if the area was relatively safe, but if the army was active locally, the cow would be placed in the 'danger field'.[16] In the spring of 1923, the Kerry Command admitted in reports to headquarters that the distribution of messages among the anti-Treatyites, as well as the use of signals, 'is so perfect, that it is impossible to apprehend Irregulars'.[17]

The age-old phenomenon of the informer was also employed to good effect. Thomas Rohan of the Castlegregory IRA claimed that he started to associate with army officers, such as David Neligan and Paddy O'Daly, and was able to pass on information and intelligence to his company leader, Tadhg Brosnan. But Rohan was also wooed by the Free State forces: 'they wanted me to come along and join up, they offered me all sorts of things, Lieutenant's pay and all that if I would come on ... They trusted me.'[18]

One of the military strategies pursued by the Free State Army in locating and arresting republicans in rural and isolated homes or hideouts was the 'round-up'. This tactic was described by Seamus O'Connor, an IRA volunteer from Knocknagoshel, in his memoir *Tomorrow Was Another Day*:

This meant that on a certain morning early, hundreds of troops from surrounding towns would have assembled in bands of say, twenty each, at different strategic points, surrounding a parish or two. This would be complete by dawn on an appointed morning. They then started to move in more or less extended order, searching all houses and likely places in their path ...[19]

'You could do nothing,' recalled Greg Ashe of Lispole. 'One Sunday, I was up on the mountain on the back of a rock and the parish below me was all troops, searching.'[20] The sweeps were not always successful, but they often yielded results, with some eighty-six republicans captured in one week alone in October 1922.[21]

Despite these challenges, the anti-Treaty forces continued to show a capacity to mobilise in large numbers. Some seventy men were involved in an attack on Free State forces near Rathmore on 15 December, which claimed the life of Private Matthew Ferguson.[22] At Castlemaine on 23 January, about 250 anti-Treaty forces attacked the army garrison there with trench mortars, Thompson and Lewis guns and grenades, as well as rifles and revolvers. Private James McGovern from County Leitrim was killed.[23] The livestock of several local farmers in the surrounding area was injured and, in some cases, killed, in the crossfire.[24] This would be the last large-scale attack on army forces in Kerry.

+++

Writing to his future wife, Winifred Gordon, towards the end of 1922, Austin Stack remarked that, in Kerry, 'the F.S. [Free State] people have stepped into the shoes of the Auxiliaries and Black and Tans'.[25] In the months that followed, the brutality of the war in Kerry, in many respects, put the actions and brutality of the Crown

Forces in 1919–21 in the shade. In early January 1923, the O/C
Kerry Command, W.R. English-Murphy was 'put out to grass'.[26]
He later became commissioner of the Dublin Metropolitan Police.
It has been suggested that English-Murphy was out of his depth
in dealing with the IRA's guerrilla tactics, but he was also sensitive
to the ramifications of excessive levels of execution and violence
towards prisoners, which he rightly suspected would alienate public
opinion.[27] He was uncomfortable with the 'pseudo-legalistic' powers
introduced by the Emergency Powers Act of 1922.[28] In a submission
to Chief of Staff Richard Mulcahy less than three months after its
introduction, for example, English-Murphy argued that the shooting
of those found guilty of offences had already had 'a salutary effect'
and suggested that only those 'caught actually firing or in ambush
should alone be executed'.[29] Four republican prisoners – Tom
Devane, Con Casey, Matt Moroney and Dermot O'Connor – had
been sentenced to death at the end of 1922, but English-Murphy
resisted plans to carry out the sentences, arguing that their deaths
would be counterproductive. The matter was considered by the Army
Council and the Judge Advocate General and the death sentences
were eventually suspended.[30]

Whereas English-Murphy had often resisted the carrying out of
executions, his successor as head of the Kerry Command had no
such qualms. Paddy O'Daly assumed full control of the army in the
county on 2 January 1923. He was in charge of almost 2,300 soldiers
at twenty-one different barracks and outposts across the county.
Shortly after he was promoted, O'Daly made publicly clear his
intention to step up the military campaign against his opponents by
ordering the executions of four prisoners: James Daly, John Clifford,
James Hanlon and Michael Brosnan. As they awaited their death on
the morning of 29 January, they were forced to stand beside their
open coffins for thirty minutes until the officer in charge arrived.[31]

Before the execution, Brosnan, from Rathanny, Tralee, wrote to his family: 'I am leaving the world at 8 o'clock in the morning ... Father, do not blame anyone for me, cheer up ... I thought we would not part as soon ... I am now going to say my rosaries for the morning. Cheer up now father, brothers and sisters, it's all for Ireland. From your fond son. Michael Brosnan.'[32]

Following a resolution passed by Tralee Urban District Council demanding that the death sentences hanging over other prisoners be commuted, O'Daly responded angrily to councillors, writing that the executions would stop 'when train-wrecking, murder and highway robbery cease and when the people you represent and work for are allowed to enjoy the freedom they sacrificed so much for'.[33]

O'Daly's new regime of brutality was not confined to executions. He oversaw interrogations that were particularly vicious. Men in custody were often 'clubbed unconscious with hammers and rifle butts'.[34] One of the officers based at Ballymullen Barracks recalled that Daly's office was on an upper floor and that 'the roars [from the office] could be heard all over the barracks and that they got on everyone's goat, the roars'.[35] O'Daly's right-hand man was Colonel David Neligan, intelligence officer of the Kerry Command. A native of west Limerick, he too had been part of Michael Collins' inner circle. Neligan was accused of presiding 'at all the beatings and tor-turings'.[36] A 'favourite trick' of Neligan's, Johnny Connor recalled, was to 'belt you across the shins with a rifle'. When one prisoner told Neligan he had an injured knee, Neligan 'kicked him hard then on the bad knee'.[37]

Even O'Daly must have been aware of how volatile and violent Neligan could be. In a rare intervention to protect prisoners in custody, O'Daly is said to have sat outside the cell of prisoners, which included Tom Daly of Fries, who were being detained at the

Great Southern Hotel in Killarney, to prevent them being attacked by Neligan. Neligan had just murdered seventeen-year-old Bertie Murphy outside the hotel and 'wanted to shoot' Tom Daly.[38] O'Daly sat with a gun on the stairs, warning that he would shoot any soldier who came near the prisoners. Tom Daly's sister, May, recalled that her mother was allowed to see her son and that O'Daly 'was very nice to me'.[39] O'Daly's actions may have had more to do with the fact that he knew Tom Daly from their shared membership of the Irish Republican Brotherhood in Dublin than any humanitarian concern for his prisoners.

The descent into 'localised butchery' under the regime of O'Daly, Neligan and others had predated the former's appointment to the head of the Kerry Command but intensified in the spring of 1923.[40] The treatment of republicans in custody, in particular, came to exemplify the actions of the Kerry Command at this time. An officer of the 5th Battalion of the IRA in west Kerry, Daniel 'Bob' McCarthy, was brutally tortured and murdered in March 1923 by a contingent of the Free State Army under Denis Griffin of Dingle and Colonel James Hancock. Hancock would later preside over the siege at Clashmealcon caves in April 1923. McCarthy endured three days of torture and an 'awful death'.[41] Dorothy Macardle recounted what occurred when his sister visited McCarthy in prison: 'The soldiers were kicking a football about and her brother was among them. They were forcing him to kick the ball. He was swaying on his feet and was all stained and dusty. When she went to him he stared and seemed not to know her. His eyes were half closed and there was blood on his head.'[42]

According to Gregory Ashe of the Lispole IRA, the army 'spent three days killing him':

They put him in a corner and they pegged stones at him. About 80 soldiers pegged stones at him. He was outside in the corner of a field and they got their soldiers to do that. They pulled him down after them from Gleann na nGealt [near Camp], and pulled him from the top to the end after a lorry. In Ballymullen Barracks, they thought he was dead and they put him in a coffin. Paddy Shea [prisoner] heard him stirring and he told an officer there was something stirring inside and the officer fired a couple of shots in through the coffin.[43]

In a similar incident, John Savage of Castleisland was beaten and tied to a truck before being dragged through the main street in the town in a tactic that combined humiliation and torture.[44] Meanwhile, as a group of prisoners was being taken from Cahersiveen to Killarney in March 1923, one of them, Frank Grady from Glenbeigh, attracted the attention of Free State Army captain Michael 'Tiny' Lyons. It was believed that Grady had been involved in blowing up a bridge near Glenbeigh a few weeks previously.[45] Denis Daly from Cahersiveen – later a Fianna Fáil TD – looked on as Lyons confronted and shot the prisoner at close range. Grady's brains were 'scattered on my arm', Daly recalled, while another officer 'put a couple of bullets into him as he was wriggling on the ground'.[46]

The violence directed towards republicans could also be redirected to within the ranks of the Kerry Command when there was indiscipline, desertion or leniency towards the enemy. Billy Mullins was in Ballymullen Jail when a number of Free State officers were brought to the prison in custody. They had abandoned the Free State garrison in Castlemaine on 23 January 1923, when it came under sustained assault by republicans. Mullins witnessed their fate:

Soldiers who had run away from an ambush in Castlemaine were put in the clink in Tralee barracks ... the soldiers were ordered to strip off. They were flogged with Sam Brown belts ... I saw the soldiers lying on the bare floor with their backs streaming blood ... Then a stretcher was got, white sheets spread over the beaten prisoners ... Paddy [O']Daly was [in] on the beating up of the soldiers ... One of them was an Englishman and he wouldn't cry out until he got 21 lashes.[47]

The actions of O'Daly's men were hugely consequential for the ranks of his command, who continued to be killed in large numbers throughout the early months of 1923 in a series of retaliatory attacks by the IRA. Such was the nature of the injuries sustained by eighteen-year-old Private James Byrne in an IRA ambush in Duagh in October 1923 that his remains could not be positively identified after he died at the infirmary in Abbeyfeale. He was wounded by 'explosive bullets, his features blackening and swelling abnormally in consequence'.[48] A local priest was able to hear his Confession as he lay on the road where he was ambushed, but he was unable to receive Communion as 'this made him inclined to vomit'. He was, Fr Harrington added, 'naturally, in great pain ... He was quite resigned to die, and gladly forgave those who had so foully done him to death.'[49] Byrne's family was only informed of his death several months after he had been buried in Glasnevin Cemetery in Dublin.

It would be wrong to suggest that O'Daly's reign of terror in Kerry was implemented in a political vacuum. Great political pressure was being brought to bear on the army to bring the war to an end. There was no shortage of rhetoric from the political authorities, which constituted official sanction for what was being done in Kerry. As early as August 1922, President W.T. Cosgrave was using provocative and emotive language. The Free State, he said, would not hesitate in pursuing its opponents and, if necessary, would 'have to exterminate 10,000 Republicans' if it was to survive.[50] In a message to the Kerry Command in February 1923, Cosgrave stated that he appreciated 'most heartily the very honourable action' of army officers in the county.[51] It was, perhaps, no wonder O'Daly famously remarked that nobody had asked him to 'take my kid gloves to Kerry and I didn't take them'.[52] The euphemism, Gavin Foster argues, was a rather blasé summary of what was to come: an 'array of ugly tactics, including torture during interrogations, routine abuse of prisoners and a pattern of extra-judicial murders', which contributed to the reign of terror of the Free State Army in Kerry in the early months of 1923.[53] The worst, however, was yet to come.

CHAPTER 7

'Human flesh scattered in all directions'

Paddy 'Pats' O'Connor wasn't at home on a Sunday evening in December 1922 when a 'large body' of anti-Treaty IRA members came knocking. O'Connor's parents, Patrick and Hanora, both in their seventies, were at home in Knockaneatee, a rural townland near Castleisland. The men came, they said, to look for Paddy 'Pats'. Not finding him, they proceeded to 'rob and plunder'. The raiding party, some of whom were wearing Free State Army uniforms, carried off the family's cattle and a pony and trap, as well as 'a pair of boots, 2 overcoats, a pair of leggings, a bicycle, two hundred weight of bacon, and £36.10 in cash'.[1] The grudge held by the republicans towards Paddy 'Pats' O'Connor, his brother claimed, centred on his refusal to 'join their organisation'.[2] The reality was more complicated, however, and, as Doyle has observed, the raid on the O'Connor home grew out of a 'combination of personal animosity, local rivalry and the desire for revenge [which] crossed over from the civilian sphere into the military arena'.[3] Matters developed quickly as a 'blood feud'.[4]

Among the raiding party that night were members of the local anti-Treaty IRA, including Patrick Buckley, a former RIC officer who was much loathed by republicans in east Kerry in the years before the War of Independence, but who later embraced the IRA cause.[5] Patrick O'Connor, the seventy-three-year-old father of Paddy 'Pats', had fallen out with Patrick Buckley and another IRA member, John Daly. O'Connor was suspected of having tipped off the Free State Army that the IRA was planning to ambush an army convoy travelling between Brosna and Castleisland.[6] The IRA had also occupied a field belonging to Paddy 'Pats' for use as a dugout and they refused to leave, preventing him from saving some of his hay.[7] When the Free State Army conducted a sweep of the area, Patrick was suspected of providing information to local army officers. He was taken away by the IRA for several days, 'kept on his knees' and blindfolded.[8] Accused of being an informer, O'Connor denied any such charge. He was released but fined £50, a fine he refused to pay.[9] An army report later claimed that O'Connor Senior was 'immensely terrified'.[10]

Following the raid on the family home on 16 December 1922, and furious about how his father had been treated, Paddy 'Pats' O'Connor walked into Castleisland Army Barracks, which was located at Hartnett's Hotel, and enlisted in the Free State Army at the rank of lieutenant. The hotel, which was 'virtually impregnable' and the highest building in the town, was known to host horrendous abuse of republican prisoners.[11] O'Connor quickly developed a reputation for mistreating prisoners, and the local IRA alleged that he 'made a hobby of torturing inmates'.[12] He also spearheaded a series of raids for republicans in the Knocknagoshel area, targeting those who had knocked on his father's door that night in December. Among those arrested in the sweeps of the area were John Daly and Patrick Buckley, as well as Michael O'Connell of Castleisland. O'Connor's enlisting in the army would trigger a series of events across Kerry in March 1923 that ensured it became known as the

'Terror Month' in the county. It also made the name of Knocknagoshel known 'the length and breadth of the land'.[13]

+++

The landmine, as Seán Enright has observed, had, by the beginning
of 1923, 'become part of the anti-Treaty weaponry. Left on lonely
bridges and culverts and detonated from a safe distance, the
landmine wreaked devastation. The technology was later developed
to include trip mines: when a search party moved a heavy stone
a hidden trigger detonated the mine.'[14] Explosion followed the
release of pressure on a wire attached to a detonator, or when it
was stepped on. The trip mine was not the first tactic considered
by the IRA of Castleisland and Knocknagoshel as they plotted their
next move against Paddy 'Pats' O'Connor and his fellow officers.
Seamus O'Connor recalls a plan to 'shoot up the officers' from the
barracks in Castleisland 'whilst they were at their lunch in a hotel in
the middle of the town'.[15] But, having failed to lure O'Connor from
the safety of the barracks in Castleisland, the IRA decided to pursue
a booby-trap strategy. A bomb packed with explosives and shrapnel
was prepared by IRA leaders Jeremiah O'Leary, Johnny Nolan and
Mick McGlynn. An anonymous letter penned by two members of
Cumann na mBan, Kathleen Hickey and Kathleen Walsh, was then
delivered to the barracks, claiming that there was an IRA arms
dump at Burke's field at Barranarig Wood near Knocknagoshel.[16]
The bomb was prepared, placed and primed.

Convinced of the potential to deprive his opponents of a cache
of guns and ammunition, O'Connor led a detachment to the site
just before 2 a.m. on the morning of 6 March. One of the few first-
hand testimonies about what happened at Knocknagoshel – and
which was corroborated by his fellow officers – was that of Sergeant

Matthews of the Dublin Guard. He told the army inquiry into the matter that he proceeded to Knocknagoshel with Captains Dunne and Stapleton and others, leaving Castleisland at 1.40 a.m.:

> Captain Dunne left me in charge of the Crossley [Tender] and 2 Vols. [Volunteers] at Talbot Bridge and proceeded in the direction of Baranarig [*sic*] Wood with the rest of the party to search for a Dump supposed to be in or around the wood. After about a quarter of an hour on the bridge something in the nature of a heavy Mine exploded. Immediately I ran in the direction to find out what happened and on arriving near the scene of the explosion I found Captain Dunne and Lieut. O'Connor dead. I then made a search of the place and found Vol. M. Galvin, Vol. O'Connor and Captain Stapleton almost dead. I asked Captain Stapleton if I could do anything for him and he told me to take the Crossley back to Castleisland and report the matter to H.Q. and also to get a priest, which I did; but on arrival of the priest, Vols Galvin and O'Connor were dead. Captain Stapleton was alive and after receiving the last rites of the Catholic Church he expired.[17]

'Portions of their mangled bodies were found hundreds of yards away,' according to *The Cork Examiner*.[18] Paddy 'Pats' O'Connor was decapitated and died instantly. His head was discovered in a stream by a local schoolgirl, Bridie Lyons.[19] A lower limb was found 'some 100 yards away', and it was impossible, the *Irish Independent* reported, 'to know to what body the different limbs belonged. Sunk deep into all the bodies were portions of stone, gravel, and grass.'[20] According to some reports, Stapleton's Lewis gun was 'atomised' and body parts were 'strewn in all directions'.[21] The remains of Michael Dunne, who like Stapleton was a member of the Dublin

Guard and who, it is believed, triggered the mine, 'fitted into his tunic afterwards'.[22] Also killed were Laurence O'Connor, of Lissycurry, Causeway, and Michael Galvin of College Street, Killarney, bringing the number of fatalities to five. Another soldier, Joseph O'Brien, sustained serious leg and facial injuries. On being taken to Tralee, his two legs were amputated below the knee. His 'left eye was practically blown out of his head, and his right eye is so badly damaged that he will probably never recover its use'.[23] The IRA members who set the mine were hiding in a dugout about a mile away. Hearing the explosion, one of them uttered: 'The Lord have mercy on their souls.' Then they turned over and went back to sleep.[24]

The five fatalities at Knocknagoshel represented the highest daily death toll among the Free State forces in six months.[25] In Dublin, the funerals of Captains Edward Stapleton and Michael Dunne were described by the *Evening Herald* as among the biggest witnessed since that of Michael Collins.[26] On learning of the deaths, particularly those of his colleagues in the Dublin Guard, Paddy O'Daly had to be physically restrained by fellow officers at Ballymullen Barracks. He declared that, from then on, prisoners would be used to clear obstructions or barricades suspected of being mines or booby traps. 'The tragedy of Knocknagoshel must not be repeated,' he warned his men, 'and serious disciplinary action will be taken against any officer who endangers the lives of his men in the removal of such barricades ... the taking out of prisoners [to remove suspect mines] is not to be regarded as a reprisal, but as the only alternative left us to prevent the wholesale slaughter of our men.'[27] Few could have predicted the ferocity of the retaliation which followed. Knocknagoshel, as Diarmaid Ferriter has described, unleashed a 'lust for revenge'.[28]

+++

The atmosphere at midnight in the guardroom at Ballymullen Barracks was described as 'menacing'.[29] It was almost twenty-four hours after the explosion at Knocknagoshel, and fury pervaded the mindset of the troops of the Kerry Command. Nine prisoners, many of whom had been tortured and beaten with a hammer, were selected by Colonel David Neligan to clear an obstruction on the Tralee to Killorglin road at Ballyseedy Cross. They included Patrick Buckley of Scartaglin, a former RIC officer at Farranfore; John Daly of Ahaneboy, Castleisland; Pat Hartnett of Gortnaminch, Listowel; Michael O'Connell, Castleisland; John O'Connor, a former RIC officer from Innishannon, County Cork; George O'Shea, Tim Tuomey and Stephen Fuller, all of Kilflynn; and James Walsh of Churchill. Daly was taken on a stretcher owing to a back injury.[30] A tenth prisoner, John Shanahan, had been so badly beaten that he was unable to walk and was left behind. It was contended that one of the reasons these men were selected from a wider group of prisoners was that they had no known links to the Catholic clergy or hierarchy, so their deaths would not antagonise the Church, which was actively and vocally supportive of the Free State and its leadership.[31] The selection of Patrick Buckley was also believed to have been motivated by his refusal, as a former RIC officer, to join the Free State Army. Before being removed from the prison, Stephen Fuller was shown into a cell which contained nine coffins: 'This is yours,' he was told.[32]

The nine men were led out of the barracks by a group of soldiers, including Commandant Edmund (Ned) Breslin and Lieutenant Joseph Murtagh, and were placed in a truck which was driven to Ballyseedy Cross where a barricade was blocking the road. They were ordered to stand round the barricade, their hands were tied behind their backs and they were tethered to each other. Stephen Fuller described what happened in the moments before the explosion:

They tied us then, our hands behind our back and left about a foot between the hands and next fellow. They tied us in a circle then around the mine and they tied our legs then and the knees as well, with a rope. And then they threw off our caps and said we could be praying away now as long as we like.[33]

A few moments later, the mine was detonated from nearby, causing a loud and enormous explosion. Three army officers were injured by shrapnel from the blast, including Capt. Breslin, Lt Murtagh and Sgt Ennis.[34] The bodies of the prisoners were then shot with automatic weapons to ensure they were dead, among them Patrick Buckley, who had been 'blown in two at the waist'.[35] Not all of his fellow prisoners died instantly: according to an IRA report to GHQ 'one prisoner who was still alive was finished off by Comdt. Joe Leonard', who 'fired into him as he lay moaning on the ground'.[36] Stephen Fuller, who was listed in press reports as having been killed, was blown into a stream by the force of the explosion and managed to reach the nearby home of the Curran family, where he was treated.[37] He was taken from there the following morning to the home of the Daly family at Knockaneacoolteen and later spent several weeks hiding in a dugout.

That Fuller survived the explosion at Ballyseedy was extraordinary. According to May Daly, who looked after him, his back 'was all tattooed with the gravel of the road and his hands also'.[38] For a few days, Fuller was unconscious but gradually recovered. A clue to his subsequent psychological trauma came from Daly's observation that he 'got nervous'. Medical assessments in subsequent years detail the effects of the explosion at Ballyseedy. Dr Edmond Shanahan, the first doctor to tend to Fuller, wrote ten years later that he was suffering from nervous shock: 'a chronic neurasthenic and I have no doubt but his present condition is due to the explosion ... all his back was burned with gunpowder and dozens of small pieces of grit embedded under the skin ... The scars from same are still to be seen today.'[39]

A local girl who later passed the site of the explosion described a 'shocking site. There was a hole in the middle of the road and human flesh scattered in all directions, debris and everything scattered all over the place.'[40] The *Cork Examiner* reporter described how the prisoners were 'mangled almost beyond recognition; portions of their limbs and flesh, with pieces of clothing, were found adhering to trees and strewn along the roads and fields over a hundred yards [from the scene]'.[41] An IRA report claimed that 'some of the Colonials [army officers]' returned to the site at dawn and 'laughed and jeered as they threw the pieces of flesh, boots, and clothes over the hedge on either side'.[42]

When the dismembered remains of the eight men who died were placed in coffins and returned to their families at Ballymullen Barracks, there was a dramatic furore. Bill Bailey, a native of Ballymullen, was one of the Free State officers on duty and recounted the events of the day to Ernie O'Malley years later. At about four o'clock in the afternoon, it was decided to release the remains to the families, who were waiting outside the barracks with an estimated 400 people. Bailey described how, as the 'procession of corpses' made its way through the barrack gates, the army band began to play lively music: 'the band lined up and playtime ragtime [music] inside [the] gate – "I'm the Sheik of Araby" etc on either side of the main gate. Completely shocked and dazed the people.'[43]

The families reacted furiously, throwing stones at the soldiers and smashing the army coffins on the ground as they placed the deceased in coffins they had brought themselves.[44] The remains, many of which could not be clearly identified, had been placed indiscriminately in the coffins: the sister of Michael O'Connell discovered his body in a coffin bearing the name 'Stephen Fuller'.[45] Patrick Hartnett's mother arrived from Listowel and was handed one of the coffins but insisted on opening it, stating, 'I won't want anyone's son, only my own.' One of the coffins was opened and Mrs Hartnett was only able to identify her son by a 'small bit of his black curly head'.[46] She brought his remains back to Lixnaw before his burial the following day at Dysert cemetery. The family of John Daly purchased a new coffin for his remains from John Brosnan, an undertaker in Castleisland, at a cost of £10. A further £3 was spent at J.K. O'Connor's Emporium on a 'hearse, 2 cypresses, and 1 Habit'.[47]

Cumann na mBan members throughout Tralee circulated posters and handbills decrying the deaths at Ballyseedy:

> When Coffins were opened
> Mutilated Corpses were seen by horrified thousands in
>   Kerry
> 'Disgraceful Scenes' (So says an Official F.S. [Free State]
>   Message to the Censored Press)
> The F.S. Murder Gang
> In Future will Cover their Tracks!
> There must be no more Disgraceful Scenes!
> There must be no more Evidence!
> Mutilated Dead will be Buried Secretly!![48]

The funerals which followed prompted an outcry and condemnation of the actions of the Free State Army. As a result, it was decided that, henceforth, prisoners who died in military custody in the Kerry Command areas would be buried by troops where they died rather than in their own parish.[49] The real reason for the order, the republican newspaper *Éire* declared, was to ensure that 'O'Daly and his butchers are given a free hand to murder their prisoners and to cover up the evidence of their butchery.'[50] Meanwhile, the police authorities moved quickly to absolve themselves of any connection with the deaths at Ballyseedy on the basis that it wasn't reported to the Civic Guard in Kerry. The area was under curfew (11 p.m.) at the time and no patrols were undertaken after this hour. 'In any event,' noted the superintendent of Tralee, 'in the Ballyseedy area at that time there were a considerable number of Irregulars, which rendered it unsafe for the Guards to patrol there'.[51]

+++

The explosion at Knocknagoshel indirectly claimed another life before the 'Terror Month' of March 1923 had ended. Acting on information that the casing for the mine used to kill the Free State soldiers had been made in his forge at Knocknagoshel, the army arrested Dan Murphy along with his brother, John 'Coffey' Murphy, on the morning of 23 March. Dan had received a warning from Con Brosnan, a Free State Army officer, that his life was in danger, but he decided to remain at home until the following morning.[52] A group under the command of Lieutenant Jeremiah Gaffney – who would leave a significant impact on Kerry during and after the Civil War – arrived early in the morning, searched the forge and found nothing. Gaffney attempted to shoot John Murphy, but another soldier grabbed the barrel of his rifle and saved John's life.[53] Gaffney and others then marched Dan Murphy through the village to a field close to Barranarig, where the trip-mine explosion had occurred. What followed was witnessed by a young Bridie Lyons, who watched from a distance and described her experience to Pat Butler for his television documentary *Ballyseedy* in 1997.[54] Murphy denied having any involvement in the construction of the mine. He was shot several times and rose briefly onto his elbows before being shot again, this time fatally. His mother, Katie, plugged the twenty-one bullet holes in his body as he was prepared for burial.[55] The bullets had been used on the wrong man: Dan Murphy had not been present when the mine casing was manufactured; it had been made by his brother, John.[56]

+++

The only official refutation of the evidence given at the army inquiry about what happened at Ballyseedy in March 1923 might not have emerged at all, but for the persistence many years later of journalist and publisher Dan Nolan. Nolan, a native of Castle Street, Tralee and a cousin of one of the founding directors of *The Kerryman* newspaper – also Dan Nolan – was managing director of *The Kerryman* until the late 1960s. He founded Anvil Books in 1964, which fulfilled his passion for publishing.

While local lore in north Kerry and beyond was replete with accusations of the premeditated murder of eight republican prisoners at the hands of Free State soldiers in the early hours of 7 March, it was to be many years before any officer formally disowned the official army version of events. Nolan was aware that retired army captain Niall Harrington was contemplating writing an account of his experiences during the Civil War in Kerry. Harrington had spent many years researching what happened in Kerry in 1922–23, but he would never have published his account if not for the persistence of Nolan, whose lengthy correspondence with Harrington is held in the National Library. Nolan recognised the value of an account from a Free State soldier as a counterbalance to Dorothy Macardle's strongly pro-republican *Tragedies of Kerry* published in 1924, which, he remarked, could be quoted 'at length' by many people in Kerry.[57] He was conscious, too, of the need to achieve balance in the Harrington story and provided much information that ensured the final publication offered the perspectives not just of those, like Harrington, who arrived at Fenit on the *Lady Wicklow*, but also many of the combatants on the anti-Treaty side.[58] Nolan, who lived in Dublin in later years, spent much time in contact with IRA men such as Mick McGlynn and Con Casey, and he gathered up an array of republican accounts from the period. Harrington died in 1988, but his book, *A Kerry Landing*, was published by Anvil Books in 1992 with the support of his daughter, Nuala Jordan.

During the writing of the book, a handwritten note contained in Harrington's papers emerged and is the only known record of a Free State Army officer clearly disputing the official account of events at Ballyseedy. It was attached to a copy of the report of the Court of Inquiry, which had been held on 7 April 1923 and was a whitewash investigation into the murders at Ballyseedy and elsewhere. In the note, which is undated, Harrington was explicit and definitive about what had occurred:

> The attached copy of an alleged Court of Enquiry held into the Ballyseedy slaughter is in my personal knowledge, totally untrue. The mine was constructed in Tralee under the supervision of the principal officers, Captains Eddie Ed Flood and Jim Clarke, and with complete knowledge and encouragement of Major Gen Paddy Daly ... Ballyseedy was a reprisal for Knocknagoshel. It was planned and carried out by a group of Dublin Guard officers.[59]

It was not to be the only such premeditated attack on republican prisoners in the county.

CHAPTER 8

'It is a murder gang that is going around'

Daniel Sugrue was a man of divided loyalties. Like so many who felt compelled to join the Free State Army, whether through political conviction, military experience or financial necessity, Sugrue enlisted in October 1922.[1] A tailor from Dominick Street in Tralee, and later living at Brewery Lane in Killarney, he became the tailor for the Free State Army garrison in Killarney, which was based at the Great Southern Hotel.[2] Daniel's wife, Mary, believed that her husband, in joining the army, was defending the recently established Cumann na nGaedheal administration against the anti-Treaty IRA: he had 'the good of his country at heart' and did 'his utmost to prevent the overthrow of the present Government'.[3] But sources from the period suggest Sugrue held a more nuanced attitude towards his role as an army private and the spiral of violence which typified the Civil War in his native county. Sugrue was one of those in the new army, who, if not sympathetic to republicans and their cause, was at least willing to treat opponents and anti-Treaty prisoners with some dignity. Though he had no known involvement in the IRA during the War of Independence, Sugrue may well have known some of those who were in jail in the cellars of the Great Southern Hotel, and he faced the dilemma of many of those in the army in 1922–23 about how to treat those in custody.

Sugrue's actions in the spring of 1923 certainly belie the notion that all Free State soldiers in Kerry treated republican prisoners with universal cruelty and disdain. At a minimum, Sugrue treated prisoners in the Great Southern Hotel with a kindness they were denied by so many of his fellow soldiers. Conditions in the cells were grim: 'the walls were moist and the blankets, the only thing in the cell, were soaking'.[4] In March 1923 Sugrue's superiors discovered that he was smuggling in the occasional bottle of stout to the prisoners, as well as 'what news he could', but had warned them not to reveal his kindness for fear of his life.[5] The decency of Sugrue was unusual and is starkly juxtaposed with accounts of the abuse and torture that took place in the prison cells – one detainee, Tadhg Coffey, was beaten unconscious with an iron poker – often signified by screams heard by local residents in the early months of 1923.[6]

Official records state that on entering the tailor's room in the barracks on the evening of 14 March, Private Sugrue began to 'play with a revolver', which was accidentally discharged, and he was killed instantly.[7] He was attended to by Dr Murphy, the battalion's medical officer, but the gunshot wound proved fatal. Sugrue's widow, Mary – who was left impoverished and 'exhausted' after his death – claimed that no death certificate was issued and the Free State garrison 'took all charge of all funeral arrangements'.[8] In the absence of an inquest, it will never be possible to know precisely what happened to Daniel Sugrue, but other accounts suggest that there was no accident and that he met his death at the hands of his fellow soldiers.[9] A week after his colleagues murdered four IRA prisoners on the outskirts of Killarney, Sugrue appears to have been loose-lipped about what had occurred, and it was alleged that he may have been providing information to republicans.[10] A report prepared for IRA headquarters offers a very different perspective about what happened in the Great Southern Hotel on the evening of 14 March:

> A tailor named Sugrue from Killarney who was working in the Free State Barracks was murdered by an officer there on Wednesday evg [evening] 14th inst. He had been speaking to some of his friends in the town and was explaining how the Prisoners were murdered [at Countess Bridge] and how they were arrested – they were tortured by 14 of the Staters. When he returned to Barracks, he was shot dead. Of course, it appeared in the Press as the usual 'accident!'[11]

The account was supplemented by the testimonies of families, which were gathered by Dorothy Macardle for her book *Tragedies of Kerry*.[12] The death of Private Daniel Sugrue at the hands of his fellow soldiers represented a new and further descent in the downward spiral of indiscipline and violence within the ranks of the Kerry Command, but also exemplified the litany of cover-ups which came to characterise the policy and approach of the Command in the spring of 1923.

+++

Sugrue's death came just a week after another of the atrocities that typified the violence and mayhem of March 1923: the murder of four Republican prisoners on a railway bridge near Killarney. Among them were some of those to whom Sugrue had brought porter in jail before they were executed. Writing two decades after the Civil War, Fionán Lynch, TD for Kerry and a senior figure in the Free State Army which prosecuted the war against the republicans in his native county, noted that the murder of four men at Countess Bridge was 'one of the very tragic incidents of the Civil War in Kerry'.[13] If there was any sense that Ballyseedy would be the extent of Free State Army retribution for the trip mine fatalities at Knocknagoshel, it was shattered just a few hours later. About twenty-four hours after the explosion at Ballyseedy Cross on 7 March, five prisoners – Stephen Buckley, Tim Murphy, Daniel Donoghue, Jeremiah O'Donoghue and Tadhg Coffey – were taken from their cells in the Great Southern Hotel and marched a short distance to Countess Bridge, where officers had placed a mine within a barricade on the road.[14] The soldiers were led by Colonel David Neligan. One of his officers told the prisoners that the barricade was the work of 'the Die-Hards'.[15] Dorothy Macardle recounted what happened, based on interviews with families and witnesses:

> There was a low barricade of stones across the road. They [the prisoners] were ordered to move the stones and throw them inside the fence. They saw a soldier at the far side of the fence bending down. They saw the rest of the soldiers draw the bolts of their guns. The prisoners ran to the barricade and jumped over it: they thought they were to be shot while they were removing the stones. There was a moment's pause. Some of the officers began whispering together and arranging something with the man at the fence. Then, suddenly, the soldiers scattered and ran and threw themselves down under cover. 'My God, lads, this is a death-trap!' [Tadhg] Coffey cried and he bent down to look for a wire. A stone was flung. It must have been a signal. Instantly the explosions came.[16]

Unlike Ballyseedy, the men were not tied to each other or around the barricade which contained the mine before it was detonated. Three of the prisoners were injured but not killed instantly, and Tadhg

Coffey and Jeremiah O'Donoghue crawled away. The soldiers then began to fire upon the prisoners and threw grenades at them. Coffey, the only survivor of the attack, managed to escape and, despite a knee injury, climbed over a high gate and ran about 200 yards along an open road under machine-gun and rifle fire until he outdistanced his attackers; he eventually reached shelter at the home of Jack Moynihan in the parish in Kilcummin several miles away.[17]

The use of prisoners to clear roadway obstructions in which explosives had been placed occurred in south Kerry too. Tensions had been rising in the Cahersiveen area following the deaths of three Free State soldiers in a series of engagements near Gurrane and in the surrounding area just a day before the trip-mine explosion at Knocknagoshel. Free State officers Timothy O'Shea from Cahersiveen, Jeremiah Quane from Ardfert and William Healy from Valentia were killed during a sweep of the area in a search for republicans on 5 and 6 March.[18] The army claimed that republicans fired on a Red Cross ambulance and two local priests as they tended to the wounded.[19] Dan Clifford of the Kerry No. 3 Brigade of the IRA was shot dead in a cow house 'in circumstances that have never been explained'.[20] A large number of IRA members were taken into custody and they were detained at a Famine-era workhouse at Bahaghs, which served as a Free State barracks and prison. A relative of one of the soldiers killed near Gurrane fired a shot through a cell door in the workhouse, injuring one of the republican prisoners, Peter Brady, in the face and hand.[21]

A week later, in the early hours of 12 March, five prisoners were taken from Bahaghs in the middle of the night to clear a barricade on the road nearby. The men were asked, 'Would you like to come for a drive?' and may have assumed they were being transferred to jail in Tralee.[22] Willie Riordan,[23] Daniel Shea, Eugene Dwyer, John Sugrue and Michael Courtney had been arrested while attending a wake and had been brought before a military tribunal a few days before, but they were not made aware of any sentence.[24] A Department of Defence account of the incident claimed that, earlier that day, a party of Free State soldiers on the way from Cahersiveen to their barracks at the workhouse had been 'ambushed' by anti-Treaty forces when they came across a barricade on the road. Having 'beaten off the attackers', they proceeded to the workhouse and brought five prisoners to clear the barricade.[25] No evidence has ever been produced to verify whether the troops were ambushed or that republicans had placed a mine within a barricade on the road, and the claim was subsequently denied in a statement issued by the local IRA brigade.[26]

Reminiscent of what occurred at Ballyseedy and Countess Bridge, the five men were told that they would have to remove the barricade and 'take the chance of it containing a mine'.[27] Unlike Ballyseedy and Countess Bridge, from which two prisoners had escaped, the soldiers present – some of whom were said to be intoxicated – set out to ensure that there would be no such recurrence.[28] Before they were blown up, the five prisoners were shot in the legs. All five were then blown to smithereens, some beyond subsequent recognition.[29] Such was the force of the explosion that some of the soldiers received minor injuries and 'had the overcoats blown off them'.[30] A local doctor and ambulances attended the scene. Early the following morning, two local nurses went to Bahaghs: 'They found clumps of earth and grass flung everywhere and gaps in the road; cartridge cases were lying about. They picked up a chain of rosary beads – it was soaked in blood. They came to the shambles then and saw what it would not be right to describe.'[31]

The remains of the families were initially refused to the families at the workhouse, but following the intervention of the clergy, funerals took place and the five were interred together at Kilnavarnogue graveyard. The army was later forced to deny claims that soldiers had bragged about the killings in a local hotel bar after the incident.[32]

+++

What followed was a blatant cover-up.[33] The immediate political response to the deaths at Bahaghs sought to implicate the victims in their own deaths and to deny any culpability on the part of their assailants. Documents held in the Military Archives and the National Archives, some of which were only released seventy-five years later, betray a concerted effort not only to cover up the actions of Free State Army soldiers, but also to deny the relatives of the deceased any compensation as part of the effort to protect the instigators of the killings.[34] The inquiry into the events at Bahaghs heard claims that the bomb in the barricade had been 'placed there by Irregulars'. Comdt J.J. Delaney claimed he came across a barricade on the road at Bahaghs and took five civilian prisoners from the workhouse to clear it away: 'I told them that mines were being laid and that some of our officers and men had been killed in this way, and that they would have to remove this barricade and take the chance of its containing a mine.' The prisoners, he said, made no objection, but were 'nervous'. The inquiry concluded that 'no blame is attached to any officer or soldier engaged in the operations in which these prisoners lost their lives', and allegations of the mistreatment of prisoners were 'untrue'. Echoing findings which would also be made in relation to both Ballyseedy and Countess Bridge, the inquiry report added that 'in view of the abnormal conditions which have prevailed in this area, and of the inordinate and malignant nature of the fight carried out against the Army in their effort to restore peace, the discipline maintained by the troops is worthy of the highest consideration'.[35] In the Dáil, the Minister for Defence, Richard Mulcahy, justified the actions of his officers by noting that 'efforts were being made by rather numerous groups of Irregulars in the Cahirciveen area to take Cahirciveen out of the hands of our troops'.[36]

Files released by the National Archives in 2008 revealed the truth of what occurred at Bahaghs and exposed the government and army cover-up. A note from a senior official in the Ministry of Home Affairs dismissed the findings of the inquiry and queried why no evidence had been procured from the army garrison at the workhouse. It added that there were discrepancies in the statements of witnesses, whose examination was 'lacking in strength'.[37] Correspondence from the police also vigorously disputed the official version of events based on their own examination of the incident. The Assistant Commissioner of An Garda Síochána, Éamonn Coogan, insisted that the prisoners had been shot and blown up by army officers, writing that 'Evidence of these facts can be procured.'[38] The Secretary of the Department of Justice, Henry O'Friel, believed a full investigation was required and that charges against the relevant officers might be necessary.[39] He suggested to Minister for Justice Kevin O'Higgins that he 'discuss the matter personally' with Minister for Defence Richard Mulcahy, adding: 'There is a paramount duty on the civil authorities in the State to protect the public from military irregularities either by direct action or by representation to the Minister responsible for the Army.'[40]

The government, however, pulled up the drawbridge on the issue. At an Executive Council meeting chaired by W.T. Cosgrave on 22 January 1924, it was decided that if there was 'prima facie evidence of complicity in an attack against the State on the part of an applicant', this was a bar to compensation claims from the families of the deceased and that the onus was on the claimants to provide evidence of allegations of wrong-doing on the part of army officers.[41] No evidence of complicity in any attack was presented in the case of any of these victims. Moreover, the compensation claim of the father of twenty-year-old Daniel Shea – a labourer earning £2 and supporting a family of eight – was dismissed on the grounds that he could not be deemed eligible for compensation because of his involvement with the anti-Treaty IRA in subverting the state. The relatives of the other victims faced similar decisions. Despite appeals from the parish priest of Caherdaniel on behalf the family of Willie Riordan, his father, Maurice, was denied a payment because of 'complicity' with forces opposing the Free State Army in the area.[42] Maurice was later described as a 'waster' in official documents.[43] The Director of Intelligence, Colonel Costello, told Mulcahy that another of those killed, Eugene Dwyer, was engaged in 'Irregular complicity' and no claim from his father should be entertained.[44]

The political and military reverberations continued. Disgusted by what had occurred, the commanding officer at Bahaghs Workhouse, Lieutenant McCarthy, resigned from the army.[45] Dorothy Macardle quotes McCarthy as saying:

> They [the prisoners] were murdered on the road this morning by the men who took them out. I myself am putting in my resignation this night ... There was no attempt to escape, as the prisoners were shot first and then put over the mine and blown up. It was a Free State mine, laid by themselves ... It is a murder gang that is going around trying to keep on the war. We ourselves will support the Free State Government and fight for it, but we will not fight for murder.[46]

Another Free State officer, Niall Harrington, later wrote that the mine used at Bahaghs, as well as those set at Countess Bridge and Ballyseedy, had been 'constructed in Tralee under the supervision of two senior Dublin Guards officers'.[47] They were Commandant J.J. Delaney and Lieutenant Patrick Kavanagh. Harrington sought an immediate transfer from Kerry after the Bahaghs incident, a request that was granted.[48] He was not the only soldier who was apparently disgusted by what had occurred there. Timothy Jones of Killorglin, who had joined the Free State Army in May 1922, requested a discharge: 'I did not feel like soldiering no more,' he wrote.[49]

+++

In the days after the killings at Ballyseedy, Countess Bridge and Bahaghs, the battle for control of information about what had occurred was intense. A telegram for the press, disputing the official account of events, was prepared at the home of Peg Cahill of Cumann na mBan in Killarney.[50] Sinn Féin councillor Kate Breen was arrested at Killarney post office as she tried to send an account of the events at Countess Bridge to the national newspapers.[51] The army also visited Breen's home on the night of the funerals of those killed at Countess Bridge and warned they would 'burn the place'.[52]

The army, meanwhile, sought to save face by holding the official inquiry into the events at Ballyseedy, Bahaghs and Countess Bridge, which has been described variously and accurately as a 'sham', 'monumental charade' and a 'tissue of lies'.[53] Presided over by Assistant Adjutant General Eamonn Price from GHQ, and Major General O'Daly and Colonel Jim McGuinness of the Kerry Command, it was held in Tralee on 7 April 1923 and, as Tom Doyle suggests, 'purported to be an even-handed evaluation of the circumstances' surrounding the deaths of the seventeen republican prisoners.[54] It was anything but. The defence put forward the story that soldiers were merely acting on orders by getting prisoners to move obstructions on the roads, that it had been necessary to use prisoners to remove obstructions on public roads, that the propaganda of those 'Irregulars' about the incident was false and misleading, and that 'the civilians in question lost their lives while removing obstructions on the road, placed there by Irregulars'.[55] In the Dáil a few days later, General Richard Mulcahy reiterated and defended the findings of the inquiry and commended the discipline of his troops in Kerry.[56] He told the Dáil:

> The troops in Kerry have had to fight against every ugly form of warfare which the Irregulars could think of. They have lost 69 killed and 157 wounded, and their record there is such that it is inconceivable that they would be guilty of anything like the charges that are made against them in the Irregular statements which are at the present moment being circulated in profusion in connection with these occurrences. On the other hand, the Irregulars in Kerry have stooped to outrage of every kind.[57]

Before the Dáil adjourned that evening, the Labour leader, Thomas Johnson, insisted on a new non-military tribunal of inquiry into events in Kerry: the recent investigation had alienated many in Kerry who had been 'won over to friendship with the Army and the State'.[58] Johnson insisted he was not listening to anti-Treatyite statements on the matter: his information came also from 'friends of the Government, friends of the Army, friends of the Free State, not from enemies of the Government or the Army or the Free State'. Mulcahy maintained that the Kerry Command had his fullest confidence. Johnson pressed the Minister for Home Affairs, Kevin O'Higgins, about an inquest into the deaths at Ballyseedy, which had not taken place. O'Higgins committed to considering the matter, but efforts to ensure that an inquest be held were rebuffed within government, as department records reveal:

> It is the Coroner's emphatic opinion that an inquest should not be held as the demand for it is solely inspired by people with a view to propagandist purposes and to give local rumour a wider circulation and that if an inquest be at all desirable it should be decided by the question whether [survivor, Stephen] Fuller has any evidence to give.[59]

A report submitted to army headquarters a week after the massacre suggested that Fuller 'has become insane'.[60] Fuller, despite suffering enormous psychological damage for many years, had not gone insane and he did have evidence to give, evidence which would never be heard by any government or army inquiry. It would be almost sixty years later when Fuller, seated in the kitchen of his north Kerry home, gave his evidence, as the BBC's Robert Kee and his cameraman looked on.

+++

The 'Terror Month' of March 1923 claimed thirty-nine lives in Kerry. Twenty-nine republicans died in their native county, among them the seventeen victims of the mine explosions at Ballyseedy, Bahaghs and Countess Bridge. The figure for Kerry republican deaths rises to thirty-two if the execution of Daniel Enright, Timothy O'Sullivan and Charlie Daly (brother of Tom and May Daly) at Drumboe in County Donegal on 14 March are included.[61] Ten Free State soldiers died, among them six who were native to County Kerry, including Paddy 'Pats' O'Connor, Laurence O'Connor and Michael Galvin, who were blown up at Knocknagoshel. Despite the bloodshed and a sense that matters were rapidly spiralling out of the control, the war continued unabated in Kerry. Major Leeson Marshall of Callinafercy dreaded that, if what he heard of the atrocities was true, 'things will get more bitter'.[62] At the end of March, a report to IRA headquarters noted that the number of republican prisoners 'murdered officially and unofficially in Kerry' had reached thirty-three. The writer wondered, in an eerie play on the words of Michael Collins, whether if 'there are more "Stepping-Stones" needed, the list of Martyrs for this County will reach fifty'.[63]

CHAPTER 9

'They'll be executed when we have time'

The farewell dinner held in Killarney on 21 April 1923 was described in the army newspaper as a 'great send-off' and a 'great success'.[1] Though times were 'tough enough down here' in Kerry, the report in *An t-Óglach* continued, 'we find time for a little celebration now and again'. The subject of the send-off was Colonel David Neligan, who had been a central figure in the Kerry Command since the arrival of the Dublin Guard at Fenit in August 1922. Neligan, a key figure in Michael Collins's intelligence network during the War of Independence, was being recalled to Dublin to take up the position of director of intelligence, and his colleagues gathered to pay tribute to his service in Kerry:

> Everyone – military and civilians, were more than anxious to give expression to their appreciation of all 'Dave' had done to 'enforce the will of the people' in Kerry ... Major General O'Daly presented the guest of the evening with a gold watch and chain on behalf of the Officers in the Kerry Command ... It was a splendid but most deserving tribute to one of the finest soldiers in the Army.[2]

Neligan's appointment in later years to the Land Commission infuriated Fianna Fáil activists locally, who accused him of being involved in 'murders at Kerry [*sic*]' towards the end of the Civil War.[3] He worked as a detective in later years with An Garda Síochána, and helped to established the force's Special Branch. His influence in policing in Ireland was 'considerable' for many years.[4] Interviewed in retirement in the early 1970s, Neligan was said to be 'proud of his patriotism. He was clear he had done the right thing for his country,' during his career in the army and the gardaí.[5]

Three days after the farewell dinner, Major General O'Daly prepared a report for army headquarters in which he hailed the 'excellent' morale among the Kerry Command. There was, he wrote, a 'victory smile' on all their faces.[6] Neither Neligan, O'Daly nor other senior ranking officers with the Dublin Guard and the Kerry Command would ever face official sanction for their own actions or those of their colleagues in Kerry. After leaving the army in 1924, O'Daly was awarded a pension of £280 per annum.[7] He worked as an overseer at the governor general's residence in the Phoenix Park and lived in one of the cottages on the grounds with his wife, Brigid, who died in 1930 while giving birth to a stillborn child.[8] He re-enlisted in the army during World War II at the rank of captain. His brother, Frank, who had taken the republican side during the Civil War, also joined the army at the same rank and the two reconciled their political differences in later years. Not so Paddy's sister-in-law Maisey, who found it difficult to speak to him because of his role with the Kerry Command. When she eventually challenged him to explain the explosions and executions, O'Daly said it had been a long time ago and he had no control over his soldiers.[9]

In August 1924, a year after the landing of army forces at Fenit, O'Daly posed with colleagues for an anniversary photograph on Fenit pier. The group included Colonels Jim McGuinness and David

Neligan, as well as the army chief of staff, General Seán McMahon. With the passage of time, Dominic Price has argued, it has become 'a photograph of those responsible for grave misconduct, torture and murder'.[10]

+++

If Neligan's departure for Dublin and what O'Daly believed to be the excellent morale among his troops might have been expected to herald any relaxation or alteration in the military strategy and approach to the anti-Treatyite campaign in Kerry, any such expectations were misplaced. Four days after Neligan's farewell celebration, three more men would face a Free State Army firing squad.

In the middle of April 1923, the final climactic episode in the Civil War in Kerry unfolded on a rugged cliff face overlooking the Atlantic Ocean. Several days after the IRA's Chief of Staff, Liam Lynch, was killed in County Tipperary – ushering in the end of the conflict – three IRA men and two Free State soldiers died in dramatic and controversial circumstances at Clashmealcon in north Kerry, in an incident which made a lasting imprint on the history of the conflict and local folklore.[11] Following engagements between anti-Treatyites and the army, and a gun battle in the townland of Meenagohane, six IRA men decided to hide out at Dunworth's cave on the cliff face near Clashmealcon on the night of 15–16 April. It was as inhospitable a hideout as it was difficult to access, and the men assumed they would be able to evade capture in a place unknown to the Free State forces.[12] They were led by Timothy Lyons, better known by his nickname 'Aero', and the group included Edward Greaney, Thomas McGrath, Patrick O'Shea, James McEnery and Reginald 'Rudge' Hathaway, a former British soldier and Free State Army enlistee who had joined the IRA. Though armed, the men had decided not to take food rations with them.

However, their hiding place quickly became known to the authorities. Jim McGrath, Thomas's brother, who had been arrested during the clashes at Meenagohane, was tortured at Ballymullen Barracks – some accounts suggest he was forced to dig his own grave – and he revealed that there was a hideout at the Clashmealcon caves.[13] On the morning of 16 April, four Free State officers, under Lt Henry Pearson from Limerick, descended the treacherous cliff face and, as they removed a barricade at the cave's entrance, the IRA fired on them: Private James O'Neill was killed instantly, while Pearson was seriously wounded in the leg. O'Neill, who had fought with the Irish Citizen Army in Dublin during the Easter Rising, remained on a beach below the caves for several hours until his remains were removed by the Red Cross.[14] Pearson later died of his injuries.

Burning hay and turf was used in an attempt to smoke the men out of the cave. In the dark, lamps were lowered, but they were shot out by the men inside. Without food and fearing capture, first cousins Patrick O'Shea and Thomas McGrath decided to swim for it in the dark. They were never seen again, nor were their bodies ever recovered. The four remaining men – Lyons, Hathaway, Greaney and McEnery managed to move to an adjacent cave as Free State Army reinforcements arrived. A news report speculated that they were not likely to emerge 'until starved into submission'.[15] Some thirty hours into the siege, Lyons is said to have gestured for a rope to be lowered on condition that the IRA men would be allowed to go free. As Lyons was ascending the rope, which had been lowered by the Free State soldiers just before noon on 18 April, the rope 'either snapped, or was cut, and he fell onto rocks below. While he lay there, he was riddled by machine-gun fire.'[16] The republicans insisted that the rope had been severed deliberately and an IRA report on the incident stated that Lyons was killed by Colonel James McGuinness.[17] Though the official army report on the incident stated that the survivors were 'hauled up by ropes', some sources suggest the soldiers boasted afterwards about having cut the rope.[18] Lyons's body was swept out to sea and washed up on the coast three weeks later, his remains said to be identifiable only by the shoes a local shoemaker had made for him.[19]

At 8 a.m. on 25 April, the three IRA members to survive the siege at Clashmealcon – Reginald Hathaway, Jim McEnery and Ned Greaney – were executed in Tralee. As a deserter from the Free State Army, Hathaway had been singled out for particularly vicious treatment while in custody. Fr Thomas McEnery, a brother of Jim McEnery, returned from England on hearing of the events and of his brother's detention. He was denied access to the jail and was warned he could face charges as an accomplice to murder. Major General Paddy O'Daly told the priest: 'They'll be executed when we have time.'[20] In a final letter to Fr Thomas, Jim McEnery wrote that he was 'proud that I'm dying a soldier of the Irish Republic. I never expected this would be my fate, but welcome be the will of God.'[21] The first that Elizabeth Quinlan, the adoptive mother of Ned Greaney, learned of his death was a letter received from a local officer 'then in charge of the Tralee area'.[22]

These were the last such authorised executions to take place in Kerry. It has been pointed out that the number of executions carried out in Kerry between November 1922 and May 1923 was high, but well below the number in Dublin, for example, where a quarter of the eighty-one executions carried out by the Free State government occurred.[23] Clashmealcon was the 'last epic struggle' of the conflict in Kerry.[24] Two days after the executions, the cessation of hostilities was announced.

+++

The last army soldier killed in the conflict in Kerry was Lieutenant Michael Behan of Marrowbone Lane in Dublin. As he was returning from Currow to Castleisland on 23 April with Lieutenant Jeremiah Gaffney and two Civic Guards, they were forced to remove a tree which was blocking the road. As they did so, they were held up by armed men. In the running fight which followed, Behan was shot and died instantly.[25] Doyle notes that Behan was the seventy-second member of the Free State Army killed in Kerry during the Civil War.[26] Including an estimated fourteen army soldiers who died in accidents and non-combat incidents, the war in Kerry claimed the lives of eighty-six members of the army.[27] The number of fatalities among republicans has been placed at seventy-three.[28] Orson McMahon has identified forty-two IRA members who were the subject of extrajudicial killings.[29] When fourteen civilians who died are included, the entire death toll in Kerry, including combatants and civilians is approximately 173. As Gavin Foster notes, this figure represents a higher death toll in less than one year in Kerry than the entire two and a half years of the War of Independence.[30] With estimates for the national death toll ranging between 1,500 and 2,000, Kerry fatalities, including combatants and civilians, represent somewhere between 8.5 per cent and 11.3 per cent of casualties nationally.[31]

The number of civilian casualties in Kerry between June 1922 and April 1923 is difficult to quantify from official records and newspaper accounts, but Tom Doyle has identified at least twelve non-combatants who died.[32] Three innocent civilians died within two months of each other in Milltown and were literally in the wrong place at the wrong time. Their deaths account for a quarter of all the civilians killed in the county.[33] The first of them was fifty-three-year-old farmer and father of ten, Jeremiah Hanifin, who was standing at his front gate at Knockreigh near Milltown talking to a neighbour, Thomas Quirke, on 23 September 1922.[34] Jeremiah's wife, Julia recounted what happened next:

> A number of National Troops guarding a 'convoy' to Killarney came from the direction of Milltown and turned up a cross-road called Farran Cross. This cross is about 300 yards distant from where my husband was talking to Quirke. The main body of the troops had passed when a shot came from the direction of the Troops and wounded my husband in the stomach from the effects of which he died.[35]

There was no apparent motive for the shooting of Jeremiah Hanifin, but if members of the Free State Army were often trigger-happy, they also sometimes fired indiscriminately when confronted by anti-Treatyites. When a cycle corps of Free State troops was passing through Milltown on 7 November 1922, they were fired upon by republicans. It was recorded that a local man, Jeremiah McKenna, ran at the army patrol with a hatchet and was shot dead outside his home. His mother, Mary, ran to his aid and was shot also. Both died of their injuries.[36]

+++

In April 1923 *The Times* of London claimed that Austin Stack and Éamon de Valera had become 'converts to the peace movement' and that Humphrey Murphy was among those who had been working hard for the acceptance of peace proposals which had been put forward by the Catholic hierarchy.[37] The mortal wounding of the IRA chief of staff, Liam Lynch, in the Knockmealdown mountains in County Tipperary on 10 April focused many minds. Shortly after Lynch was killed, Stack called leaders together to 'sign a statement

[but] they all refused to take the responsibility, despite agreeing that it was "neither politic nor sensible to carry on the war"'.[38] Stack was captured with the document in County Tipperary shortly afterwards: the fact that he was bearing a piece of paper which heralded the ending of the conflict 'probably saved his life'.[39] Three weeks after Lynch's death, on 30 April, de Valera issued an order to the 'Soldiers of the Republic' stating that the Republic could no longer be 'defended successfully by your arms'. Four weeks later, on 24 May, Frank Aiken, Lynch's successor as chief of staff, issued the order to dump arms.

Despite the end of the hostilities, the Civil War was to claim another victim in Kerry, an anti-Treaty leader with direct ties to the tragic massacres of March 1923. Jeremiah O'Leary of Mount, Scartaglin, who had joined the Irish Volunteers 'on the night of the Rising' in 1916, was among those who had constructed the trip mine which killed five Free State soldiers at Knocknagoshel. He was captured at Kilmurray House in Cordal – where the trip mine had been packed with explosives – on 28 May and taken to the barracks at Hartnett's Hotel in Castleisland.[40] The following morning, O'Leary was ordered by an officer to close a gate and was shot in the back while doing so.[41] The official report on the case – redolent of the typical 'shot while trying to escape' misrepresentations of the Kerry Command at the time – claimed that O'Leary was making a run for it while in custody. James O'Leary, who happened to be in Castleisland when his son was killed 'by three officers of Cosgrave's army', met the priest who anointed Jeremiah.[42] With his friend Con Browne, James went to Ballymullen Barracks to retrieve his son's remains. Local women were denied access to wash and dress the body. 'The deceased was my only son,' O'Leary's father later wrote, 'and I relied principally on him for the maintenance of my farm.'[43] His loss, he added, 'was great … it broke up my family altogether'.[44]

James O'Leary would spend many years pleading with successive governments for compensation for his son's death. It was a grim reminder that, though the guns had fallen silent, the death and suffering continued.

CHAPTER 10

'A couple of tarts getting a few lashes'

A knock on the door of a medical doctor's house in the early hours of the morning was not unusual in 1923, even in the days and weeks after the Civil War had ended. Local doctors were used to being available to their patients at all hours of the day and night and, with very limited access to telephones, the only way in which the doctor could be called to tend to a medical emergency in the hours of darkness was to visit his home to rouse him from his sleep. At Dr Randall MacCarthy's home, 'Erinville', in Kenmare, there was an improvised surgery on the first floor where he regularly saw patients.[1] A few minutes before 1 a.m. on Saturday, 2 June 1923, Dr MacCarthy and his household were woken from their sleep by loud banging on the door, which was answered by twenty-one-year-old Florence (Flossie) MacCarthy, the doctor's daughter.[2] A man 'wearing a white mask' rushed in.[3] He flashed a torch in her face and threatened her with a revolver. Two other men entered, one of whom was wearing black goggles and a trench coat. Flossie thought she recognised the first man, despite his mask. He had a Dublin accent. 'Is that you, Captain Flood?' she asked. Edward (Eddie) Flood was an officer in the local Free State Army garrison who had recently danced with Flossie at an army ball. The man didn't respond. Flossie was 'dragged out of the front door, screaming'.[4]

Also roused from her bed, Florence's sister, nineteen-year-old Jessie, was descending the stairs to the hallway as 'a man rushed up the stairs and he caught me by the top of the head and he pulled me down the stairs. When we got to the door, I had a struggle with him. He then put his hand over my mouth and dragged me along the ground outside.'[5] Flossie and Jessie were manhandled and dragged into the garden at gunpoint. They were flogged with a Sam Browne belt across the back, 'with nothing to protect them but their pyjamas'. Flossie stated that her sister was lying on the ground, 'one man standing on her, the other beating her with the Sam Browne belt, which I distinctly saw. The man who was beating her was shouting "Now you will be Free Staters again."'[6] The sisters had 'a thick motor grease' or 'dirty motor oil' rubbed into their hair and faces.[7] The smearing of hair with grease was 'a known toxic formula' akin to tarring.[8] Grease was not only difficult to wash away with water but also caused hair to 'fall out in clumps'.[9] Symbolically, however, the greasing or cutting of hair was designed to humiliate and to mark women out as whores and prostitutes.[10] During the struggle, one of the assailants sustained a cut lip and Jessie 'had a red mark on her face'.[11] Captain Flood is alleged to have said, 'We will plug ye yet.'[12] Jessie scratched one of her assailants on the face. It was claimed that the women were 'black and blue and covered with weals'.[13] It is also alleged that there was a sexual element to the assault: one Free State Army officer, Bill Bailey from Tralee, later claimed that the sisters were raped, though this is the only known such allegation in this case.[14]

When she heard the commotion, the girls' mother grabbed a police whistle in the house and blew it repeatedly, prompting the assailants to flee.[15] Later that morning, army officers visited the scene and discovered a Colt revolver in the grounds of Erinville. It belonged to Major General Paddy O'Daly. That the most senior army figure in the Kerry Command was implicated in the brutal assault on two young women set off a chain of events that contributed to a conspiracy and cover-up at the highest levels of the army and the government, and provided clear evidence that the Kerry Command of the Free State Army remained a law unto itself even in the weeks after the Civil War, when the military conflict had ended.

+++

What could possibly have provoked such a horrific attack on two women in the dead of night? Flossie and Jessie MacCarthy had, it was alleged, been 'friendly with some members of the British Crown Forces' during the War of Independence.[16] This was said to have enraged Paddy O'Daly.[17] The girls subsequently socialised with two local Free State soldiers, Lt Michael Higgins and Capt. Niall Harrington, who later wrote *A Kerry Landing*.[18] The MacCarthys were invited to a dance organised by the Kerry Command, but they declined the invitation, insisting: 'We will not have anything to do with murderers.'[19] This remark may have related to several attacks by the army on the home of the staunchly republican Hartnett family on Main Street in 1922–23, some of whose members were implicated in the murder of the Scarteen brothers a few months previously. They were deliberately targeted by O'Daly and his men, and the Hartnett house and pharmacy was burned on the night of 7–8 December on O'Daly's orders.[20]

O'Daly, embarrassed by the relationship between his soldiers and the MacCarthys, forbade Higgins and Harrington from having any further contact with them, but the soldiers and the sisters

continued to fraternise.[21] Richard Mulcahy's biographer, Pádraig Ó
Caoimh, suggests that what most antagonised O'Daly was a sugges-
tion that Higgins and Harrington had been involved in burning of
the Hartnett home and that Dr MacCarthy had been loose-lipped
about his dislike of their conduct and the conduct of soldiers in the
Kerry Command, much to O'Daly's chagrin.[22]

The women's assailants, according to an investigation by the
Civic Guard, were Captains Jim Clark and Edward Flood, as well
as O'Daly, whose revolver had been discovered at the scene.[23] All
three were identified by another soldier who was on sentry duty
at the army barracks on the night and saw the three men leave.[24]
Captain Flood's initialled goggles, with 'the fur torn on one', were
identified by one of the MacCarthys.[25] Flood fled Kenmare the day
after the assault, with 'scrape marks about his face'.[26] What gave the
accusations against Clark and Flood an added political potency was
the fact that they had been implicated in the massacre at Ballyseedy
and had, according to Harrington, constructed the mine used in the
explosion.[27]

Dr MacCarthy, his daughters and other witnesses were invited to
Dublin on 8 June to a hearing on the matter hosted by State Solicitor
for Kerry Terence Liston and the Civic Guard. Suggesting that intimidation of the witnesses might have occurred if their evidence was
heard in Kerry, Liston was anxious, according to one source, to have
the hearing outside of the county as one of the accused, O'Daly, was
'still in command in Tralee'.[28] The witnesses remained in Dublin for
several days at their own expense.[29] Apart from the investigation
by the Civic Guard, Minister for Defence Richard Mulcahy established a military court of inquiry, which sat at O'Connor Barracks
in Kenmare between 26 and 28 June. Seventeen witnesses gave evidence, including Flossie and Jessie MacCarthy. It was alleged that
one of the sentries on duty at the army barracks on the night of the

assaults was denied the opportunity to testify that he had seen the three accused washing grease from their hands in a tent at the barracks on their return from Erinville.[30] Dr MacCarthy subsequently alleged that soon after the inquiry, one of the sentries 'has since been drowned' and another had gone to Canada.[31] It was also alleged that on the eve of the inquiry, other army personnel who were to give evidence were 'whisked away to distant parts of a country'.[32] The investigating officers found Flood guilty of the charges, but O'Daly and Clark were declared innocent.[33]

The case quickly prompted a full-scale political crisis at the highest levels of government. On being presented with the file on the matter by the army's adjutant general, Gearóid O'Sullivan, Judge Advocate General Cahir Davitt was told, 'This is the worst yet.'[34] Davitt insisted the matter could not be 'hushed up' amid fears that a civil suit by the MacCarthys or a police prosecution of the three soldiers would have a 'disastrous' impact on public opinion. On 3 July 1923, Davitt was asked to prepare court-martial charges against the three and argued for a full court complement of seven senior officers with an army major general as president. Davitt was clearly cognisant of the wider political implications of the case:

> One of the main reasons justifying the commencement of the Civil War was the necessity to stop unlawful interference by force with the rights of ordinary citizens. Here [in the Kenmare case] we had a glaring instance of that kind of conduct inspired by the same sort of mentality. Much blood and money had been expended in putting down 'Irregularism'; was it going to be tolerated in the Army itself?[35]

The answer to Davitt's question was yes. Minister for Defence Richard Mulcahy – who was also commander in chief of the army

– resisted any attempt to convene a court martial, citing O'Daly's military record during the revolution and claiming O'Daly had told him he had nothing to do with the matter.[36] Despite Davitt's protestations, Mulcahy insisted that with so little evidence and such a 'low charge', he was reluctant to degrade O'Daly by making him face such an investigation.[37]

Minister for Justice Kevin O'Higgins was incensed and in a state of 'considerable agitation', not only about what had occurred, but also about Mulcahy's intransigence.[38] O'Higgins, as John M. Regan argues, was disgusted by a crime perpetrated against his 'own caste: a provincial doctor and his family', and was becoming increasingly anxious about the action of soldiers in Kerry; he used the Kenmare case to highlight the phenomenon within government.[39] O'Higgins raised the matter directly with President W.T. Cosgrave on 17 August, writing:

> I feel bound to define my position with regard to the Kenmare scandal. If this case is not dealt with in a perfectly clean straight way, I could not agree to join a future Government and I think it fairer and decenter [sic] to say that now than to wait until such time as the matter might arise in a practical way.[40]

He twice insisted that unless the matter was properly dealt with, he would leave government, but he later withdrew the threat.[41]

The Executive Council decided to seek the advice of Attorney General Hugh Kennedy. His nine-page report prepared for the government and dated 27 September 1923 followed his detailed examination of the case, including the testimony of the seventeen witnesses.[42] The report oozes misogyny, hypocrisy, arrogance and 'latent snobbery'.[43] It betrays not only a clear attempt on the part of the government to portray the MacCarthy sisters as somehow deserving of their fate, but is also indicative of the tolerance at the highest levels of criminal behaviour on the part of the army in County Kerry. Kennedy accepted that the girls' hair had been greased, as this had been corroborated by other witnesses. But in respect of their physical injuries, he noted that there had been no 'independent medical examination' and the case rested on the girls' evidence only. Nor had they sought medical attention, which was peculiar given their claim that they had been 'very badly beaten and severely bruised'. Kennedy seemed to ignore the fact that the girls' father was a medical doctor, adding:

> It is said that these girls were in their pyjamas and it is positively asserted by one of the girls that one of the men stood on her sister. The men were fully dressed apparently, with boots on and it is perfectly obvious that if an average man, fully dressed, stood in his boots on the body of a girl attired in pyjamas, the physical consequences would have been such as to render medical and surgical treatment for a prolonged period absolutely necessary.[44]

It was in considering the character of the victims, however, that Kennedy's scorn for the MacCarthys was most apparent:

> They are not city people ... We all know the type of Catholic bourgeoisie which existed in Irish country towns and villages under the British regime ... This group had distinctly British leanings ... [British soldiers] were cultivated by the ladies of this social type ... many of the girls of this social stratum were easy associates ... It seems clear that the MacCarthys were of this type ...[45]

Kerry Sinn Féin councillor Albinia Brodrick (right) who heckled Fionán Lynch TD during the Dáil debate on the Treaty, pictured with Mary MacSwiney TD. (Courtesy of University College Dublin Archive)

Members of the anti-Treaty IRA take control of Ballymullen Barracks in Tralee in January 1922. (Courtesy of Martin Moore)

First Southern Division delegates at the IRA Convention at the Mansion House, Dublin, 9 April 1922, including Kerry delegates Tadhg Brosnan, Tom Daly, Tom McEllistrim, Dan Mulvihill, Denis Daly, John Joe Rice and Humphrey Murphy.
(Courtesy of Kilmainham Gaol Museum/OPW, KMGLM.20PC-1A26-22)

Brigadier General Fionán Lynch with Michael Collins in Tralee in August 1922.
(Courtesy of the Lynch family)

Fionán Lynch TD (second from right) and W.R. English-Murphy, head of the Kerry Command (right) with senior Free State Army officers including Eoin O'Duffy (fourth from left). (Courtesy of National Library of Ireland)

Captain Ned Breslin, Kerry Command, Free State Army. (Courtesy of South Dublin Libraries/Brophy Collection)

Colonel David Neligan, Kerry Command, Free State Army.

Free State Army soldiers disembark from the *Lady Wicklow* at Fenit on 2 August 1922. (Courtesy of the *The Kerryman* Archive)

Free State Army soldiers in Listowel in August 1922. (Courtesy of National Library of Ireland)

Free State soldiers marching in Listowel in August 1922. (Courtesy of National Library of Ireland)

Niall Harrington, an officer in the Kerry Command of the Free State Army and author of *A Kerry Landing*.

Brigadier General Tom O'Connor Scarteen, killed in Kenmare on 9 September 1922.
(Courtesy of the O'Connor-Scarteen family)

Unidentified Free State soldiers in east Kerry in 1922.
(Courtesy of the Daniel Dennehy Collection, Military Archives)

Group of Free State Army soldiers in Kerry from the album of J.J. Greene.
(Courtesy of National Library of Ireland)

Members of the Free State Army in Kerry *c*. 1922 including John 'Jack' Lynch (back, centre), later a Fine Gael TD for Kerry North.
(Courtesy of the Lynch family, Listowel)

Republican prisoners in Tralee Jail in 1922.

Austin Stack, Sinn Féin TD for Kerry 1919–27.
(Courtesy of the Stack family)

Major General Paddy O'Daly, head of the Kerry Command of the Free State Army from January 1923. (Courtesy of South Dublin Libraries/Brophy Collection)

Unidentified Free State Army soldiers pictured at Rathmore Railway Station.
(Courtesy of the Daniel Dennehy Collection, Military Archives)

Clockwise from top left: James McEnery, IRA, who was executed following the siege at Clashmealcon Caves in April 1923; Tom McEllistrim, Kerry No. 1 Brigade, IRA, and TD for Kerry 1923–69; Dan Mulvihill, Kerry No. 2 Brigade, IRA, who said, 'There was no middle path during the Civil War'; John Joe Rice, Officer Commanding Kerry No. 2 Brigade, IRA and Humphrey Murphy, Officer Commanding Kerry No. 1 Brigade. (Rice and Murphy courtesy of Kilmainham Gaol Museum/ OPW, KMGLM.20PC-1A26-22)

Soldiers survey the damage to a train which was derailed near Ardfert in January 1923 causing the death of two railway workers.
(Courtesy of the Irish Railway Record Society)

Members of Killorglin Cumann na mBan.
(Courtesy of Killorglin Archive Society)

Clockwise from top left: Joan O'Brien of Cahersiveen Cumann na mBan, who went on hunger strike in 1923; Jeremiah (Jer) O'Leary, IRA, who was shot dead in Castleisland in May 1923; Johnny 'Machine Gun' Connor, IRA, Farmer's Bridge; James Daly, IRA, Killarney, who was executed in January 1923; Cornelius (Con) Lucey, IRA, Caragh Lake.

Stephen Fuller (right), the only survivor of the Ballyseedy massacre, campaigning in the 1938 general election.

Stephen Buckley, killed at Countess Bridge on 7 March 1923.

Jessie (left) and Flossie MacCarthy who were assaulted by Free State Army soldiers at their home in Kenmare in June 1923. (Courtesy of Patsy Healy)

The attitude of the most senior legal officer in the land was that if the MacCarthy sisters were perceived 'not as innocent, respectable women in their home who were violated but instead [as] the sort of ladies that embarrass Ireland by consorting with soldiers, therefore what happens to them isn't a crime but a punishment, then it becomes okay not to seek justice'.[46] Kennedy did accept that the greasing of the girls hair had been 'a shameful outrage' but concluded that accusations of a flogging were not 'credible'.[47] There was 'not one shred or tittle of evidence' against O'Daly and Clark, and that evidence against Flood was of the 'flimsiest and contradictory' character.[48] As neither the army nor the government could or should pursue a prosecution of Captain Flood, Kennedy suggested that the MacCarthys could pursue a civil case for assault, though he noted they had taken no such initiative, adding: 'I do not anticipate that any more will be heard of the matter.'[49]

The Executive Council met the following day. If the attorney general needed an advocate for his position, he found it in Minister for Finance Ernest Blythe, whose attitude was, in the words of Diarmaid Ferriter, 'dripping in misogyny'.[50] Blythe believed that 'no great harm was done' and 'the outrage was more an indignity than anything else'. It seemed to him that it was merely a case of 'a couple of tarts getting a few lashes'.[51] Kevin O'Higgins and Richard Mulcahy engaged in 'bitter exchanges' on Kennedy's report. At one point during a meeting of the government, O'Higgins rose and walked out of the meeting, refusing to attend cabinet meetings for several days. Kennedy was asked to draft a letter to Dr MacCarthy, in which Cosgrave suggested that the family could initiate legal proceedings of their own if they so wished.[52] There would be no formal inquiry.

+++

Later that summer, Dr MacCarthy's wife and daughters were at the cinema when two army officers, one of whom was drunk and was a brother-in-law of one of the assailants, came in and sat behind them. The intoxicated officer whispered to the MacCarthy sisters: 'What oil do you use for your hair? Is it motor grease?'[53] The incident prompted the family to leave Kenmare for a break in England as Flossie and Jessie, who had endured 'mental torture', were 'unable to sleep and were in constant dread of other attacks at night'.[54] Several years later, the family were still pursuing their campaign for justice. In 1927 there was an angry exchange of letters between Dr MacCarthy, who was a supporter of Cumann na nGaedheal, and Kevin O'Higgins. MacCarthy insisted again that justice had not been done. He had gone to Dublin with his daughters to be interviewed by the state solicitor in 1923, and four years later still had related out-of-pocket expenses which had not been paid: 'When I see your title [Minister for Justice] as above I wonder what justice you meted out to me and mine. It is now over 3½ years since 3 prominent officers of the Free State Army brutally assaulted my daughters and up to this no compensation has been tendered by you …'[55]

MacCarthy alleged that witnesses at the inquiry were threatened by O'Daly that they would be 'done in' at Brennan's Glen [near Killarney]. Most controversially MacCarthy warned O'Higgins:

The beating of my daughters was not an isolated case of the General's bravery – he stripped and painted several girls in Killarney – and many other acts of the hero have come to my knowledge. Yes, I waited over three years hoping that I might get some justice from the Free State Government when it was established but my hopes were in vain.[56]

+++

Dr Randall MacCarthy's quest for justice was never satisfied, but the case highlighted a phenomenon of significant levels of violence against women during the Civil War in Kerry. The assault on the MacCarthy sisters was by no means a stand-alone or unusual episode. Accounts from the period point to regular assaults on women who were members of Cumann na mBan, relatives of IRA combatants, or were perceived to be either friendly or sympathetic to the republicans or antagonistic to the Free State Army. The type of assaults which were often committed during the War of Independence, invariably involving beatings, hair-cropping and the humiliation of women, continued to be a feature of the Civil War in Kerry.

In September 1922 the *Irish Independent* reported on an incident in Killarney – to which Dr MacCarthy had referred – in which a group of women were stripped and smeared with paint: 'On Friday night last the residences of six young ladies in the town, who are known to have sympathy with the Irregulars, were visited by armed and masked men. Finding the young ladies in bed, the raiders painted their bodies with green paint.' The report offered little else by way of detail but added that the outrage was 'universally condemned' and that Major General Paddy O'Daly – who led the assault on the MacCarthy sisters in Kenmare nine months later – 'has promised to mete out extreme measures to the culprits'.[57]

Schoolteacher Kathleen Walsh and her sisters were also on the receiving end of army brutality. Walsh had penned the note which was sent to Hartnett's Hotel in Castleisland in March 1923 to lure the soldiers to the trip mine hidden at Barranarig Wood. After her role in the incident was discovered, Walsh and her sisters, Bridie, Joan and Eileen, were tortured by Free State Army officers and their hair cropped.[58]

The pension applications of members of Cumann na mBan in Kerry provide ample evidence of physical abuse by Free State soldiers and, occasionally, even if not explicitly stated, assaults which appear to have had a sexual motive or component. At the beginning of 1923, Bridget O'Sullivan of Ballineanig in Ballyferriter was dragged from her home in early hours of the morning because it was known that she had 'information in connection with the boys' in the local IRA. On the last Saturday of January, at 1 a.m., 'they took me out of my bed in my night dress, the wettest night that ever came and took me a few hundred yards from my house and abused me, twisted my hands and beat [me], endeavouring to find out where the boys had their dug-out. Although I knew, I did not tell.'[59]

After Ellie Cotter's brother in the IRA was arrested on 7 January 1923, anti-Treaty fighters no longer stayed at her home at Dromada in Knocknagoshel, but they occasionally came for food. The house was raided twice and Ellie claimed that she was threatened with a gun 'to the jaw' in an effort by Free State soldiers to extract information about the location of an arms dump: 'They offered to release my brother if we'd show them the dump. One of them tapped me in the Chest with a revolver and another Stater put the revolver to my jaw wanting me to give away the dumps.'[60] Mary Barron of Ballyduff often accommodated men overnight, including Timothy 'Aero' Lyons. She helped a man called Paddy Healy escape to safety and claimed she was questioned by members of the Free State Army about Healy and was 'roughly handled'.[61] Katie Mannix of Cordal 'was beat[en] by two Free State soldiers in Castleisland'.[62]

Tending to the wounded and the dying also made targets of women. Annie Mary O'Connor's decision to tend to the wounded Jack Galvin, who was shot dead at Ballyseedy in September 1922, was followed by much abuse from local soldiers. While trying to get word to local IRA commanders, 'I was ill-treated by a Free State Colonel (name supplied if necessary) who tried to get information from me ...' Annie and her family were 'continually, indeed almost daily harassed by Free State soldiers'.[63]

That soldiers were sometimes under the influence of alcohol is a feature of many testimonies. Lizzie O'Donnell and Nora Brosnan were arrested and taken to the local schoolhouse in Castlegregory, where the 'Free State troops kept coming in, some of them in a very drunken condition and we were in terror of our lives as they had guns on every side of us.'[64] When they were placed on a boat to Fenit, there were only 'a lot of drunken soldiers with us'. Drunkenness as a feature of violence was frequently used to vilify the Kerry Command. One IRA report from the time spoke of a Free State officer in the county as 'having all the earmarks of a drunkard, the traitor, the wife-beater, the tramp, the tinker and the brute'.[65] Even the Kerry Command itself admitted at one point that it had managed to reduce alcohol consumption and drunkenness in the ranks by three-quarters, but it does not provide a reference point for what it had been theretofore.[66]

The case of the MacCarthy sisters would not be the only legacy incident in Kerry in the months after the Civil War. Two other tragic episodes in the autumn and winter of 1923 offered a reminder of the deep scars which endured, and how febrile and toxic the situation remained.

CHAPTER 11

'Have a heart: love a die-hard'

Twenty-two-year-old Hannah O'Connor was in 'the midst of gaiety' as she made her way home from a dance in Glenbeigh in the early hours of 2 September 1923.[1] The farmer's daughter had earlier walked from her home at Lickeen, in rural Glencar, to enjoy music and dancing with her friends. The Civil War had been over for several months and social occasions such as dances and other gatherings had been taking place with increased frequency as largely peaceful times prevailed. After spending about an hour and a half at the dance, Hannah left with two cousins, as well as a young soldier, Sgt Jim Shea, who was off duty for the night.[2] When the group encountered three other Free State Army officers on the road, they engaged in conversation with them: they were 'all joking'.[3] One of the trio remarked to Sgt Shea that he had a lot of girls with him, to which Shea replied, 'They are all Free State girls.' Hannah O'Connor replied, 'No, I'm a Die-Hard ... Have a heart; love a Die-Hard.' One of the soldiers, Lt John Hunter, a member of the Armoured Car Corps with the Kerry Command of the army, drew his revolver and a shot was discharged.[4] O'Connor was shot in the abdomen and died the following day.

The jury at the inquest decided that it had not heard sufficient evidence to satisfy itself whether the shooting was accidental or intentional. At trial, Lt Hunter entered a guilty plea and expressed regret, insisting that he believed his weapon was not loaded. Prosecution counsel admitted that O'Connor's remarks 'had no political significance' but was rather 'a cant in the neighbourhood'. The prosecution decried the 'loose use of firearms' as a matter 'that those in authority should carefully see to'.[5] Finding Hunter guilty of manslaughter rather than murder, the jury acknowledged that he had helped in getting the injured girl to a doctor and had accompanied her to Killorglin where she spent the night. Mr Justice Pim bound Hunter to the peace for three years. While the evidence and verdict amounted to an acceptance of Hunter's account of events, and the incident had all the appearances of an unfortunate accident, the political undertones to the case were apparent, which was indicative of the tensions in the county in the months after the Civil War, and the rancour and bitterness they had engendered. The killing of Hannah O'Connor would not be the only such death in Kerry in the months after the conflict, and the maintenance of law and order remained a significant challenge and problem in the county.

The establishment and normalisation of the Civic Guard – which became An Garda Síochána in August 1923 – in communities across the country was a key priority. In his history of the force, Conor Brady notes that it was not universally accepted in counties such as Kerry – officers attending Mass in Rathmore were spat at by a girl in the congregation. Brady attributes much of the success in the bedding down of the new force in counties like Kerry to Commissioner Eoin O'Duffy.[6] In September 1923, for example, the commissioner – who would come to have a long and difficult relationship with the people of Kerry – visited Ballybunion, 'at one time one of the most disturbed districts in Kerry', and complimented his officers on their 'knowledge of police duties and general proficiency'.[7] In October 1923 the Kerry Division of the Civic Guard reported to O'Duffy that 'the greatest respect for the Courts and the Garda prevails', despite the fact that over half of the litigants in the local courts at the time were 'of Republican sympathies'.[8] The Civic Guard had been singled out by the local IRA as a legitimate target, however. In a proclamation issued by Humphrey Murphy following the establishment of the force, he described it as 'a continuance of the RIC' and instructed that, from 1 January 1923, measures would be taken 'to prevent this body from functioning'. Members were warned to leave the force to avoid assisting 'the enemies of the Republic'.[9]

The sinister warning manifested itself dramatically before the end of 1923. The sensational murder of a member of An Garda Síochána in rural east Kerry in December – and the subsequent and related murder of a local civilian – sent shock waves through Kerry, as well as the police and government. Twenty-two-year-old James Woods, a native of Lisdoonvarna in County Clare, was the first garda sergeant killed in the line of duty following the establishment of An Garda Síochána.[10] He had joined the force in November 1922 and been posted to the new garda station established in the village of Scartaglin in May the following year. The station was part of the house occupied by Jeremiah Lyons and his family and, until December 1923, relations between the five gardaí and the local community 'were of the most friendly character'.[11] Woods was described as 'exceedingly popular' and was not 'over-zealous' in his duties.[12]

On the evening of Monday 3 December, two garda officers were out on patrol when, at about 8 p.m., six armed men whose faces were blackened in disguise entered the station at Scartaglin. Garda Spillane, who was on duty with Sgt Woods, was ordered upstairs and told to remove his clothes.[13] The assailants broke open garda boxes in the room, from which they retrieved uniforms and money. Alerted to the commotion, Sgt Woods left the day room and was quickly ordered up the stairs. An official report detailed what happened next:

> The Sergeant in compliance with this order put his hands up, and proceeded to go up the stairs, when he was on the second step ... he was struck on the back with the muzzle of the rifle by the man who had ordered him upstairs ... a shot rang out and the Sergeant fell dead, shot through the head.[14]

The Liberator newspaper described how Woods' skull 'was split in twain'.[15]

The authorities initially believed that robbery was the motive of the assailants and that the killing of Sgt Woods was not intentional or necessarily politically motivated. The death of Woods prompted a series of furious reprisals in the locality, however. A party of Free State soldiers under the command of Lt Jeremiah Gaffney was dispatched from Tralee to investigate. Gaffney had something of a notorious reputation and had, just a few months previously, been involved in raiding the home of a local man and firing shots over his head.[16] As Gaffney and his men conducted a sweep of Scartaglin the day after the shooting of Woods, they were drawn to the O'Connor home at Dromulton, where there were 'five men sleeping'. The men were dragged into the yard and a young servant boy, Con Horan, was shot in the back but not killed. During the melee, Mrs O'Connor and her daughter Alice were injured by being repeatedly struck with the butts of the soldiers' rifles. Alice's teeth were loosened when she was repeatedly slapped in the face.[17] Lieutenant Gaffney, described as smelling of whiskey, visited the garda barracks, telling Garda Spillane that he had '"creased" a couple of fellows' at Dromulton.[18]

The wounding of Con Horan prompted many residents in the locality to flee their homes in fear.[19]

With no arrests in the immediate aftermath of the death of Sgt Woods, and amid accusations that the perpetrators were republicans, the local IRA leadership was forced to publicly deny any knowledge of the attack or attackers. Writing to the *Irish Independent* and other newspapers, the O/Cs of Kerry I and II Brigades, Humphrey Murphy and John Joe Rice, sympathised with Woods's family and repudiated any allegation that any 'Republican soldier was implicated in the crime' or that 'hidden arms' were used in the attack.[20] The local and national press roundly condemned the murder, insisting that it was the 'bounden duty of the Free State Government to leave no stone unturned to trace the authorship of crimes which must shock civilisation'.[21] At Sgt Woods's graveside, Commissioner Eoin O'Duffy promised that his 5,000 officers would remain undaunted and 'yield only in death'.[22]

Gaffney and his fellow officers had not completed their reprisals in Scartaglin, however. Three days after Woods died, nineteen-year-old Thomas Brosnan was found shot dead on the roadside a short distance from his home in the village.[23] Brosnan was a dispatch carrier and intelligence officer with the local IRA.[24] He was shot six times in the back with a 'Peter the Painter' gun by a group of soldiers led by Gaffney. The soldiers had been drinking whiskey in the pub owned by Brosnan's father, Cornelius, before they proceeded to kill Thomas.

The attack on the boy prompted as much confusion as it did revulsion. It was suggested by Kerry gardaí that Brosnan was certainly 'friendly with the Civic Guards' but was also 'playing a double game' and was in league with 'the irregular element'.[25] Gaffney also believed Brosnan was 'in possession of certain information as to the perpetrators of the murder' of Sgt Woods.[26] Other accounts suggest there was a more personal matter at play and that Brosnan was targeted by Gaffney because of a row between the Brosnan family and the lieutenant over Gaffney's relationship with a member of the extended Brosnan family.[27] The Brosnan family would be denied compensation for their son's death: the authorities concluded that there was insufficient evidence to prove Thomas Brosnan's active service with the IRA, an essential eligibility requirement.[28] Regardless of the motive, the murder highlighted the fact that 'army indiscipline and extrajudicial killing in Kerry continued long after the civil war had officially ceased'.[29]

Lt Gaffney and six army soldiers – Michael Shea, Denis Leen, Robert McNeill, Daniel Brosnan, Michael (Micky) Shea and James McCusker – were questioned by their superiors in connection with the murder of Brosnan. Leen absconded and was arrested in Liverpool en route to Canada.[30] McNeill was immediately discharged from the force after being quizzed about the murder.[31] He appears to have objected to Gaffney's killing of Brosnan and the real cause of his discharge was believed to be his refusal at the time to 'perform obnoxious duties'.[32] Gaffney dramatically escaped from custody while being detained in Tralee but was subsequently arrested in Dublin with the assistance of Major General Paddy O'Daly.[33] Commissioner O'Duffy, who visited Scartaglin soon after the murders, was furious that Gaffney had escaped and suspected the connivance of a garda inspector in Tralee.[34] Gaffney was found guilty of the murder of Thomas Brosnan and hanged by the British hangman, Albert Pierrepoint in Mountjoy Prison in March 1924.[35] Private Denis Leen was also found guilty and sentenced to death, but was subsequently reprieved and his sentence commuted to penal servitude for life.[36]

The fact that two senior soldiers were tried and one executed represented something of a shift in the approach to army outrages

in Kerry and stood in stark contrast to the cover-ups which typified
Bahaghs, Countess Bridge, Ballyseedy and elsewhere. But a residual
indiscipline and sense of untouchability among many senior officers remained. A critical report on the murder of Thomas Brosnan,
which was co-authored by local District Justice Richard Johnson,
State Solicitor for Kerry Terence Liston and Chief Superintendent
James Hannigan, concluded that Brosnan had no connection with
the killing of Sgt Woods. In a damning indictment of the army, it
concluded: 'The conduct and attitude of the Officers of the 7th
Infantry Battalion ... has been such that we believe their removal
from this area would be in the interest of the peace and good order
of this County.'[37]

Six men, meanwhile, were arrested in connection with the murder of Sgt Woods: Daniel Casey, Paddy Óg Lyons, John Kelly, Tim
Riordan, Denis Nolan and Con Cronin. Local gardaí also suspected
the involvement of others, including Michael Healy, Tim Healy, Denis
Sullivan, Lawrence Kelly and Edward Marshall, and concluded that
the 'plot was hatched' at the home of Paddy Óg Lyons.[38] There were
allegations that the accused, prior to their detention, had called to
people in the locality and 'warned them not to mention their names'
in connection with the outrage.[39] Of those arrested, Tim Riordan
was released immediately, and the five others, who were detained
in Cork Gaol, protested their innocence. Daniel Casey, for example,
insisted that he could prove he was elsewhere when the shooting
occurred.[40]

There was a sustained local campaign in support of those jailed.
A sister of Lyons implored the Minister for Justice to sanction his
release, insisting that even 'the staunchest Government supporters in
East Kerry consider his treatment hard and unjust'.[41] Professor John
Marcus O'Sullivan, a Cumann na nGaedheal TD for Kerry, queried
whether there was 'any evidence' against Lyons and argued that

local opinion held that he had no role in the killing of Sgt Woods.[42] A peace commissioner who visited the prisoners in Cork Gaol added that each protested their innocence and that Lyons' farm at Knockreigh, Scartaglin 'is going to ruin, during his internment' and that all of the men were willing to swear they had 'never fired a shot'.[43]

The garda case gradually unravelled amid efforts by the local gardaí to continue to detain the five prisoners without issuing charges, while other suspects remained at large. In July 1924 one of those arrested, Denis Nolan, was deemed not guilty by local police.[44] Another suspect, Lawrence Kelly, was released from custody: the Labour leader, Thomas Johnson, insisted his detention following a raid on his home without a warrant was 'very irregular'.[45] Garda Commissioner Eoin O'Duffy was censured by the Department of Justice and warned that gardaí should 'submit all the facts in their possession' when seeking internment orders from the department.[46] In January 1925 Michael Healy of Knocknagree on the Cork–Kerry border, a lieutenant in the anti-Treaty IRA, went on trial at the Central Criminal Court for the attack on Scartaglin Garda Station. He was identified by Garda Spillane by his aquiline nose and broad build.[47] But the charge before the court was one of armed robbery, which he denied, and not murder. Healy was acquitted.[48] Nobody was ever prosecuted for the murder of Sgt James Woods.

CHAPTER 12

'Wipe them out for once and for all'

Dorothy Macardle paused before stepping into the kitchen of the Shea family in their small cottage at Islandboy on the slopes of Inny Valley near Waterville in rural south Kerry. It was the spring of 1924 and the family were still mourning the death of their second eldest child, Daniel (Dan), one of the five republican prisoners blown up and killed by the Free State Army at Bahaghs on 12 March 1923. His parents, James and Mary Shea, welcomed the stranger who had come from Dublin to interview them about what had happened for her book on the darkest days of the Civil War in Kerry, which would be published at the end of 1924. A republican activist and journalist, Macardle had travelled to Kerry to meet with the families of republicans who died during the conflict and to record their experiences. If she was a stranger to the Sheas, Macardle was no stranger to the worst excesses of Free State Army brutality in Kerry. When Tadhg Coffey, the only survivor of the Countess Bridge atrocity escaped to Dublin after the war, he was supported and looked after by Macardle and Countess Markievicz, who sought medical treatment for his injuries.[1]

Macardle's *Tragedies of Kerry* became not only the first published book on the Civil War in Kerry, but also a totemic reference point for the republican narrative of the war. Despite the fact that, as Macardle's biographer Leanne Lane has noted, the book was 'highly fictionalised' in places, it represents a valuable contemporaneous account of what Macardle herself described as the story of 'some of the soldiers of the Republic, men of Kerry, who, during these months, met with lonely and violent deaths'.[2] She innovatively used not just the personal stories of those who died, but also published photographs of their relatives, particularly those of the mothers of those killed, including, for example, the mother of Timothy 'Aero' Lyons who died at Clashmealcon, and the mother of Stephen Buckley, blown up at Countess Bridge. This approach was indicative of Macardle's efforts to highlight the brutality towards women at this time and the invasion of the domestic space by enemy forces.[3] 'Shea's mother, father and two young sisters stare out of the photograph,' explains her biographer, 'forcing the reader to contemplate the manner in which whole families were affected by the violence against republicans in the county.'[4]

The most evocative and vivid descriptions in *Tragedies of Kerry* were reserved for the Ballyseedy massacre. Macardle charted what happened to Stephen Fuller when the mine was detonated:

> He turned over; he was not hurt; he was lying under a ditch in the wood. His clothes were scorched and torn to shreds … The soldiers had no means of counting their victims. They went back to their breakfast and Stephen Fuller crawled away to safety over the fields. The military thought him dead; his name was on one of the nine coffins which they sent out.[5]

It was another of Macardle's dramatic descriptions of this event which resonated even further, however, and became a mantra for evoking the extent to which the depths of depravity had been plumbed in the spring of 1923. For days after the explosion, she added: 'the birds were eating the flesh off the trees at Ballyseedy Cross'.[6]

Macardle's macabre and chilling evocation was used to great effect by another republican writer, Ernie O'Malley – who spent years collecting the stories of combatants – to illustrate the attitude of the Roman Catholic Church to events in Kerry and across the country in 1922 and 1923. 'The thundering pulpits,' O'Malley wrote, 'were strangely silent about what the crows ate in Kerry.'[7]

O'Malley's cynical claim had a ring of truth to it. The prevailing attitude in the hierarchy of the Catholic Church in Ireland and in Kerry during this period was one of vocal and vehement hostility towards those on the anti-Treaty side. Reassured by the relative stability which the new State had brought – and with it the restoration of the place and status of the Catholic Church in Irish society – the Church aligned itself politically to Cumann na nGaedheal and strongly supported the Anglo-Irish Treaty.[8] The Bishop of Kerry, Dr Charles O'Sullivan, was vocal in his support for the Treaty from the outset. In his Lenten Pastoral in March 1922, he hailed the agreement as making 'the Irishman a master in his own house', adding that it would enable Ireland to 'renew our old and highly developed Gaelic civilisation'.[9] O'Sullivan, a native of Ballyfinnane and a cousin of Professor John Marcus O'Sullivan, the Cumann na nGaedheal TD for Kerry from 1923, remained a strong supporter of the government of W.T. Cosgrave. When the president visited Tralee during the 1923 general election campaign, O'Sullivan published a letter welcoming him to Kerry and emphasising the need for 'stable and national government'.[10]

Before the outbreak of the Civil War, support for the Treaty and its political advocates was also evident among the clerical rank and file. As the debates on the Treaty came to a head in Dáil Éireann, the senior ranks of the Catholic Church in Kerry were setting out their official position on the matter. At a meeting held in the grounds of the cathedral in Killarney on New Year's Day 1922, Fr P.J. Fitzgerald advised parishioners that 'if the Treaty is rejected, there seems to be no alternative but to return to the warfare, bloodshed and strife through which we passed before the coming of the Truce'.[11] Fr Fitzgerald's comments were a neat summation of both the dilemma and the position in which the Catholic Church found itself after the War of Independence, during which its authority and power had been challenged by the turmoil and mayhem of war. With that conflict now ended, the Church sought to re-establish its political and pastoral influence through ensuring the restoration of the essential ingredient for the exertion of that power – stability. The 'return to warfare' – either between the IRA and the Black and Tans, or between the pro- and anti-Treaty IRA – therefore, could not be countenanced. Those who would take up arms against the Treaty in Kerry, and thereby threatened the new stability and homogeneity in which a powerful Church could operate, would face the full wrath of the majority of clerics from the pulpits in the years ahead.

Clerical support for the Free State government and the Treaty manifested itself, too, at public meetings. Canon Browne of Cahersiveen welcomed Fionán Lynch to a pro-Treaty rally in March 1922, appealing to parishioners to support the government.[12] The parish priest of Listowel led his parishioners in calling on Kerry TDs to vote in favour of the Treaty.[13] In private, too, the Church in Kerry nailed its political colours to the mast. In a letter to Deputy Piaras Béaslaí days after he had spoken in favour of the Treaty, Bishop O'Sullivan commended his local TD: 'Allow me to convey to you an expression of huge appreciation of your speech on the Treaty. In letter and in spirit, to my mind, it left nothing to be desired. I feel, I can say, with truth, that it expressed the sentiment and convictions of 95% at least of the people of Kerry.' The bishop concluded by quoting Abraham Lincoln at Gettysburg: 'We here highly resolve that these dead shall not have died in vain, that this nation, under God, shall have a new birth of freedom, and that government of the people, by the people, for the people, shall not perish.'[14]

During the Civil War, members of the clergy in Kerry were increasingly hostile towards republicans, often using the pulpit to condemn the chaos and murder which the IRA was causing in the face of efforts to build the new State in a safe and secure manner. Cumann na mBan members also came in for plenty of condemnation. Fr Maurice Costello, the curate in Listowel, insisted they were 'immoral'.[15] Lady Gordon, who lived near Killorglin, recalled:

> For several Sundays, the priest denounced our local Republicans as murderers and thieves, apparently without greatly disturbing their susceptibilities. Eventually he alluded to them as *bosthoons* (an untranslatable Irish term of contempt). A fusillade of shots fired round his house at night showed that the thrust had gone home … at the reading of the Bishop of Kerry's Pastoral in several churches, the Irregulars marched out as protest of the denunciations it contained of them.[16]

As that pastoral letter, which condemned the IRA killing of two army medics on Innisfallen Island, was being read in Kerry churches in September 1922, an IRA leader in the congregation at Curraheen church stood up, blew a whistle and led a walkout of his comrades.[17] At the same church on Christmas Eve 1922, the priest facilitated the arrest of twenty-two local IRA members, some of whom were hiding behind the altar.[18] Other churches which saw protests and walkouts of this nature, *The Freeman's Journal* recorded, included Ballmacelligott, Abbeydorney, Clogher and Currow.[19] Jeremiah

Murphy was among those who went to Mass in Kilgarvan in the autumn of 1922: 'The church was so crowded with armed men that the regular congregation could not enter … The parish priest told us to the leave the church and he loudly denounced us. Dan Hayes, one of our group, argued violently with the priest, who was a Free State sympathiser no doubt.'[20]

+++

Condemning the anti-Treaty IRA from the pulpit was one thing, but the more public humiliation of republicans within the walls of the chapel was another method employed to embarrass IRA members. In October 1922 the Catholic hierarchy made clear that the activities of republicans were 'without moral sanction' and those who participated in the 'Irregular' campaign were 'guilty of grievous sins and may not be absolved in confession nor admitted to the Holy Communion if they persist in such evil courses'.[21] Fr Burke of Knockaderry observed not only the spirit of the diktat, but also implemented the rules to the letter, denying the sacraments to local women who were suspected of having republican sympathies.[22] Thomas Rohan of the Castlegregory IRA decided to resign from the anti-Treaty IRA in October 1922 after his local parish priest refused him Communion: 'When at the Altar Rails for Communion, the priest asked me if I was a gunman. I answered "Yes." He asked me if I was going to sever my connection with the "Irregulars." I said "No." Then he refused to give me Holy Communion. This thing got me afterwards, and as I pondered a lot over it, I resigned.'[23]

Rohan returned to his involvement with the republicans months later, but his treatment by his parish priest not only highlights a clear attempt by a cleric to publicly embarrass his parishioner, it also shows the crises of conscience among those who were fighting the forces of the Free State when they were forced to choose between their politics and their faith.

Many of those killed on the anti-Treaty side were denied funeral rites by the clergy. When Michael Flynn died near Derrymore in November 1922, his parish priest refused to admit the remains to the church and the Bishop of Kerry forbade priests from affording him a funeral Mass.[24] The funeral of James Walsh, who was shot in a field near Cordal in March 1923, arrived to Kileentierna church, but there was no priest present to offer the Requiem Mass. A cousin of the deceased rang the church bell in defiance and a priest ultimately said prayers at the burial, albeit outside the walls of the graveyard.[25] At the funeral of Denis O'Connor in Knocknagoshel, an IRA volunteer was ordered to ring the bell at his funeral and the parish priest physically tried to stop him from doing so.[26]

There were other sinister attempts to intimidate republicans and deprive them of any of the compassion and forgiveness they have might have expected from the leaders of their Church. When the men who were executed in an explosion at Countess Bridge were in prison in Killarney, they were visited by a Franciscan priest, Fr Fidelis, who asked them: 'How much nearer to the republic are we now than when we started? We had the country destroyed,' they were told, 'our leaders had cleared off to America and left us fools to fight for them.'[27]

However, hostility to republicans was not universal among the lower ranks of the clergy. There were occasional incidents of kindness by priests towards the IRA that seem to have been motivated less by politics and more by basic humanitarianism. Poppy Healy from Kenmare was arrested by the Free State Army and jailed in the local workhouse in February 1923. He claimed he had been destined for 'a good hiding' but for the intervention of an unnamed priest who secured his release from prison.[28] Some priests were also known to visit republican prisoners in jail. Among them was Fr Ayres, a Dominican priest who travelled to Dublin in 1923 to visit members of Cumann na mBan from Tralee who were interned in Kilmainham. Hanna O'Connor, one of those in jail, remembered that he was refused admission to the prison:

> I remember getting up on a table in my cell and trying to reach the wee window high up and the other Tralee girls put a stool on the table and I was able to look, and sure enough I saw poor Fr Ayres in the distance – he seemed to be on a bridge and was waving his hand. The window had very tiny panes and one was broken and I can remember the girls put a handkerchief on a piece of wire or timber (a coat hanger) and I pushed it through trying to wave it.[29]

Not all republicans tolerated the public pressure and diatribes from the Catholic clergy. Apart from walkouts from churches, the clerical condemnation of the IRA was occasionally met with angry correspondence to the bishop. The mother of IRA leader John Joe Rice, for example, wrote to Bishop O'Sullivan in November 1922 complaining about a homily directed at her son in the parish church in Kenmare. The bishop was not popular in the Rice household and was called 'a tyrant' by John Joe.[30] In her letter, Mrs Rice claimed that republicans had to sit in the pews every Sunday to listen to the Treaty being 'rammed down our throats' and to be humiliated and insulted from pulpit:

> I could not sit there and listen to insults flung at my son who is the 'Leader' and who can stand a better test of character than Fr Lynch in the town of Kenmare ... until you take up the matter we will stay outside the Church: and if the welfare

of our souls are in your keeping I trust you will instruct the Archdeacon to pay the same respect to his Republican flock as he is to his 'Free State' flock.[31]

Fr Lynch, she suggested, was an alcoholic who 'knew all the brands of whiskey better than any barmaid' and was a much poorer character than Rice and his comrades.[32] Mrs Rice's letter was, however, a rare attempt to call the clergy to account for their hostile pulpit rhetoric. From within the ranks of the clergy itself, documented rumblings about the position of the bishop do not exist in the archives of the Diocese of Kerry. It fell to a priest from outside the diocese to point to a hypocrisy on the part of the hierarchy. Fr Thomas McEnery, whose brother Jim was executed after the siege at Clashmealcon Caves, was based in England but returned to his native county on hearing of Jim's arrest. In a letter to Bishop O'Sullivan, he wondered how: 'the very priests who made these young fellows swear a solemn oath of fealty to the Republic are now enjoying comfortable incomes as chaplains to the Free State [Army]'.[33]

+++

Censures were not always without consequences for the priest and the prevailing deference to the clergy in Ireland at the time did not mean priests and their property were immune to violence. The parish priest in Kilmoyley, Fr Patrick Barton, repeatedly denounced the 'misconduct of the Irregular forces'. Soon after one of his sermons, a window was smashed in the western gable of the parish church.[34] When Fr Timothy Trant of Ballymacelligott denounced the burning of the home of Colonel Nash at Ballycarty in January 1923, the priest's hayshed was burned and the national school at Rahavannig was damaged. Fr Trant believed his comments had prompted the retaliation, but a wider conspiracy against him was also suspected because of his failure 'to appoint a certain person to a teaching position'.[35] In Kenmare, Archdeacon Marshall had 'three of his fat bullocks' stolen when he criticised a fracas that followed the removal from the altar of a copy of a statement of the Irish bishops.[36] Another prominent priest, who was a 'strong supporter' of the Cumann na nGaedheal government, had his boat set ablaze near Milltown. Fr Alexander 'Sandy' O'Sullivan was a former chaplain with the British Army during World War I and had tended to the wounded during the Ballymacandy ambush in June 1921.[37] While walking near the demesne owned by Sir William Godfrey in Milltown in early September 1922, he was fired upon by republicans. *The Freeman's Journal* reported the incident under the dramatic headline 'Priest pursues men who fired at him':

> The Rev. Alexander O'Sullivan, of Milltown, Kerry, was fired at on Saturday evening while proceeding towards Castlemaine. He is a strong supporter of the Irish Government, a big man physically, brave, and experienced to the dangers of war, having served as chaplain in France. He vaulted the wall of Sir [William] Godfrey's demesne, from which four shots had come, and pursued his assailants.[38]

In subsequent years, Fr O'Sullivan remained a target for the anti-Treatyites. Less than a year after the war ended, while cycling from Tralee to Milltown, he was stopped by up to a dozen men at the railway bridge in Castlemaine.[39] Among them was Seán 'Bertie' Scully from Glencar, who was described in a Free State Army report as 'one of the most active Irregular leaders in the south of Ireland'.[40] The men demanded that the priest stop so that he could be searched, and he was asked if he was carrying dispatches for the Free State

Army. Fr O'Sullivan subsequently insisted in court that he was a supporter of the Free State government, but that he now bore no enmity towards Scully as a result of the incident.[41] Scully's defence counsel insisted that the charges of assault and attempted robbery were politically motivated. Scully was returned for trial, but the matter ended when the charges were withdrawn.[42]

+++

While the Catholic clergy was overwhelmingly supportive of Cumann na nGaedheal, there was a small minority of priests who aligned themselves publicly with the other side. During the War of Independence, an RIC County Inspector had been prompted to observe that just four young priests in Kerry 'were really active Sinn Féiners'.[43] Likely included in that list were priests and brothers Joseph (Joe), John and Frank, brothers of Kate Breen, who was a prominent republican county councillor.[44] Fr Joe Breen was among a small number of priests who refused to read the bishop's letter on the sacraments in his church in Millstreet, County Cork, part of the Diocese of Kerry.[45]

However, of greatest political influence at the time was Fr Myles Allman, described as one of the 'most dedicated Republicans among the Kerry priests'.[46] From Rockfield near Killarney, he was a brother of Daniel Allman, who was killed at the Headford Junction ambush during the War of Independence. Fr Allman was prone to engaging in fiery rhetoric during election campaigns and meetings in particular. During the general election campaign of August 1923, An Garda Síochána reported him to the Bishop of Kerry for remarks included in a letter he sent to a republican meeting in Ballyheigue, which was read from the platform: 'The few remaining true soldiers of the Republic have died and shed their blood for Ireland. Why not trample on the Free State now that you have the opportunity and wipe them out for once and for all and re-establish yourselves. The true spirit still lives and shall not be quenched.'[47] This language of exterminating the enemy was inflammatory stuff, but for years after the Civil War, Fr Allman would remain a prominent republican. A 'skilled political strategist', he became chairman of the Comhairle Dáil Cheantair (Constituency Executive) of Fianna Fáil in 1929 and was the party's director of elections in 1933.[48]

Despite Allman's remarks, support for Cumann na nGaedheal from the majority of priests was evident during the general election campaign of 1923. Almost every Cumann na nGaedheal platform featured the local parish priest, which lent the party a significant degree of respectability and authenticity. Anyone brave enough to heckle a priest got a verbal bashing in return. As a group of women and girls tried to interrupt a Cumann na nGaedheal meeting in Glenbeigh by 'shrieking while the speeches were being delivered,' Fr William Byrne, who was chairing the meeting remarked, 'If this is a specimen of your republic, may God help you.'[49] Fr Troy of Listowel – who had made efforts to negotiate peace on the opening day of the war in Listowel in June 1922 – attacked Éamon de Valera for his claim that Irishmen would have to wade through each other's blood as a 'comic opera'.[50] After the election, Fr Troy said Ireland had redeemed its name internationally by backing men like Fionán Lynch – 'Kerry has partly redeemed herself in the eyes of civilised people by your [Lynch's] victory,' he wrote in a letter to the *Irish Independent*.[51] In a similar vein elsewhere, voters were warned of a grim future under republicans; the prospect of the type of disruption and misery which had been experienced during the Civil War, destruction and chaos, higher taxes, and loss of land and property:

If you want your bridges down, your roads torn up, your markets idle, the grass growing on your streets, your taxes redoubled, then vote against the Government. If you want your land handed over to your neighbour who has a revolver, your cattle taken by him and sold under your noses by order, moryeagh [*sic*], vote against the Government. Young men who have no hope in your country rise up and out of her ashes and ruins, to see God's holy laws observed – not the law of the looter – to see your country march in the front rank of nations, bearing her burthens and prosperity proudly; to save your country from utter ruin, and make her a place worth living in, you will cast your votes for the men who saved your country from dissolution and death.[52]

The influence of the clergy during the first election campaign after the Civil War was a foretaste of the political power which the Catholic Church would continue to exert during the remainder of the twentieth century.

CHAPTER 13

'The Black and Tans were only a rumour'

The soldiers who forced Lizzie O'Donnell and her fellow prisoners onto a boat in Tralee Bay on a cold night at the beginning of 1923 were drunk. O'Donnell and the other women were 'in terror of our lives of being drowned'. The prisoners were taken to Fenit and kept there on a boat for two days and nights without any proper sleeping quarters. They spent a week in Tralee Gaol, which was 'just dreadful ... The place was simply filthy and the food very bad and we were allowed no visitors,' O'Donnell recalled. The journey in an 'old battle boat' to Dublin was 'a terrible voyage ... the whole lot of us were seasick'.[1] She would spend almost a year in prison in Dublin in Mountjoy.

Conditions on ships which were used to transport republican prisoners from Kerry to prisons in Dublin were dreadful. Seamus O'Connor from Knocknagoshel was one of hundreds of prisoners on the *Arvonia*, which, though overcrowded, was anchored in Dublin Bay for a fortnight while prison accommodation was sought: 'The air was unbelievably foul. After a while, we fell into a stupor ... Over a hundred got covered with a revolting growth of black ulcers. The food was scarce which was just as well. Some prisoners' legs swelled up, and on leaving they were unable to walk off the ship.'[2]

The prisons themselves were no less grim. Kerry prisoners in Cork jails reported that the 'butter is not good, tea is very bad, plank beds'.[3] The improvised jail at the Great Southern Hotel in Killarney was no better. 'We were,' Denis Daly remembered, 'eaten with lice and dirt while we were there ... There were a few old, dirty blankets. We used to have competitions by searching sheets to see who would find most lice.'[4] Illness was common: Timothy Herlihy of Gortatlea, for example, developed pleurisy while in Maryborough Gaol in Portlaoise.[5]

The conditions in which republican prisoners were detained were compounded by the often violent treatment that they endured, which contributed to what would become a mass protest in the autumn of 1923. When Johnny Connor from Farmer's Bridge was jailed on Holy Thursday in 1923, he found many of his cellmates in Ballymullen Barracks had 'their arms in slings and they had bandages on their heads', while the prisoners' morale had been 'beaten to a frazzle there by torture'.[6] Denis Quille from Listowel recalled the hardships in Maryborough Gaol: 'our lives were continually in danger. I was threatened several times and of course we were fired on, on many occasions.'[7] In Mountjoy Prison, Tadhg Brosnan from Castlegregory was on the receiving end of a 'terrible crucifixion' at the hands of a Free State officer identified as Bob Halpin. Johnny Connor of Farmers' Bridge witnessed how Halpin

> struck Tadg [sic] Brosnan as he was being slung along trying to keep his head up so that it would not be bumped off the floor as his carriers were trying to bump it, anyhow Halpin hit him an unmerciful skelp on the head and the blood burst up like a fountain so that Tadg was soon a mixture of blood and water.[8]

Officers were regularly 'sodden with drink' and would use the buckles of their belts to beat prisoners.[9] 'Oh God,' said Denis Daly, 'you would not recognise them when they had come back to us.'[10] 'When you were "interrogated",' according to Johnny Connor, 'you never came out the same door, but you saw a body carried out covered with a sheet on which red ink had been spilt.'[11] On one occasion, he witnessed an unconscious prisoner who was 'dumped out in the lavatory' and was badly beaten.[12]

Female prisoners were not immune to such treatment. Sheila Nagle of Ballygamboon was 'dragged down an iron stairway in Kilmainham Prison'. Dr Shanahan of Farranfore reported in 1937 that on her release from jail she was 'suffering from suppurating glands in the groin and as far as I remember some form of womb trouble'.[13] The conditions in the cells in Tralee Gaol were 'damp' and there was no proper sunlight or ventilation. After six months in the prison, Tralee Cumann na mBan member Nora Hurley suffered bad eyesight and pulmonary tuberculosis for many years, but when she applied for a pension payment, the Board of Assessors refused to accept that her illness was linked to her imprisonment. Her mother, Ellen, mused that the department must have been getting advice from 'those enemies of mine – those Black and Tans and Free State neighbours that tried to injure me'.[14]

Dan Mulvihill, who was jailed for much of the Civil War, singled out the brutality of the army prison in Killarney for particular mention in his memoir of the period:

Killarney, under the Dublin Guards, was probably one of the most dangerous places in Ireland ... knock a fellow across a table, get four fellows to hold hands and legs, another held nostrils until he had to open his mouth to breathe. Officer was waiting and shoved a packet of red paper down his throat. I saw this done to Florrie Donoghue from Glenflesk. I met him later on and asked him what he thought of it. He said 'Christ, Dan, the Black and Tans were only a rumour.'[15]

+++

By the middle of the summer of 1923, there were over 11,000 republican prisoners in custody in Irish prisons. Among those behind bars were the three Kerry anti-Treaty deputies: Austin Stack, Paddy Cahill and Thomas O'Donoghue. The fourth republican TD, Thomas McEllistrim, had evaded arrest but was on the run.[16] As a protest against the conditions and the continued detention of republicans, hunger strikes commenced in many prisons. On 13 October, hundreds of prisoners at Mountjoy, including many from Kerry, began to refuse food. The mass hunger strike would last for forty-one days and included prisoners at ten locations.[17] Not all participants were in favour of the approach and the proposal met with opposition from some Kerry prisoners, including Billy Mullins from Tralee:

> In order to have a successful hunger-strike, you must have dedicated and sincere men who are prepared to go a long way … I fought tooth and nail against such a move, pointing out that it could not possibly succeed … I pointed out to the [Prisoners'] Council that there would be men running to the cookhouse after two, three and four days … I was overruled.[18]

Sinn Féin rubbished claims made by W.T. Cosgrave that Austin Stack was opposed to the hunger strike and that the prisoners were being well treated.[19] The *Irish Independent* carried the Sinn Féin invective: 'It is false that Austin Stack was opposed to the hungerstrike [*sic*] … He [Cosgrave] states that the prisoners in Mountjoy had received proper treatment. Is hosing, beating, kicking, exposure of men in a saturated state for 37 hours, and finally confinement without exercise for a month proper treatment?'[20] Stack joined the hunger strike in Kilmainham Gaol in mid-October.

The health implications for members of the IRA and Cumann na mBan who went on hunger strike while in jail were frequently long-lasting and profound. 'I felt like a lamb to the slaughter,' wrote Dan Mulvihill. 'I was fourteen stone when it started, I was nine when it ended. I went in with a good stomach, came out with a bad one.'[21] Denis Daly's 'head swelled' while he was abstaining from food and he underwent surgery in hospital.[22] Lizzie O'Donnell of Stradbally, a cousin of the former MP for West Kerry, Thomas O'Donnell, was arrested while carrying a 'bag of bombs' and spent eleven months in jail. She came back, her comrade Bridget Coakley-Kennedy wrote, 'a complete wreck after a long hunger strike'.[23] While on hunger strike, Austin Stack wrote of the conditions in Kilmainham Gaol and the deteriorating health of prisoners:

I have so far been getting up each day when cells open to have a chat with others. Needless to say, we don't walk much. Most of the fellows remain in bed however ... I feel quite fit and surprisingly so. I have grown very thin however. Seán Buckley still gets worse. He was anointed last night I believe and received an injection. Ernie O'Malley is weak also ... It will be terrible should they die like this ...[24]

There were seventy men on hunger strike in Tralee Gaol.[25] A Sinn Féin statement described the conditions:

Batt Fogarty, Caherciveen; John Curran, do [ditto]; Dan O'Sullivan, Tralee; have all received the last sacraments, and are liable to die at any moment. There are 60 men now on hungerstrike [*sic*] in Tralee Gaol, this being their 24th day. Ten men went off strike on the night of the 9th in consequence of promises of release within two days if they took food. The majority of men are in a very weak condition. The place is in a filthy condition with the rain beating through glassless windows into cells. There are no heating arrangements, the hot water pipes being cut off and the conditions generally are horrible.[26]

In a letter to those in Tralee, Éamon de Valera referred to those on hunger strike as embodying 'the whole future of our cause' and he told them that they were 'repositories of the NATIONAL FAITH AND WILL. When you get free, you can leaven the whole people.'[27]

These hunger strikes provided a critical focus for republicans in Kerry in the months after the Civil War. The Free State Kerry Command reported that 'Irregulars' in the county were 'more aggressive and emboldened' in October 1923.[28] Large meetings and vigils – including one described by the Kerry Command of the Free State Army as a 'monster meeting' – gave the anti-Treaty organisation the opportunity to mobilise and to counter some of the apathy in the republican movement after defeat in the Civil War.[29] The Sinn Féin club in Castlegregory led a march through the village, which was followed by hymns, and speeches calling for the immediate release of prisoners.[30] Among the speakers at Kerry meetings was County Councillor Albinia Brodrick – she adopted the Irish name Gobnaít Ní Bhruadair – who continued to campaign against the Treaty and for the cause of those of jail: she would read letters from the prisoners to rallies in the county during the winter of 1923.[31]

In November, Sinn Féin organised a plebiscite in east Kerry, which claimed to have 16,229 signatories demanding the release of all internees.[32] Meanwhile, members of Tralee, Listowel and Killarney Rural District Councils had each passed a resolution calling for the release of the prisoners, with the members in Killarney explicitly demanding the attention of the 'representatives of Kerry in Parliament' in that regard.[33] Other bodies, including the Kerry County Committee of Agriculture, made similar calls: 'There must be majority rule,' insisted one member, but he also suggested that if those in prison and those who represented them saw fit to enter the Dáil, 'they should be admitted'.[34] Paddy Cahill was released from jail in December 1923 and Thomas O'Donoghue the following month.[35] Stack was one of a number of imprisoned TDs who remained in detention.[36] Writing to Winifred Gordon in February 1924, he implied that political prisoners were being kept behind bars and out of sight for a very sinister reason: 'I should like if I could put away thoughts as to release, for I feel some of those F.S. [Free State] people intend to keep a few of us as long as they possibly can. They dread something that they imagine stalks them daily and they think they require hostages to protect them from ghosts.'[37]

The hunger strikes ended towards the end of November, with many prisoners having refused food for over forty days. The effects were long-lasting and heralded premature death in many cases, caused by the long-term toll taken on the body. Tom Daly of Knockaneacoolteen died in 1929 at the age of just forty-one, wracked by pulmonary tuberculosis.[38] Austin Stack, too, died prematurely in 1929, partly as a result of the deprivations he suffered in prison.

CHAPTER 14

'Even John Bull did not attempt this'

The small fishing boat with its thirty passengers bobbed up and down in the choppy waters of the Atlantic Ocean. Most of the occupants of the vessel were women and children who experienced 'great hardship and suffering' during the journey from Dingle to the port of Cobh in County Cork. Described as 'emigrants from County Kerry' in the short report in *The Cork Examiner* of 23 October 1922, the group was travelling from west Kerry to Cobh to board one of the many ships which carried emigrants to the United States at the time. The necessity of leaving Ireland, as well as the difficulties in travelling on land via road and rail, which were greatly compounded by the destruction of roads and railway lines during the Civil War, had forced these women and children to take to sea: 'The only accommodation on the boat afforded was a small cabin containing two bunks, which were given to two women and four children, the remaining passengers, nearly all women, having to remain on deck. Heavy seas caused by a strong easterly gale swept her deck from stem to stern.'[1]

Emigration – by both civilians and combatants – was one of the most significant social and economic impacts of the Civil War in Kerry, and is a recurrent theme in the pension application files and accounts from the time. The population of Kerry fell by almost 10,000 between 1911 and 1926, with an estimated 20,000 people leaving the county in the same period.[2] This was exacerbated not only by the War of Independence, but by the disruption and hardships of the fratricide of 1922–23. In Kerry, the only choice for many was 'either a life of poverty or emigration'.[3] In a letter to *The Liberator*, a Cahersiveen resident contended that emigration was 'better than starvation', adding that 'patriotism has little meaning to a hungry man'.[4]

It has been pointed out that the reasons for emigration were manifold and primarily related to the prevailing economic situation and a lack of employment opportunities. However, the economic problems wrought by the war only made life more difficult for those trying to make ends meet and source employment. The new state offered little by way of employment prospects, particularly for those who had fought with and supported the anti-Treaty cause.[5] Many of the republicans released from jail in 1923 left Kerry 'in droves', in what Jeremiah Murphy called another Flight of the Earls.[6] Snippets from the newspapers in the mid-1920s are a testament to the exodus. The Kenmare correspondent of the *Kerry News* mentioned the case of Ned Shea in 1924:

> For the past few weeks there is a constant stream of emigrants leaving this area for foreign countries ... Among the last batch to leave was Ned Shea. If any man has cause to think badly of his own countrymen it is Ned ... He took the Republican side in the Civil War and consequently lost his job. Now, he has to go and seek employment under an alien flag.[7]

In many cases, entire families were impacted by emigration. 'Our sons are gone away to America. They loved the Irish Republic,' wrote Margaret Linnane of Lisselton in 1934. Her son, Seán, was shot dead by the Free State Army at a dugout in Duagh in April 1923, and his siblings had emigrated, among them Tom Linnane, who, like his brother, had served time in jail and on hunger strike towards the end of the Civil War. Tom and his brother Timothy were 'trying to exist in New York City'. Margaret's daughter, Ellie, was a missionary nun in South Africa and another son, Paddy, worked as a shop assistant in New Jersey, where he lived with a wife and two children.[8] Margaret and her husband, John, were elderly and reliant on a tiny income from a few acres of bog and 'poor land' in Glouria, a rural townland near Lisselton. The couple had two cows, a pony and twelve fowl, with no crops and 'turf not sold'.[9] The departure of all of their children for foreign shores deprived them of any other source of income save for £5 sent most Christmases by Tom and Tim.[10] In a letter to the Minister for Defence, Frank Aiken, Mrs Linnane wondered if anything could be done so that one of their sons 'could come home from America and stay with us in our old age as we are both alone'.[11]

In the years after the Civil War, there was little relief from this exodus abroad. Four years after the conflict, 'a dozen of the ablest boys and a dozen of the comeliest girls' left the small parish of Brosna.[12] Noel Ó Murchú details how an estimated 40 per cent of IRA volunteers in west Kerry, the vast majority of whom were anti-Treaty, emigrated between 1923 and the early 1930s.[13] IRA headquarters was informed of efforts by Kerry commanders to dissuade or prevent jobless IRA members from leaving the county in the years after the Civil War, fearing their military capabilities would be restricted.[14] 'Emigration must stop and we must officially stand out against it,' one senior officer reported in March 1924.[15] The extent of the problem was evident in a report prepared by local IRA captain Tomás Ó Dálaigh, who indicated that forty-four members of Kerry brigades had recently emigrated: 'As can be seen from the figures given elsewhere in the report, the number of Volunteers who have emigrated is very large. In compiling the figures, I only took the number of those who had been actually engaged in the recent war. Numerous others intend emigrating ...'[16]

IRA volunteer, John M. O'Connor of Ballylongford, described the flight of young men from his parish: 'But those who had fought on the Republican side in the Civil War had no hope left. Before December 1925, 85% had emigrated ... of the Ballylongford [football] team of 1924, eleven had emigrated before 1926 including Thomas O'Connor, the holder of an All-Ireland junior medal.'[17]

A list from the 1930s of former members of the Lauragh IRA company offers another stark indication of the level of emigration among republican combatants. Of the seventy-two names listed, two were deceased, and of those living, thirty-three or almost half, had addresses in England or the United States.[18] Elsewhere, several members of the Firies Company of the IRA were abroad in the years after the Civil War, according to records in the Military Archives. The addresses provided tell their own story:

> James Riordan – Allors, Queensland, Australia
> Timothy Sullivan – 6471 St., Green St, Chicago
> William Kerrisk – Present address unknown, Chicago
> Patrick Kelliher – 503 W 169 St., New York
> Michael Griffin – Present address unknown, USA
> James Woods, 662A, 4th Ave., San Francisco, California
> John Woods, 662A, 4th Ave., San Francisco, California.[19]

The women of Cumann na mBan also left Kerry in large numbers. In 1936 Bessie Cahill was tasked with supplying the Department of Defence with names and addresses for all Cumann na mBan veterans.

However, it was nearly impossible to locate such data for the Keel Branch, 'as the majority of them have imigrated [sic] and the others have changed their addresses'.[20] A member of the same branch of Cumann na mBan told the department that a 'good number' of the fifty members of the Keel company had left for Australia, New Zealand and the US by the late 1930s.[21] Síobhra Aiken has estimated that in rural areas like Dungloe, County Donegal, Ventry, County Kerry, and Beara, County Cork, between 60 and 70 per cent of Cumann na mBan members had emigrated by the mid-1930s.[22]

The fact that many veterans of the period were abroad presented its own challenges in terms of the payment of pensions and allowances. Edward (Ned) Langford of the Callinafercy Company, who took part in fighting against Free State forces in Castlemaine and Killorglin, spent many years in the United States at up to eight different addresses in New York and California.[23] The constant relocation meant Langford was forced to write to the Department of Defence several times in the 1930s and 1940s to check the whereabouts of his most recent payment. He was just one of many republican fighters 'who ultimately could not afford to remain in the country they fought to free'.[24]

+++

Unemployment and acute poverty were as much a feature of life in Kerry during and after the Civil War as emigration. In a report on Kerry at the beginning of 1923, the *Voice of Labour* newspaper noted, 'severe unemployment had followed in the wake of the war, and, as usual, the workers have suffered most'.[25] In 1922 a member of the Thomas Ashe Sinn Féin Club in west Kerry told the Minister for Home Affairs, Eamonn Duggan, that there had been 'unimployement [sic] and acute distress for the last three years' in the area, with no relief for those out of work. He appealed to the minister for grant support from Dáil Éireann 'to get these men working again'.[26]

Unemployment did not only affect those who had taken up arms against the new State. It also impacted the families of those who had served in the Free State Army. The surviving siblings of Corporal Con Sullivan from Knockeenahone, Scartaglin, who was killed in combat in County Limerick in 1922, faced significant financial distress in the years after the war. His mother, Mary, told the Department of Defence that the loss of her son was compounded by the 'badness of the times, and the widespread unemployment, and whenever a day's work is to be had in this district, a boy of mine will not be the first to get it'.[27]

The age-old Irish political tool of the boycott as a form of intimidation also impacted employment: in one instance, Madge O'Connor of Cahersiveen Cumann na mBan, who ran a grocery store and boarding house, was 'subject to severe boycott' because of her politics. She had to 'abandon [the] business and boarders and go to London to earn a living'.[28] Unemployment, as will be considered in further detail later, was exacerbated by attacks on and damage to infrastructure like roads, coastguard stations, retail premises and railway lines. In February 1923 the gas supply in Tralee was cut off following a republican attack on the gas works: 'The town is in darkness. Hundreds of users of gas cookers are terribly handicapped, while bakeries and other industrial concerns dependent on gas for power are crippled … This will leave the inhabitants short of bread supplies, and will throw industrial concerns idle, causing further unemployment, and adding to the already severe sufferings of the people.'[29]

Financial hardship was endemic. A dispensary doctor described the situation in Kerry and other rural counties where his colleagues were 'working among the peasants with small uneconomic holdings, who are unable to pay a fee sufficient to cover the cost of the medical officer's travelling and are not yet poor enough to be entitled to charitable medical relief'.[30] Diarmaid Ferriter cites a petition from a group of tenants in Ardfert to the Land Settlement Commission in 1922, which not only evokes the starvation and poverty that many endured, but also the challenges faced by an Irish government preoccupied with fighting a civil war:

> The provision of milk for our children is one of our great difficulties. It is impossible to get grazing for a pony and a pony is a necessity for most of us … We live right on the edge of this land and have to look at the bullocks of the Grazier for years while our children pined for milk. There are among our children 19 children either babies or little beyond the baby stage … They haven't a perch of land.[31]

While the Civil War took its toll on the civilian population in many ways, not least in terms of the damage and disruption to infrastructure, public services, transport and communications, which made normal social and commercial activity increasingly difficult as the war intensified, the most salient impact came from the significant interference by republicans with the rail network. Throughout the conflict in Kerry, the anti-Treatyites pursued an active policy of disrupting railway services.[32] The main objective was to disrupt troop movements and force army transport and convoys onto the roads, making them more vulnerable to ambush.[33] Tadhg Coffey, who escaped the explosion at Countess Bridge, took part in the destruction of Ballybrack railway station and the adjacent railway line, and was also involved in preventing repair crews from restoring the line. Coffey claimed that the objective was to prevent supplies from reaching Free State garrisons: the republicans wanted to 'starve them out, we had them almost starved out, we had the railways torn up'.[34]

Just ten days after he had arrived in Kerry, Major General Paddy O'Daly was among the passengers on a train which was ambushed near Farranfore.[35] A day later, catastrophe was narrowly averted when a train commandeered by republicans was driven at high speed towards Tralee railway station. A railway worker switched the tracks at the critical moment and the train avoided the main station, but it crashed through a buffer and ploughed across the main Tralee to Listowel road before bursting into flames. Remarkably, there were no casualties.[36] At the beginning of 1923, the destruction of a recently reconstructed railway bridge at Currans severed most of the key rail arteries in mid- and south Kerry, while Lisselton railway station near Listowel was burned to the ground. The destruction was excoriated by the *Voice of Labour* newspaper as having been carried out by 'people with no end in view but a vision for the soul and a vacuum for the stomach'.[37]

Whatever about the ambition of disrupting the movements of the Free State Army and the delivery of food and goods to their barracks, civilians also suffered significantly from the IRA campaign to damage railway lines. Lady Gordon of Ard na Sídhe in Caragh Lake observed sarcastically that a journey on the Mallow to Killarney railway line was precarious and 'varied with the possibility of losing one's luggage, if not one's life'.[38] But this was the reality for many rail passengers. Railway journeys, where they could be taken, were fraught with danger. *The Irish Times* reported the vandalism of a train by armed men in January 1923:

> The 5pm train from Ballybunion was 'held up' by about 15 armed men on Friday evening, 26th inst. The driver and

fireman were ordered off the footplate and told to go back to Ballybunion. The raiders then removed all the passengers from the carriages and held them prisoner alongside the railway. The engine was smashed with crowbars and hammers ... The mail bags were taken from the van and opened ... The passengers were allowed to walk to Listowel, a distance of nine miles.[39]

The most shocking consequence of tampering with railway lines also came in January 1923, when anti-Treaty forces sought to derail a trainload of Free State Army troops bound for Tralee. But what they thought was a train carrying troops was instead a goods train. By the time the IRA men under Tom Driscoll of Kilmoyley discovered this, a section of the track had already been removed. Driscoll and his men fired warning shots as the train approached, but the driver, Patrick O'Riordan, assuming it was an attempt to hijack the train, maintained his course. On a steep embankment at Liscahane, the train derailed and toppled over. O'Riordan, a father of five from Tralee, and his fireman, Daniel Crowley from Cork, the 'sole support of his mother and his widowed sister', were crushed and scalded to death.[40] A *Freeman's Journal* report on the incident stated that 'the callousness with which the wrecking of the train was planned is revolting beyond description'.[41] In a far more trivial aspect to the tragedy, the Rowntree's chocolate company in England later claimed compensation for the loss of 'one box of confectionary' in the crash.[42] At the inquest, Patrick O'Riordan was described as 'the little man with a big heart'. Major General Paddy O'Daly used the opportunity to remind people what his men 'were up against', adding that O'Riordan and Crowley 'who were endeavouring to feed the people of Tralee had been murdered'.[43]

A few days later, engine drivers Dan Lynch and Daniel Daly were shot (Daly fatally) outside Tralee railway station. Daly, a member of the local IRA, was alleged to be involved in a plot to disrupt railway services.[44] The army claimed the killings were carried out by republicans because the men had refused to destroy railway stock.[45] But the assailants were Free State soldiers: Corporal Niall Harrington saw the three killers leave their barracks in plain clothes and return shortly after the shootings.[46]

The destruction of and tampering with railway lines not only impacted on commercial activity and travel, it also had significant consequences for those working on the railways. The compensation applications in the National Archives detail a total of eighty-one claims from engine drivers, pavers, porters, guards, signalmen, milesmen and other staff owing to the destruction of the Great Southern and Western Railway lines in the county for varying periods in 1922 and 1923.[47] Timothy Jones, whose father worked at Killorglin railway station, was forced to join the Free State Army in May 1922 because of the financial impact of the disruption of railway services in the area. His father was 'a railway man at that time, no work, money' and the family was 'destitute'.[48]

The disruption meant that trade and commerce were largely stagnant and supplies of many materials and foodstuffs ran low. The prices at fairs were poor: butter was 'down 1s 2d, eggs 10/-' in Killorglin, and the town's annual Puck Fair in August 1922 was the 'smallest ever seen' with 'only one bunch of cattle' sold.[49] Commodities such as tea, eggs, bacon, butter and flour were frequently intercepted and looted by anti-Treaty forces while they were being transported. Jerome Slattery, a merchant from Blennerville, had stocks of butter stolen by republicans in various parts of the county on an extraordinary twenty different occasions in 1922.[50] The knock-on effect for civilians was often severe. Killarney Mental Hospital, for example, was forced to reduce its daily rations of bread, sugar and tea for its 540 patients.[51] The wider population suffered, too, as *The Cork Examiner* explained in a stinging vilification of the IRA:

> One wonders if those responsible for this temporary hold up of the people's chief article of food in parts of Kerry are proud of this achievement, or do they believe that they are helping Ireland's cause by inflicting loss and inconvenience on the helpless classes? ... Even John Bull did not attempt this. The sad part is, it is old people, sick people, lunatics and growing children are the ones being most put out by short rations.[52]

+++

Trains were not the only means of transport disrupted during this period – those travelling by road also faced hazards. The cutting of roads to hinder the transport of goods as well as troops – a familiar feature of the war against the Crown Forces – continued to be employed by republican forces. The cost of the destruction of roads and bridges in Kerry alone has been estimated at £500,000.[53] Jeremiah Murphy of Headford recalled that the order from his commanding officer at the end of 1922 was simple: 'Destroy all available bridges.'[54] Seamus O'Connor recalled that the destruction of bridges was 'a form of occupational therapy'.[55] At Castlemaine, three mines were placed in the arch of the bridge across the River Maine, and although just one exploded when they were detonated, this was enough to limit access to pedestrians and the few carts that used the bridge.[56] Apart from the very obvious destruction caused to vehicular and other traffic by such attacks, they also had consequences for those in the immediate vicinity. When a bridge near Castleisland was blown up by the IRA, the explosion killed two goats belonging to a nearby farmer.[57]

Civilians facing disruption from such destruction often took it upon themselves to repair bridges and roads. A bridge destroyed near Abbeydorney was repaired by locals, who were fired at as they did so, 'but they pluckily completed the repairs'.[58] Those who had motorcars took to the roads at great risk. Edmund Burke from New York, an Irish-American travelling around Kerry in his Ford car in August 1922, was fired on by republicans who assumed the car was part of an army convoy, and had to have his arm amputated as a result of the gunshot wounds sustained.[59] Possession of a motor car itself became a hazard: dozens were stolen or commandeered by republicans and Free State troops, and the compensation records from the period also include seventy-seven claims for the theft of a bicycle.[60] Lady Cuffe of Caragh Lake had her motor car taken by both republicans and army personnel, the latter returning her car in 'an excellent condition'.[61]

A side-effect of the interference with road and rail transport was the impact on communications, particularly the postal service, which faced not only disruption to deliveries but also a series of sinister attacks on its staff. The postal service was already playing catch-up when the Civil War began. As the War of Independence came to an end, the postmistress in Milltown told her customers that she had seventy-bags of unopened mail to sort through because of disruption to train services, and that it would take five days to clear the backlog.[62] Republicans were particularly active in preventing the delivery of mail as they attempted to stifle government and army communications. Postmen were held up from time to time and warned 'under direct penalties not to deliver any more mails in the district'.[63] In one month alone, three different postmen in the greater Killarney area were 'deprived of letters' and one was warned that 'if he delivered any more, he would be shot'.[64] The home and business of John McSweeney at Kilnabrack, Glenbeigh was targeted by republicans several times because his wife was postmistress and handled 'official cash'.[65] Indeed, the money handled by post offices often made them a target for robbery.[66] Telegraphy workers were confronted, too: in March 1923 telegraph wires were severed at Headford and workmen carrying out the repairs were held up by anti-Treatyites and 'relieved of [their] working implements'.[67] In March 1923 the Commissioner of the Civic Guard, Eoin O'Duffy, advised the Minister for Home Affairs that letters from Dublin to Cahersiveen were not being delivered for between two and four weeks, which was affecting not only the ordinary civilians but was also proving disruptive to the work of the police.[68] The General Post Office in Dublin noted that such difficulties were attributable to the 'disturbed conditions prevailing' in the county at this time.[69]

Disruption to schools and education services was also significant, particularly where fighting was more intense. Two months after the Carnegie secondary school in Killorglin had been commandeered by the Free State Army during fighting in the town in September 1922, students were still unable to return to their classrooms. Commandant General Fionán Lynch insisted that his soldiers would not be able to vacate the school as long as the war continued. Efforts to find alternative accommodation for the school failed to procure anything suitable, and the four teachers and the headmaster, John Dwyer, remained out of work.[70] Elsewhere, when the principal of Banna National School refused shelter to anti-Treatyites, its windows were smashed and the wall enclosing the school was knocked down, with the rubble being used to build an obstruction across the Ballyheigue to Ardfert road.[71] A more sinister fate befell the Boys and Girls National School in Knocknanure at the beginning of 1923. Early on the morning of 19 January, the school was 'maliciously, wantonly and wilfully set on fire'.[72] The reason for the arson attack is not specified in official records, but a report in the *Irish Independent* noted that the school principal, Mr O'Callaghan, 'has been in custody for some time'.[73] Restoration works took several years.

In a county in which agriculture was the backbone of the local economy, the suffering of farmers was particularly acute. The burning of creameries had been a central part of the modus operandi of the Black and Tans during the War of Independence. The purpose was not only to inconvenience farmers themselves, but to disrupt the supply of milk and produce to market.[74] In July 1922, persons unknown destroyed creameries and machinery at Ballylea and Parknageragh.[75] Goods, machinery, butter and bacon were also taken from creameries in Abbeydorney, Causeway, Ballyheigue, Stradbally and Kilquane, while the creamery at Dromartin, Ballyduff, was 'knocked down and taken away' by armed men in January 1923.[76] The compensation files held in the National Archives detail several examples of the seizure of large quantities of butter and cream while in transit from creameries or seized directly from creameries in Castlemaine, Farmers' Bridge, Castleisland, and Firies.[77] The creameries owned by the Watson family came in for particular attention from the anti-Treaty forces, but the family's creamery at Ballyheigue bore the brunt of occupation by both republicans and Free State soldiers. Republicans took over the premises in November 1922, and when they left it was occupied by the army a few months later, who undid the repairs the family had undertaken in the interim.[78]

Farms and crops were sometimes weaponised for political ends. Free State soldiers stationed at Barraduff prevented anyone from working on the Kennedy family farm at Brewsterfield. Jeremiah Kennedy, a senior figure locally in the anti-Treaty IRA, was on the run, and his brother and father had been arrested at the beginning of 1923. The family were told that unless Jeremiah surrendered, no farm labourers would be permitted onto their land, and as a result 'there were no crops planted in the spring of 1923,' depriving the family of a critical source of food.[79]

+++

The actions of the Free State Army in Kerry in the early months of 1923 infused local politics and political culture with a deeply held revulsion for the government and its military representatives in the county, but the actions of the republicans also became increasingly unpopular as the conflict escalated. Some republicans were acutely aware of growing hostility from civilians towards the disruption and chaos which the destruction and looting was causing, even if that admission was rarely vocalised. At the beginning of 1923, Dan Flavin of the Listowel IRA noted that the 'Causeway district was getting tired and the people wanted to get the IRA to stop the fighting'.[80] A report for army headquarters in March 1923 cited a 'sense of relief' that the Kerry Command was getting a grip on the guerrilla warfare in the county, and it also summarised the isolation being felt as a result of the war: 'The people have been living in complete isolation for months – their connection with the outside world had been cut off and their feelings of isolation had accentuated their fear of the Irregulars ... [the people were] unaware of outside happenings, and depended on the Irregulars for information of outside events.'[81]

Another missive to headquarters claimed that some farmers in north Kerry welcomed the death of Timothy 'Aero' Lyons during the incident at the Clashmealcon caves, 'though they are cautious about expressing this, or showing their joy on their faces'.[82] Tom Garvin noted that while 'everyone remembers Ballyseedy', nobody remembers 'the welcome given to Free State troops in areas too long occupied by uncontrollable, self-appointed bands of armed men', including in Kerry.[83] One diarist recorded that 'Killarney people gave

FS troops a great reception'.[84] An army report recorded 'a sense of genuine relief' when garrisons were established in the county: 'On coming into actual contact with them [the people] the impression of hostility immediately evaporates ... people seemed glad to have troops in their locality.'[85] Ultimately, that welcome from many in the county transformed quickly into hatred and disgust and would be forever negated in the public memory by the actions of many army leaders and officers in the Kerry Command during the tragic early months of 1923.

CHAPTER 15

'She got mental and is definitely mental since'

Thirty-two years after his legs were amputated as a result of the trap mine explosion which killed five of his fellow soldiers at Knocknagoshel, Joseph O'Brien was provided with a commode because he found it difficult to walk across his back yard to his out-door toilet. Private O'Brien, a father of three from the North Wall in Dublin, was the only survivor of the massacre in the early hours of 6 March 1923. Such was the extent of his injuries that both of his legs were amputated '4" below the knee joint' and he lost most of the sight in his eyes because of epiphora, a traumatic cataract and related sight loss.[1] The first that his wife, Annie (Margaret), learned of his catastrophic injuries was a telegram dispatched from the adjutant general at Portobello Barracks in Dublin shortly after the incident: 'Regret to inform you that Vol. Joseph O'Brien No. 1596 lies badly wounded at the Infirmary, Tralee. Should you desire to visit him, a free voucher will be issued.'[2]

The family pleaded with army headquarters to have O'Brien moved from Tralee to a hospital in Dublin, and he was admitted to St Bricin's Hospital at the end of April 1923. An application for a wound pension was lodged but had still not been paid when O'Brien was discharged from hospital in June 1924. His plight was raised in the Dáil by Alfie Byrne TD, who questioned the President of the Executive Council, W.T. Cosgrave, on the matter. O'Brien, Byrne told the Dáil, was

> sent home to his wife, who resides at 35 St. Mary's Road, North Wall, where he is confined to bed and cannot see; that he is not in receipt of any allowance or pension; that his wife has three children to support, and if in view of this he will see that an immediate payment is made in order to enable her to provide food for her children and proper medical treatment for her husband.[3]

Cosgrave replied that 'a cheque for £10 has been sent to Mr O'Brien' and that his pension application would be assessed expeditiously. The wound pension was provided, but it was the difficulty in caring for her husband in their upper-floor home that preoccupied Annie O'Brien throughout the mid-1920s. She feared he would fall on the stairs, which he was unable to climb with his prostheses, and she appealed for alternative accommodation.[4] In August 1925 Annie asked for an 'invalid chair', as it was the only way she would be able to take Joseph 'out for air each day'. The application was approved, but the wheelchair had still not been provided six months later.[5] O'Brien also required a tricycle and harness to get around and, as he became increasingly blind, appealed on a number of occasions to be readmitted to hospital for treatment.[6] He also appealed 'for a loan of a few pounds' in 1927 when Annie became pregnant.[7] For many years after, there was a need for a tricycle, stump socks, shoulder straps, replacement prostheses, glasses and other medical supports, which were provided with departmental assistance.

The family endured further tragedy when Joseph and Annie's son, James, was killed in an accident at McKee Barracks, where he was serving with the army, in March 1955. Shortly afterwards its impact and that of Joseph's ongoing disability was noted in a lengthy report by a housing welfare officer with Dublin Corporation, Miriam E. MacAuley. The report detailed how difficult it was for Joseph to get around his home, then at Gullistan Cottages in Rathmines. She recommended that a commode be provided as Joseph had to walk to an outdoor toilet so that he could fulfil his ambition to be an 'independent man'. MacAuley was moved by the couple's attitude to their adversity:

> I cannot speak too highly of both Mr and Mrs O'Brien and their courage in facing their troubles and difficulties, not only this tragedy of 30 years standing but also the very recent one of losing a son in an accident in the Irish National Army. There is between these two a touching devotion to, and respect for each other ... [please] avert this financial hardship and indignity to a man who has already given for his country more than anyone can repay him.[8]

Annie O'Brien died in October 1957, Joseph in February 1962.

+++

The story of the O'Briens, like many of the stories recounted above, is only known to us through the Military Service Pensions Collection. This collection, comprising some 300,000 records, is the most important archive of testimony from the Irish revolutionary period.[9] The government passed legislation in 1923 to provide for pensions and allowances to members of the Free State Army who had been injured during the Civil War and to the survivors of those killed. Also eligible were members of the Irish Volunteers who were injured between the Easter Rising and 1921, and dependants of those who died, but anti-Treaty IRA members who took part in the Civil War were only included under an Act of 1934, which was introduced after Fianna Fáil came to office. Members of Cumann na mBan also only became eligible for payments in the 1930s. A number of Army Pensions Acts and Military Pensions Acts incorporated various amendments up until 1953.

To apply for a pension, a certificate of service was required, and applications were considered by a Department of Defence-appointed Board of Assessors. These boards, and various advisory committees which adjudicated on pension applications over the years, included Kerry nominees, such as the former MP for West Kerry Tom O'Donnell, Fionán Lynch TD, and Kerry IRA veterans Humphrey Murphy and Dan Mulvihill.[10] The application and verification process was often tedious, onerous and protracted. The bar was set very high. For most of those who applied there was disappointment: of the 80,000 people who applied for pensions and allowances between 1924 and 1958, just over 18,000 were successful, creating a 'chronicle of great disappointment' and a record of what many perceived as 'cold, harsh bureaucracy'.[11] The pensions caused political tensions from time to time, but their value as historical documents is immense. They allow the story of Private Joseph O'Brien and thousands of others who were affected by the Civil War in Kerry to be told.

Like the family of O'Brien, the relatives of those who were killed at Knocknagoshel experienced years of financial hardship and deprivation as they battled to secure compensation from the State. The mother of Captain Michael Dunne said that she and her only daughter, Elizabeth, were 'solely dependent' on him at the time of his death, a claim confirmed by the Dublin Metropolitan Police.[12] At the beginning of 1924, the family were in 'very needy circumstances', and Catherine Dunne asked that the government pay her £3,000 in compensation for her loss as an army allowance of 30p per week was 'barely sufficient'.[13] The loss of financial support from Michael forced the family to relocate from Clontarf to the city centre. The department agreed to pay Catherine a pension payment of £1 per week, the maximum amount payable to a mother of a deceased officer under the Army Pensions Act, 1923. Mrs Dunne died two weeks before Christmas 1924, however, and Elizabeth failed to have the pension payment continued in her name. The minute of the Army Pension Board meeting which reached that decision was signed by its chairman, Cecil Lavery (later attorney general), and was as succinct as it was brutally officious:

> Elizabeth Dunne
> Claiming in respect of the late Captain Michael Dunne
> No dependency
> No award
> Cecil Lavery, Chairman
> JJ Horgan, Secretary
> 12 January 1925.[14]

Following the death of Captain Edward Stapleton from Gloucester Street in Dublin, it fell to his widow, Mary, and mother, Julia, who claimed her son was 'blown to pieces' at Knocknagoshel, to submit claims for financial support.[15] Eight months after he died, Julia, a sixty-six-year-old invalid, wrote that 'not one [sic] has come near me to see or know how I am living'. She had worked hard to rear her family but was dependent on her daughter-in-law, Mary, who had two sons, Patrick and Edward, aged three and five.[16] Young Patrick Stapleton died in July 1926. He was just five years old. The

Stapletons were awarded payments in 1924, an allowance of £90 per annum in the case of Julia and £24 per annum to Mary.[17]

For the families of the three Free State Army soldiers from Kerry who died at Knocknagoshel, the aftermath of the explosion was no less traumatic. Patrick O'Connor, whose son, Lt Patrick 'Pats' O'Connor was killed, applied to the Department of Defence for assistance. Before joining the army, Patrick had 'assisted him in every way. He was the only son who lived on and helped to manage [the] farm.'[18] After his death, the land was 'almost going to waste as they have nobody on it owing to the high cost of labour'.[19] An army report detailed what Patrick O'Connor experienced: 'Claimant [O'Connor] was immensely terrified and annoyed by the Irregulars while they waged war against the State. He was kidnapped and threatened with death. His cattle were seized and the sum of £50 was extorted from him under the guise of a fine. Payment of claim is strongly recommended.'[20] Patrick O'Connor sought compensation of £2,000 but received only a dependant's gratuity of £150 under the Army Pensions Act of 1923. He left his home and moved to Birmingham shortly after the war ended.[21] The claim was pursued further by Patrick's brother, Fr M. O'Connor of St Mary's College in Rathmines, who told army headquarters that his parents' condition 'is the saddest that can be imagined and their need is greater than can be described'.[22]

Michael O'Connor, the youngest sibling of Laurence O'Connor, who died at Knocknagoshel, was just a year old when his brother was killed in the explosion. Laurence's father, John, believed his deceased son was politically naïve and 'did not understand the difference' over the Treaty when he joined the Free State Army.[23] His mother, Margaret, of Lissycurrig, Causeway, received an initial gratuity of just £30, even though Laurence's father was out of work and they had a large family of eight children – none of whom were in employment – to support. Neighbours came together to collect £11 'in charity' for the family to help them to pay their bills.[24] Margaret, angered at the paltry award received in compensation, complained to the Army Finance Office in the summer of 1924:

> I refused to believe that you would estimate the life of a young Irishman as of less value than an Irish terrier for which I have often seen larger compensation awarded … I sincerely hope that you will be good enough to obtain a reconsideration of my case by the Army Pensions Board with a view to granting such further allowance as would enable me to provide the necessities of life for the helpless members of my family whose principal support was my poor son, who lost his life in your service.[25]

Margaret insisted that if her son had been killed in a farm accident, she would be entitled to considerably more compensation.[26] The appeal yielded an increased gratuity of £100, the maximum allowable under the prevailing legislation.

For the family of Private Michael Galvin of New Lane, Killarney, the circumstances were no more favourable. Galvin had only been in the army for four months, during which time he had sent his father, Michael, 'about £4'. Michael Galvin Senior, a tailor, had 'no home of any description' and 'no income of any sort'; one of his sons was in Killarney Mental Hospital and two daughters were in the United States. He was, a local garda sergeant reported, 'injured a good deal in his health and mind due to the loss of his son'.[27] A gratuity of £50 was eventually paid.

+++

The families of those on the anti-Treaty side experienced similar deprivations and battles to secure financial recompense for what they had endured. The family of George O'Shea, who was blown up at Ballyseedy, suffered a litany of trauma, poor health, financial deprivation and misery in the years after his death. They had been heavily reliant on O'Shea's income from his work on the roads with Kerry County Council. When his mother, Annie, applied to the Department of Defence for compensation, a payment of £150 was recommended but was 'withheld on the instructions of the late Minister [for Finance, Ernest Blythe]'.[28] No reason for this decision appears on the application file.

The impact of Ballyseedy manifested itself in other ways, too. One of George's sisters, Mollie, was in charge of an IRA dugout and often carried messages late at night in 'a perfect wilderness as the area is bleak and lonely'.[29] After Ballyseedy, according to her brother Daniel, Mollie 'got mental and is definitely mental since'.[30] She was, according to her own company of Cumann na mBan, 'hopelessly insane'.[31] She was admitted to Killarney Mental Hospital in February 1928 and, by order of the President of the High Court in July 1943, her affairs were placed under the care of the court.[32] Daniel O'Shea applied for a pension payment on his sister's behalf. Among those who wrote in support of her claim was Stephen Fuller, who stated that the Kilflynn IRA company 'deeply regret her mental incapacity which is a sad one … we insist that she is one of those who qualify for the M.S. [Military Service] Pension'.[33] Mollie received a pension of £10.16.8 in respect of just over two years' service with Cumann na mBan.

Twenty years after the Civil War, a report on the O'Shea family's circumstances was provided to the department by the local garda superintendent, who wrote: 'Mrs. [Annie] O'Shea [George's mother] who is old and invalided is in receipt of 5/– a week – Old Age Pension … The family are regarded as being in struggling circumstances;

all are inclined to be delicate and occasionally under medical care. Mollie O'Shea ... is subject to period fits of melancholia.'[34] Annie O'Shea finally received a gratuity of £112 from the Department of Defence, and in 1959 her daughter Ellen was paid a dependant's allowance. As late as the late 1980s, payments to the O'Shea's were being dealt with by the Tánaiste Brian Lenihan and his Fianna Fáil colleague Tom McEllistrim TD (Junior).

The psychological effects of what occurred at Ballyseedy impacted the family of James Walsh, too. Following the explosion, his sister, Mary, a member of Churchill Cumann na mBan, 'took charge' of her brother's remains along with Joan Flynn of Kilfenora.[35] A medical report detailed Mary's years of poor physical and mental health, including 'delirium'. She was 'emotional and evidently depressed'.[36] Described as 'destitute' by Tom McEllistrim TD in the early 1960s, Mary died in St Finan's Psychiatric Hospital in 1967.[37]

Patrick Hartnett of Gortnaminch, Listowel, was beside Stephen Fuller when the mine was detonated. His mother, who fractured her knee when she went to Ballymullen Barracks to retrieve Patrick's remains, didn't speak 'ten words in twelve months' and died in 1924, partly because of 'an injury to her knee sustained by her on a journey from Tralee after the death of her son'.[38] Two months after the massacre, Patrick's brother John died: he had been beaten by Free State officers earlier that year. Their father 'suffered a complete breakdown ... and died practically of a broken heart' in his eightieth year on St Patrick's Day in 1932, leaving 'three boys and a girl, all unmarried to bear the heavy burden'.[39] Writing from Leinster House, Stephen Fuller, a Fianna Fáil TD from 1937 to 1943, appealed for recompense for the family: 'he [Hartnett] was killed by my side ... his people are entitled to pension or gratuity'.[40] Just one of Patrick Hartnett's siblings, Mary, met the criteria for an award and was paid £112 under the Pensions Acts.

The family of Patrick Buckley was also in dire straits: a report prepared by the Ministry of Home Affairs a year after the incident, and released for the first time in 2008, indicated that his wife and six children were 'living with some friends and they have no visible means of obtaining a livelihood'. It was noted that they were being supported by small subscriptions collected for the family.[41] Separately, Tom McEllistrim TD implored the Minister for Defence to assist the family of John Daly, another of the Ballyseedy victims. In 1935 his father, Patrick, was, McEllistrim wrote, 'in very poor financial circumstances, he has no means whatsoever'.[42]

Eileen O'Connor was expecting her second baby when her husband, John, died in the early hours of 7 March. John O'Connor had grown up in Innishannon, Co. Cork and had served in the Royal Navy.[43] He bade farewell to his wife for the last time at their home in Liverpool at the beginning of 1923. His daughter Caitlín recalled: 'He told my mother that he was giving up the fight. He believed it was over. That was March 1923. He told her he was going to America. He was hoping to find work there. He would then bring my mother and I [sic] to America.'[44] However, O'Connor was arrested after a ship on which he was a crew member arrived at Fenit on 5 March 1923 and he was taken to jail. It is suggested that O'Connor was selected as one of those to be taken to Ballyseedy – despite that fact that he wasn't on active service with the anti-Treaty IRA – because another prisoner who had been chosen had been so badly beaten that he was unable to be taken from the barracks.[45] Eileen O'Connor learned of her husband's death at her home in Liverpool:

I immediately proceeded to Tralee to bury my poor husband. After the funeral I was making my way back to England, when I was arrested on the train and conveyed to the Barracks, Tralee, and searched ... I was frantic over my little child whom I left in the care of my mother who was ill and had no one to look after her. After a week in Kilmainham, I was released. The consequence of my detention is I have lost my employment, also my health.[46]

When their mother returned to Liverpool, three-year old Caitlín and her sister Eileen, who was born on 1 November 1923, were looked after by the Irish White Cross and Children's Relief Association in Dublin. In 1926 they were placed under the court-appointed guardianship of Áine Ceannt of that organisation.[47] The children went to boarding school at the Presentation Sisters Convent in Ballingarry in Co. Tipperary.[48] Caitlín and Eileen were awarded an annual allowance of £18 per year in 1935 and, following appeals from the Irish White Cross, a contribution was made towards their boarding school fees. It is Caitlín O'Connor, who was only two years old when her father lost his life at Ballyseedy, who is depicted in her mother's arms at the Ballyseedy Memorial, which was unveiled near the site of the massacre in 1959.[49] When that monument – which was designed by Uinseann Mac Eoin and sculpted by Breton Yann Renard-Goulet – was unveiled on 30 August, Stephen Fuller was not invited: he had joined and been elected a TD for Fianna Fáil (1937–43) much to the chagrin of Sinn Féin, which maintained a policy of abstaining from Dáil Éireann.[50] It was unveiled by May Daly, whose brother Charlie had been executed in Donegal in 1923. May had contested the general election in Kerry North in 1957 on an abstentionist platform but was not elected. The commemoration of the massacre would remain the subject of many rival ceremonies over the years as Sinn Féin and the more hardline Republican Sinn Féin (formed in 1986) sought to lay claim to the legacy of the incident.[51]

CHAPTER 16

'You would get that for the loss of a finger, not to mind the loss of life'

Dr Frank Murray tended to the medical needs of the people the Bronx in New York City in the 1930s. Like anyone in general practice in the bustling city at the time, he had come across a wide diversity of ailments and medical complaints in his work as a medical officer and was experienced in recognising and diagnosing a huge array of illnesses and diseases. But in his many years in medicine, he had never treated a survivor of Ireland's Civil War. In November 1934 Tadhg Coffey, the only survivor of the explosion at Countess Bridge in March 1923, presented himself at Murray's rooms at West 76th Street, New York, for an examination. Coffey, who was forced to emigrate to the US after the Civil War, was in the process of applying to the Department of Defence for financial compensation for the injuries he sustained. Applicants were required to undergo an assessment by medical professionals to establish the extent of their injuries and the nature of any physical and mental disability. Dr Murray prepared a report on Coffey for the Department of Defence, for which he was paid £3–3–0 the following year. The assessment suggests that the impact of the blast from which Coffey escaped eleven years previously had enduring physical and psychological impacts. Dr Murray found Coffey to be 'considerably underweight' with:

> Injury to lower end of spine, scar left forearm (mine explosion). Frequent attacks of dizziness (aftermath of beatings received when prisoner of Free State Troops and mine explosion in Co. Kerry in 1922 [1923] of which claimant was the only survivor of five), headaches. Unable to stand on ladders or any heights without marked tremors ... scar on chin and displaced teeth (butt end of rifle) ... History of dizziness, headaches and tremors of frequent occurrence, symptoms of Neurasthenia.[1]

Neurasthenia was a medical term dating from the nineteenth century which was used to describe a weakness of the nerves and included symptoms such as anxiety, depression and exhaustion, as well as headache, fainting and dizziness. Its modern equivalent would be post-traumatic stress disorder. Other medical assessments referred to Coffey's difficulty in crowded places: he complained of 'dizziness and confusion of mind when in crowds, this occurs when he goes to Mass'.[2] A further account from the early 1940s referenced injury to the spine, chronic pain and stiffness, and the fact that Coffey was 'feeling nervous'. Many of his various scars and injuries were attributed to 'military service in Óglaigh na h-Éireann (I.R.A.)'.[3] While an inpatient at St Bricin's Military Hospital in Dublin in 1941, after he returned to Ireland, he was sleeping '3 to 4 hours nightly'.[4] It was a mystery to Dr Edward Carey of Killarney how Coffey had 'retained his mental stability' after being blown up and shot at by Free State soldiers at Countess Bridge.[5] Ned O'Sullivan from Beaufort, who was Coffey's commanding officer claimed that he 'was not right in the head for a good bit after that'.[6]

In applying to the government for compensation, Coffey described how he was arrested on 22 February 1923 and beaten regularly in jail, including 'with a heavy iron poker on the back'.[7] He explained that he was forced to go on the run and, within a year of Countess Bridge, was recuperating at Frankfort House, the home of Countess Markievicz in Dublin. While Coffey was staying with Markievicz, the house was often raided by the gardaí, who seized 1,500 copies of the Official Handbook of Fianna Éireann, the youth wing of the IRA.[8] There was also a raid to seize copies of *Tragedies of Kerry* by Dorothy Macardle, who was staying with Markievicz. As he was still suffering from his injuries, Markievicz and Macardle took Coffey to different medics in Dublin for treatment, including a surgeon named Macaulay, who found 'serious injury to the spine'.[9] Countess Markievicz acquired information 'that they [the Free State Army] wanted to do away with' Coffey, that 'the troops had orders to get me and not bring me in'. On learning that his home in Kerry was being repeatedly raided, Coffey went to Canada in 1925, and later to the US, with orders 'by no means to go home'. He followed a path that, by the mid-1920s, had become well-worn by anti-Treatyites who struggled to find work or peace in the new Free State. There he met other IRA men, including Jeremiah Murphy from Headford, to whom he relayed all the 'gory details' of what he had endured.[10]

After Coffey married and settled in Barleymount near Killarney, he continued to endure pain and ill health. Despite the copious medical evidence supporting his claims for recompense, the doctors' reports did not prevent a reduction in Coffey's disability allowance in 1942. Dismayed and disillusioned, in February 1943 Coffey wrote to the Taoiseach, Éamon de Valera, as well as the Minister for Defence, Oscar Traynor, asking them to investigate the reduction. He reminded the Taoiseach that he was the only survivor of the

Countess Bridge incident and that 'Stephen Fuller TD was the only other case similar to mine. We were awarded this pension since ye came into power.'[11] There appears to have been no response to his plea. Mrs Elizabeth Coffey made an unsuccessful application under the Army Pensions Acts in respect of the death of her husband, who died on 26 October 1966. As late as 1969, the Fianna Fáil TD for Kerry South, John O'Leary, was urging a senior minister that Mrs Coffey should receive some of her late husband's pension 'in view of the fact that he was disabled all his life, as a result of wounds received ... and that he died from these wounds eventually'.[12] However, there was to be no further remuneration for the Coffey family arising from the tragic events of 7 March 1923.

For the families of the four men who died at the hands of their Free State Army captors at Countess Bridge, the process of securing allowances and gratuities was also complicated and distressing. Hannah Buckley told the department that her son Stephen was arrested on 3 March and brought to Killarney Barracks before he was taken to Countess Bridge. She also gave details of the arrest and treatment of two other sons, William and Timothy. After his release, William was for years 'under the care of doctors and will never be able to do a hard days' work again'. Timothy, who was jailed in Tipperary, was 'a physical and mental wreck'.[13] Ten years after the Civil War, Hannah Buckley's circumstances 'had not changed appreciably'.[14] She eventually received a payment of £112 under the 1932 Act on the basis of partial dependency on Stephen at the time of his death and the fact that he was the youngest of his family, working the family farm when all his siblings had left home. Stephen's sister, Mary, also applied for an award but was told that 'the Minister for Finance is not of the opinion, having regard to all the circumstances of the case, that you should be treated as a dependant of your deceased brother'.[15]

Daniel Donoghue, who had four younger siblings, was described as the 'mainstay of the household' and was the principal worker on the family farm, which was sixty-four acres of 'very poor land'.[16] As a result of his death, the family had to employ help on the farm. His mother, Bridget, claimed that her payment application was delayed for political reasons, because as 'ardent sympathisers of the "Irregulars", they were debarred' from making a claim under previous Acts. Matters were further complicated by the absence of a death certificate, because Daniel's death was not properly registered.[17] Like so many bereaved families, the only immediate financial aid received after the Civil War was £50 from the Irish White Cross, which supported families impacted by the wars between 1919 and 1923. The Board of Assessors decided that Bridget was only partially dependent on her son, but, 'having regard to the special circumstances in the case,' agreed to recommend a payment of £112 to the Donoghues.[18]

Timothy Murphy's death left his father, Patrick, 'a poor man', his solicitor claimed, 'and this loss has broken his health badly'.[19] While it was determined that the Murphy family was 'fairly comfortable', a partial dependency on the deceased was accepted.[20] Another victim, Jeremiah O'Donoghue, had worked as an attendant in the local psychiatric hospital and was the main financial support for his parents and seven siblings – two sisters were in the United States – in 1923. After his death, the O'Donoghue home was raided and the furniture broken.[21] To compound the family's grief, Jeremiah's father died a few months after the Civil War. His widow, Margaret O'Donoghue, told the Department of Defence that she had 'put hard times over me, at times practically hungry'.[22] She had to rely on a £100 contribution from the Irish White Cross to help her pay her bills. She was eventually awarded a gratuity of £112 in respect of the loss of Jeremiah, but in a letter to Éamon de Valera in 1942, the level of compensation was criticised by Julia O'Donoghue, sister of the deceased:

> I am writing on behalf of my mother who is 77 years of age. She thinks she is entitled to a pension for her son, RIP, that was murdered at the Countesses [*sic*] Bridge. She got 100 [£112] a long time ago but you would get that for the loss of a finger, not to mind the loss of life, and what about all the ones that got big pensions and a lump sum and they did not do anything, most of them ... It is like asking for bread and you get stones ... I hope you won't be offended at this letter but it is hard to see others with big pensions and my mother with nothing after the loss of her son, and a good son at that.[23]

The case was taken up by Fionán Lynch TD, despite him having been a senior figure in the army which had presided over the killings at Countess Bridge. Lynch told an official that he had visited Mrs O'Donoghue's home during a visit to Killarney in 1943 and found that she was 'in dire poverty'.[24] Julia O'Donoghue was awarded an allowance of £125 in 1953.

+++

The families of all of the victims of the mine explosion at Bahaghs were denied compensation in the immediate aftermath of the incident. One of the victims, Eugene Dwyer, was a labourer who earned about £2 per week. He gave most of his earnings to his parents and his death left them in 'very straightened circumstances', according to a local garda inspector.[25] Having been refused any hearing by the Cosgrave administration, Dwyer's father, Michael, implored the

Fianna Fáil government in the early 1940s for compensation and protested the way in which his means were being used to deny him a payment. He was living in a 'barren spot' with three unmarried sons at home who could not afford to get married and he was grieving 'the blowing up of my favourite son to pieces'.[26] A gratuity payment was eventually made.

Another of the victims, John Sugrue, one of twelve siblings (six of whom emigrated to the United States), had done the bulk of the work on the family farm in Ballinskelligs and had fished for herring and mackerel off the south Kerry coast. Following the creation of the Meath Gaeltacht in the mid-1930s, his family moved and settled there in the parish of Donaghpatrick. Patrick Sugrue, John's father, became unwell, however, and was, according to records in the military pensions archives, committed to Mullingar Mental Hospital in the 1940s.[27]

As with the other victims, the Compensation (Personal Injuries) Committee ruled that no compensation be paid to Dan Shea's father, James, as they did not consider him dependent on his son, a view with which the Minister for Finance concurred.[28] Ten years later, the department revised their assessment to a partial dependency, and James Shea received a dependant's gratuity of £112. Daniel's mother, Mary, who, according to John B. Healy TD, owed 'considerable sums of money' which could not be paid as James was unable to work, was further provided an allowance in the 1940s.[29]

William Riordan was just eighteen years old when he was shot in the legs and blown up by Free State soldiers at Bahaghs. His mother, Ellen, had worked as a washerwoman in hotels in the area until her son was killed. As her husband was out of work, Ellen had relied on additional income from William, the 'greater part' of his wages being given to his mother each week.[30] Another son, Peter, who lived with her, had been badly beaten in prison and was described as a

'complete wreck … unfit for any work'.[31] In 1934 Ellen felt compelled to write to Dorothy Macardle, who had published the story
of Bahaghs in *Tragedies of Kerry*. Macardle told the Minister for
Defence, Frank Aiken, that she had received a 'very distressing letter' from Mrs Riordan, who was 'desperately poor now'. She wondered if 'the families of prisoners murdered while in custody have or
will have a claim?'[32] Ellen Riordan eventually received a payment
of £112, but the money was of little solace in alleviating her poor
health. She was certified by her doctor as 'neurasthenic' over the
course of twenty years and, as a result, was never able to resume
work or 'go out and follow an occupation like women of her age
and time have done'.[33]

The awarding of pensions and allowances to one family member and not another caused divisions and frustration. John O'Shea's
brother, Patrick, drowned after leaving the caves at Clashmealcon in
April 1923. Their father received compensation of £112 and a subsequent allowance from 1941 onwards, but John was refused a payment because he failed to meet the eligibility criteria. In the 1950s,
John implied that the department was discriminating against him:

> What do ye mean by giving one relative a pension and cutting
> another relative out of a pension, didn't my brother loose [*sic*]
> his life for Ireland as well as any other one and wasn't his life
> as valuable as the rest. If ye are not going to do something
> with me in a pension, put me into some home for I am an
> encumbrance to myself and to every other one that is playing
> with me.[34]

Patrick O'Shea's cousin, Thomas McGrath, drowned in the Atlantic
with him and though his father, Peter, was denied a payment because
of his means, his sister, Mary, was awarded an allowance. The

payment came after she begged the Department of Defence not to 'send me to the poorhouse' and as her health and circumstances deteriorated.[35]

The families of those executed after Clashmealcon had very contrasting fortunes in their subsequent engagements with the pensions process. One of those put to death on 25 April, Edward (Ned) Greaney, was the adopted son of Elizabeth Quinlan. Edward's father had died at a young age and his mother moved to Australia, leaving her son in the care of their cousins, the Quinlan family.[36] Mrs Quinlan was deemed ineligible for an allowance under the 1932 Act, which made no provision for adoptive parents and because she was deemed not to have been dependent on Edward at the time of his death.[37] The parents of Reginald Hathaway (Stenning) – a former British Army officer who joined the IRA – were also unable to prove their dependency on their son. Walter and Edith Stenning were supported by their local vicar in Oxford in their application during the 1930s, but to no avail.[38] In contrast, James McEnery's wife, Hannah, and her two-year-old son, Henry, were found to be 'totally dependent' on James when he was executed and were awarded the relevant allowance of £67 per annum, reliant as they were on an income from '4 cows, 4 calves, pigs, etc' and some support from Fr Thomas McEnery, who intervened in an attempt to prevent the executions.[39] However, within two years of James' execution, his sister, Catherine, who was 'a witness to "Clashmealcon of Slaughter"' was dead.[40]

The experiences of the survivors and the relatives of those who were killed during these events left them besieged by trauma for the rest of their lives, an experience shared by many other survivors of the Civil War.

CHAPTER 17

'We are near starving'

The dugout in the heart of rural north Kerry was described by *The Freeman's Journal* as 'a cleverly-constructed room inside a hayrick'.[1] It was about seven feet square. Hiding in this sanctuary on the farm of James Costello at Trieneragh in Duagh in the second week of April 1923 were three members of the north Kerry IRA: Jack Mullaly, John (Seán) Linnane and Richard (Dick) Bunyan.[2] The trio were wanted men. Linnane had fought the Free State Army in Limerick city in July 1922, while Bunyan had been involved in an ambush in which two soldiers were killed a few months previously.[3] At about 7.30 a.m. on 13 April, Linnane, Mullaly and Bunyan were awoken by the arrival of a nine-man Free State Army search party. Details of what followed differ in the varying accounts, but what is clear is that Seán Linnane was shot and died instantly.[4] The shooting happened despite evidence from Richard Bunyan at the inquest into Linnane's death that the IRA men had surrendered and declared, 'All right, we will go out.'[5] As Linnane was shot, Bunyan noticed that he had been 'wounded in the right breast' and head, and Bunyan himself was injured by 'pieces of bone' and fragments from Linnane's shattered skull, which spattered from his body when he was fired upon.[6] Linnane's body was removed to Listowel Workhouse and, after his wounds were dressed at Costello's farmhouse, Bunyan was taken to jail in Listowel along with Mullaly. Bunyan spent time on hunger strike before he was released from jail on Christmas Eve 1923.

The physical and psychological scars of what occurred at Trieneragh in April 1923 endured. A decade after the incident, Richard Bunyan was experiencing neurasthenia, chronic bronchitis and pleuritis, headaches and 'noises in the head'.[7] His infirmity prevented him for applying for a position with An Garda Síochána in 1933. In 1940 Bunyan was certified as suffering from 'GSW [gunshot wound] to the head as well as neurasthenia, repeated headaches' and he was 'very nervous at times'. In considering Bunyan's application for a pension payment for his years of active service with the IRA, however, the Board of Assessors determined that his injuries represented just a 20 per cent 'degree of disablement' and decided that he should paid a pension of 20 per cent of the maximum allowable for a period of just twelve months.[8] There was lengthy correspondence over many years about the size of the pension which Bunyan received. His solicitor insisted that he 'returned home [from prison] completely broken in mind and in body and will be a physical wreck, as is only natural after years of hardship'.[9] He finally received a temporary wound pension of £45 per annum, but only until 1937; it was reduced to £30 thereafter. His wife, Bunyan wrote, had 'been urging me to sell out and go to England but it is the last thing I would like to do'.[10] At this time, according to Dr John Gallagher of Day Place, Tralee, Bunyan was suffering from what appeared to Parkinson's Disease and was experiencing dizziness, tremors and headaches.[11] He received no further compensation from the government and died on 2 December 1979.

The family of Seán Linnane, from Glouria in Lisselton, who died at the dugout in Duagh, also sought compensation. Sean's father, John, told the department that his son 'gave heart and soul to the

Republican cause'. The family were 'poor people of no means to live on but a few acres of bog'.[12] Seán's brother, Tom, was arrested two days before the shooting in Duagh and was refused release from custody to attend the funeral in Gale Cemetery. After the war, Tom and another brother emigrated, their father noted, 'leaving us both alone to mourn our loss'. John Linnane continued:

> Our dear son was an obedient, kind and loving son and [it] was a sorrow to our heart to see him laid on his blood in a hay shed. His mother washed the blood of my loved son and the sorrow of his father and I was pitiable on that morning. May God rest his soul and all souls. He was a pioneer and a weekly Communicant ...[13]

The Board of Assessors considered evidence that Seán Linnane contributed an income to the household of £40 per year from his job as a draper's assistant. John was paid a partial dependant's allowance of £112–10–0, and a further allowance between 1939 and his death. The money was used to pay off 'debts to tradespeople and on ordinary living expenses'.[14] When John died in 1944, his wife, Margaret, failed to secure the transfer of the payment to her own name as it wasn't provided for in law.[15] Her son, Tom, came home from the United States to care for his mother, who 'had great trouble getting money to bury her husband' and had 'a nervous breakdown since her husband's death'.[16] When his mother died, Tom tried, but failed, to secure an allowance, as he was unable to find work and in recognition of doing 'my part too in the fight for freedom doing long jail terms and hunger strike'.[17]

+++

Dugouts like the one at Duagh left men on the run with lasting ill health and ailments into their later years, and represent one of the enduring legacies of the Civil War. Many of those who sought pensions or allowances from the government identified the deprivations of the dugout as a cause of poor health. For example, Jeremiah Sullivan from Glenbeigh blamed his asthma, bronchitis and pulmonary tuberculosis on the exposure he experienced while hiding in such temporary quarters during the Civil War.[18] Michael O'Connor of Knockeen, Castleisland, also specified the misery endured in hay barns, ditches and empty sheds, along with the lack of regular meals. O'Connor had been involved in the burning of Castleisland Barracks in August 1922, as well as ambushes of Free State forces. For much of the final period of the Civil War, however, he was on the run because his home was 'continually raided' by the army.[19] O'Connor claimed that he suffered from recurring chest problems and bronchitis because of sleeping in wet clothes and not eating properly. He was unable to work and at times could not sleep 'for want of breath'.[20]

The beatings and torture which many endured in prison could also have lifelong effects. John McEllistrim from Ballymacelligott, a brother of Tom McEllistrim, had sustained a gunshot wound and lost the use of one arm during the War of Independence. Alongside his sisters, Lena and Hannah, who were members of Cumann na mBan, he opposed the Treaty and took up arms against the Free State forces in Kerry.[21] McEllistrim was arrested in Castlemaine in April 1923 and was 'badly beaten by his capturers' while in jail.[22] He developed 'a kind of pneumonia and was spitting out blood' to the extent that he was released from custody.[23] However, having a brother in the Dáil was no guarantee of preferment when it came to securing recompense. Writing from Peamount Sanitorium in Dublin in 1938, McEllistrim appealed to the Department of Defence to expedite his claim 'as I am terrible pressed by outstanding debts at present'.[24] William O'Leary, later a TD for Kerry, also claimed that he was severely beaten, including 'a knocking around in Abbeyfeale in the guard room' while he was in prison, to the extent that, on the advice of his doctor, he 'signed the form' committing not to take up arms against the State and was released at Christmas 1922.[25]

The psychological toll of combat speaks loudly, too, from the pension application files of the anti-Treaty IRA in Kerry. Michael Enright of Derrymore joined a flying column under Paddy Cahill in September 1922 and took part in sniping operations until his arrest in February 1923. He was interned in Tralee Gaol until November 1923 and was on hunger strike for thirty-one days. By 1966, when application was made for a special allowance under the Pensions Acts, Enright was a patient at St Finan's Psychiatric Hospital in Killarney and was unable to complete the application form and unable to answer any questions about his application. Tom McEllistrim claimed that Enright had been hospitalised after a nervous breakdown as a result of being beaten in prison.[26] The department determined that as the yearly income from his farm was too high, no award of a special allowance could be made.

A former British Army soldier, Thomas McLoughlin of the Kiltallagh Company of the IRA, was among the Kerry republicans who took the fight to the Free State Army in County Limerick. The impact on McLoughlin's mental health – affected not just by the trauma of the War of Independence and the Civil War, but also his service in the British Army during the First World War – was profound. In a house near Kilmallock in County Limerick on 31 July 1922, McLoughlin shot himself in the head, but was not killed. The following day, he cut himself with a razor and succumbed to his injuries.[27] Elsewhere, the toll of the war became too great for Neil O'Leary of Knockanes near Killarney. He fought against the Free State forces in east Kerry in 1922–23. When a comrade of O'Leary's, Mick 'Cud' O'Sullivan, had been shot dead at Knockanes in November 1922, O'Leary's sister, Maggie had cradled the dying man in her arms. As Tim Horgan details, Neil O'Leary became extremely unwell and took his own life in a Cork nursing home using a piece of broken china.[28]

In many cases, physical and psychological wounds were compounded by financial hardship and distress. 'When I came home [from prison] after the Civil War,' wrote Billy Mullins from Tralee, 'I came back to poverty.'[29] Like Tadhg Coffey, who escaped the bombs and bullets of the Free State Army at Countess Bridge, David Fitzgerald from Boherbee in Tralee suffered from neurasthenia in later life. In his late thirties, he was assessed as suffering from the nervous condition, as well as duodenal ulcers which, his doctor reported, were 'contracted as a result of privation and hardships suffered on active service, and during imprisonment'. He also suffered from insomnia, dizziness, a loss of power in his legs, vomiting after eating, and was unable to work 'owing to tremor of hands'.[30] Fitzgerald spent twenty days on hunger strike in prison and he was released in January 1924. Jerry Myles, his O/C, wrote that his 'condition of health is due to his IRA activities', while Eamon O'Connor, former editor of the anti-Treaty *Kerry Leader* newspaper, was convinced that Fitzgerald 'never completely recovered from the last hunger strike'.[31] Financial woes compounded the physical scars, as Fitzgerald told officials in October 1935:

> I was in prison during the most of the Civil War and was unable to work after being released. Suffering from my nerves and stomach. I have a wife + 4 young children and nothing to keep them. I would feel obliged if I could hear from you in the course of a few days as there is [*sic*] bills pressing me and rent unpaid, for 2 years.[32]

The Board of Assessors accepted in 1936 that Fitzgerald was '100%' disabled as a result of active service, and his pension payment, first drawn down in 1932, was increased to £150 per annum.

Michael O'Connell of Doolague, Castleisland, had been shot in the leg during the War of Independence but continued to be active with the anti-Treatyites during the Civil War. In 1924 the Kerry Command of the Free State Army insisted that O'Connell was capable of maintaining '8 or 9 cows' and that he didn't appear disabled 'in the least'.[33] Dr John Prendiville of Brosna disagreed, certifying that O'Connell was suffering from several conditions but also a 'general nervous and physical breakup' after the Civil War.[34] O'Connell was in dire straits a decade after that conflict: 'We are near starving, I cannot afford to pay a workman in my stead on my little farm,' he wrote in 1933.[35]

By 1936, John Francis O'Shea from Portmagee – who had been arrested by Free State troops on the Bog of Allen in Tipperary and spent twenty-one days on hunger strike in jail – was in broken health, and the fishing industry on which he relied for a livelihood was 'practically dead'. He appealed for a pension to ensure he had 'the bare necessities of life'.[36] Significant financial hardship also befell the Lucey family of Caragh Lake. Con Lucey took part in several attacks on the Free State Army, including those at Castlemaine and Killorglin. He was interned in the Curragh until two days before Christmas in 1923, spending three weeks on hunger strike. During a prolonged appeal on a decision to recognise just part of his years of service, Lucey's business suffered badly, and by 1942 he was in debt to the sum of £150, several creditors had applied for committal orders in the courts, and it was 'much more difficult,' his solicitor wrote, 'for him to carry on and maintain his wife and three children,' including a young baby.[37]

In many cases, sources of income like the pension payment were a lifeline to those without another means of financial support. By the 1950s, James Murphy from Castle Countess in Tralee was completely reliant on his annual pension payment of £32 to maintain his family and to cover rates, ground rent and a mortgage. Apart from that, he required 'help in kind from his brothers and from his people-in-law'.[38] Murphy, who went on hunger strike while in jail in 1923, was suffering from low cerebration, memory loss and headaches, to the extent that his employer, Patrick Connolly, a pawnbroker and jeweller of Upper Castle Street, Tralee, was 'reluctantly compelled to let him go in 1941' as Murphy was making mistakes with customer accounts.[39] When he was summoned for further medical examination by the Department of Defence, Murphy's wife, Bridget, was fearful that if such an examination was to take place in the Mental Hospital in Killarney, he might be detained and that 'an impediment to my children's welfare would in consequence result'.[40] A claim for a special allowance payment in 1947 was rejected by the department, but it finally acknowledged that Murphy was in permanent infirmity and he was paid an additional allowance in 1954. Murphy's trauma, and the bureaucratic ordeal which he and his family had to endure, was replicated across the county for decades to come.

CHAPTER 18

'She has become generally listless'

When the Black and Tans went on the rampage in Tralee in November 1920 during one of the most ferocious periods of the War of Independence, Sally Sheehy from Boherbee in the town was put out of work. When the printing presses of Quinnell & Sons, which produced the *Kerry News* and the *Kerry Weekly Reporter* newspapers, succumbed to the flames of the Tans' explosives, not only were many journalists deprived of their jobs, but machine operators and proof-readers like Sally also became unemployed. The Quinnell printing presses managed to begin rolling again before the end of 1920 and Sally returned to her day job, but by this time she was increasingly immersed in her work as a member of the local Cumann na mBan. When the Civil War broke out, Sally left Quinnell & Sons and became a full-time volunteer, supporting the campaign of the local anti-Treaty IRA by doing intelligence work, carrying messages and tending to men on the run. She carried weapons which had been seized from the army and was involved in an attempted burning of a Protestant Hall in Tralee.[1] This work took its toll. In the early hours of 7 March 1923, Sally was one of those who went to the site of the Ballyseedy massacre. There, with some of her comrades, she 'gathered the remains of the dead' including 'bodies, brains, clothes'.[2] A few months later, Sally tried to resume her day job at Quinnell & Sons, but at the end of 1924 she suffered a nervous breakdown. She had no doubt about the cause: 'I attribute my breakdown to my activities during the Civil War.' Repeated spells of ill health forced her to leave her job and she emigrated to the United States in 1928.

Sally Sheehy's story is not only a reminder of the enormous toll taken on the physical and mental health of members of Cumann na mBan during the Civil War, but also shows how they continued to be a significant paramilitary force in the years after independence. For countless members there was a continuity from the War of Independence and the battle with the forces of the Crown to the fight against the Free State forces between 1922 and 1923. 'I was neither afraid of tans or Staters' remarked Catherine MacKenna of Callinafercy, Milltown.[3] The work these women did – carrying messages, providing food and accommodation for IRA men on the run, intelligence work, and hiding and carrying guns and ammunition – was integral to the republican campaign in Kerry. Testimonies provided by Cumann na mBan's members in later years in support of applications for pensions offer valuable insights into their activities.

Mary Brosnan of Cordal was typical of members who provided IRA men with clothes, food and cigarettes. On one occasion she hid two cartloads of guns and ammunition, as well as first aid equipment, in her house for a month.[4] In Laughtacallow, Castlemaine, Mary Ann O'Dowd attended to men who were wounded in combat, as well as a soldier who had deserted the Free State Army. She carried dispatches to Tralee five or six times, stored arms and sent parcels of food and cigarettes to prisoners.[5] Josephine Cashman of Brookhill, Beaufort, escorted two wounded men from Killorglin to Cahersiveen Workhouse and spent several weeks nursing them.[6] Norah Keane of Tullig, Castleisland, provided accommodation for anti-Treaty fighters for weeks after the barracks in Castleisland was attacked and she 'took charge of all their private papers and money'.[7] The home of Katty Quill at Gortaloughera, Kilgarvan, became a 'de facto' barracks for anti-Treaty fighters and sometimes accommodated up to sixty-five men, among them divisional commanders like Liam Lynch, Erskine Childers and Liam Deasy. Quill was perhaps modest when she wrote: 'It was hard going.'[8]

At their home in Boolteens, Castlemaine, Nora and Nellie Corcoran ran a bespoke 'dressing station' to host wounded men 'when nobody else would' during the Civil War. Among those whom the sisters looked after was Thomas O'Connor from Milltown, after he was shot through the lung and arm in County Limerick in July 1922.[9] They dressed wounds and procured the services of doctors and nurses 'at great risk and inconvenience', and found alternative accommodation for the injured when they were tipped off about a possible raid by the Free State forces, which happened several times.[10] Soldiers fired a shot outside their home, threatened to kill one of their farm workers and took away their horse.[11]

The testimony of Hannah Carmody of Ballylongford provides a useful example of the diverse range of activities carried out by members of the organisation between July 1922 and March 1923:

> Took part in the usual activities of Derry [Ballylongford] Cumann na mBan. Procured a rifle in Listowel and brought it out to my home and handed it over fully loaded to [IRA Flying] Column men. Procured revolver and ammunition from a Free State prisoner and handed it over to Miss Mai Murphy. Procured ammunition from Dick Barrett of Listowel and gave it over to Commdt Ned Joe Walsh in August 1922. Received dispatches from prisoners who had escaped from Free State

Troops and transmitted them to IRA. During the attack on Tarbert Barracks in Sept 1922 my house at Derry was used as H/Q and prisoners kept there who had been captured by IRA ... In March 1923 I was arrested with others by Free State troops and taken to Limerick Prison where we were later released.[12]

Carmody's testimony points to the fact that the activities of Cumann na mBan members in this period often placed them at considerable physical risk and belies any notion that they were not legitimate combatants or had an inferior or secondary role in the war.

These activities were not without significant consequences for the women's health and well-being. Mental health difficulties and nervous breakdown are a common thread through the accounts of Kerry members. Úna Moriarty of Annascaul was another of those who went to Ballyseedy in the hours after the explosion. During the final months of the war, she came under fire while putting up posters and doing intelligence work. She also travelled to London to purchase arms for the anti-Treaty IRA and brought home 'a trunk full' of guns and ammunition. In September 1923 she 'collapsed with a nervous breakdown' and was tended to by Dr Michael Shanahan, the county surgeon, who had a practice at Denny Street in Tralee. He certified that Moriarty was

> suffering from an epileptic seizure which repeated itself rather frequently ... I knew her prior to 1923, she was a robust healthy young lady. I am of [the] opinion that these attacks were brought about by severe strain and the nerve racking time she went through in 1922 and some years previously ... She lost her employment through not being able to concentrate in her work and she has become generally listless.[13]

An unfortunate aspect of the role of many Cumann na mBan members in this period was their attendance at the scenes of ambushes, murders and executions to wash and dress bodies and prepare them for burial. In February 1923 Joan Flynn helped in 'washing and dressing' the bodies of Michael Sinnott and James O'Connor, who were shot dead at a dugout in Currahane.[14] Margaret Lyne O'Connell of The Spa also attended the bodies and arranged the funerals – one note in her file refers to it as 'one of the most tragic and beastly crimes committed during the Civil War'.[15] O'Connell was later said to be suffering from shock and nervousness.

Women's homes often became the frontline of battle. The home of Bridie O'Sullivan at Ballineanig, Ballyferriter, was repeatedly raided by the army, and in February 1923 her brother Thomas was shot dead. Bridie's health collapsed. She suffered from nervous fits until 1926, when she went to America, but the new environment offered no respite and she spent a year in hospital. Writing in 1936, O'Sullivan claimed that she was 'a total wreck every bit of me shaking and nothing can be done for me'.[16] Margaret Barrett of Bedford, Listowel, was also a 'physical wreck after the trouble'. She had provided information to the IRA which resulted in the killing of a Free State officer, and she was a lookout for an ambush at Bedford in August 1922. Years later, when she appealed to the Department of Defence for a pension payment, she told officials she was 'still in a bad state of nervous debility'.[17] For Bridget O'Connor of Kilcow, Castleisland, life in the years after the Civil War – during which she was arrested and jailed on three occasions – was hampered by nervousness, claustrophobia and weakness. By the early 1950s she was 'permanently incapacitated' and deemed incapable of earning an independent living.[18] Ellen Griffin, a member of Ballymacelligott Cumann na mBan, told the Department of Defence that: 'My nerves broke down after the terrific strain' of 1922–23.[19]

In a case which the Minister for Defence described as 'exceptional', Siobhán (Johanna) Cleary from Ballymore near Dingle suffered a horrific breakdown and death as a direct result of her involvement in the Civil War.[20] Siobhán, one of ten siblings who lived on a smallholding, worked as a nurse at Cork Mental Hospital and was an active member of Cumann na mBan in the city between 1920 and 1923. She was arrested in 1923 and jailed in the North Dublin Union and Kilmainham Gaol. Cleary spent fourteen days on hunger strike before being released in October 1923. Despite a very traumatic experience in prison, she returned to her work as a nurse but became very unwell in the summer of 1924. Cleary was admitted to the infirmary of the hospital where she worked. She died on 9 November from exophthalmic goitre and exhaustion from 'incessant vomiting [for] seven days'. Dr Cashman, who cared for her, was in no doubt as to why she had died so suddenly: 'shock, strain, hardship of imprisonment and hunger strike during the period of civil stress'.[21] Her mother, also Johanna, who had been supported by her daughter and had four children in America, was left to derive a living from 'merely the grass of two cows'.[22]

+++

Members of Cumann na mBan were often subjected to intimidation and suffered financially and in their employment for many years after the Civil War. Joan Nagle – whose brother, George, from Ballygamboon, Castlemaine, was killed at Derrynafeena in Glencar in April 1923 – was a commandant with Tralee Cumann na mBan and worked at a shop on Castle Street. A month after George's death, she was dismissed by her employer due to her republican 'activities and sympathies'.[23] The president of the organisation in Tralee, Lizanne O'Brien – whose brother, Billy Myles, was shot dead near a dugout at Curraheen in October 1922 – described having to 'give up my work absolutely' after the Civil War.[24] Ellen Griffin from Gortatlea was forced to sell her home and farm – which had served as a resting place for IRA leaders including Humphrey Murphy and John Joe Sheehy – because of the 'debts incurred by her in respect of fellows who absolutely eat her out of house and home'. She claimed that she and her husband were completely impoverished by 1940.[25] Griffin's neighbour, Hannah Clifford, was sacked as an assistant teacher at the Presentation Convent School in Tralee as a result of her role in the conflict, leaving her 'drifting penniless and broken in spirit'.[26] Also in Tralee, Mary Moriarty claimed that a female cousin fired her or 'had her ousted' from her uncle's business where she worked when they were told that Moriarty was using goods from the shop to supply IRA men.[27]

It was economic necessity that often drove Cumann na mBan members to apply for pensions and allowances in later years. Nora Lucey of Knocknaboola, Caragh Lake, who helped to remove some of the wounded men to safety during the fighting in Killorglin in September 1922, was reluctant for a long time to recognise the Irish Free State. 'I always held very extreme views with regard to a Republic for Ireland,' she wrote in 1952. But she acknowledged that just three years before that, there had been established 'a Republic for at least 26 counties [and] I feel justified in seeking some compensation'.[28] But Nora was motivated by necessity rather than politics to apply for a payment. She was then dependent on her brother, Con Lucey, an IRA volunteer, for support and was 'in very indifferent health'.[29] Con himself faced difficulties in his business and found it hard to pay the bills. Nora had been unable to stay in her home for several months after the Civil War, as the army 'kept raiding for our men'.[30]

For women like Nora, direct engagement with the enemy forces was common. May Moriarty of Castle Countess, Tralee, used a Red

Cross armband as a cover as she took 'guns from dead Free State soldiers who were lying in the streets'. She held up watchmen at a factory at Rock Street with a revolver while IRA men were stealing food.[31] When a Free State soldier placed his gun on the table in the kitchen of a friend's house after an ambush near Slievaddra in Ballyduff, Norah Casey and a friend distracted him and grabbed his weapon.[32] Joan O'Brien of Kilgobnet, Beaufort, who had been dragged from her house by the Black and Tans and threatened after an ambush near Killorglin in October 1921, fled to south Kerry, undeterred by the incident. While working in Cahersiveen she continued to be active in Cumann na mBan and tended to one of the IRA members injured in the ambush at Ohermong in September 1922. With four other women, O'Brien was arrested by soldiers, driven out of Cahersiveen, dropped on the side of the road and warned to stay out of the town. The women were arrested the following day and imprisoned on Valentia Island, where they took part in a hunger strike, and O'Brien later went on the run.[33] Nellie Pierce of Ballyheigue also faced expulsion from her home town when she was providing assistance to IRA men to hide in the attic of the local presbytery where she worked as a housekeeper. Not only was she was dismissed as the priest's housekeeper in February 1923 when it was discovered she was 'working for the IRA', she was also forbidden to enter Ballyheigue by Free State troops and threatened with arrest.[34]

Injuries and fatalities among Cumann na mBan members in Kerry were rare. The only known fatality was the result of an accident rather than an engagement in combat. The home of Nora and Daniel O'Leary of Knockacopple, Rathmore, was always 'open to the IRA when on the run during the Civil War'.[35] Nora was a member of the local Cumann na mBan. The thirty-seven-year-old died when an IRA volunteer, Denis Reen, accidentally discharged his gun in the O'Leary's home on 20 October 1922. Daniel O'Leary not only suffered the loss of his wife, but also struggled financially for many years and was unable to pay the cost of Nora's funeral. In 1937 his solicitor described O'Leary as being 'very destitute and is almost starving', but a claim for an allowance under the Military Pensions Acts was disallowed on the basis of ineligibility under the legislation.[36] Separately, Marguerite Fleming was injured at her home at Mileen in Kilcummin when a Free State Army detachment under Major General Paddy O'Daly arrested three men – her brother William Fleming, Dan Mulvihill and Con O'Leary – in August 1922. Marguerite was injured in the eye and both arms by the splinter of a bomb, but she 'resumed her good work for the IRA' according to a note from Denis Hegarty, O/C 3rd Battalion, Kerry No. 2 Brigade.[37]

Not all members of Cumann na mBan in Kerry were anti-Treaty. While the vast majority supported the campaign against the Free State forces, there were a small number who fully supported the government and the Kerry Command of the army. Mary Slattery from Ballymacelligott acted as a dispatch carrier for Colonel David Neligan and other soldiers. Mary's brother, Thomas, was a member of the Free State Army and was killed at Dromulton, Scartaglin, in February 1923. She arranged his funeral and also attended to other soldiers injured in the ambush. In a magnanimous gesture many years later, when Mary was applying for a pension to the Department of Defence, Fianna Fáil TD Tom McEllistrim wrote in support of her claim, despite the fact that she 'joined the Free State Army side' during the Civil War.[38]

Like their male counterparts, members of Cumann na mBan in Kerry faced lengthy delays and bureaucratic hurdles in their efforts to secure recompense. The task of successfully applying for a pension was protracted, and when they were awarded, applicants were often forced to query reductions in payments, chase up missing payments and fight to secure any additional allowances for which they became eligible. Hanna O'Connor was an active member of Cumann na mBan in Tralee and catered for the republican forces that took over Ballymullen Barracks. She had reported for duty at the Grand Hotel in Tralee on the day the Free State Army landed in Fenit, and later spent a year in prison in Dublin before her release in October 1923. O'Connor was denied a payment under the Military Pensions Acts but was sent a service medal in 1958. She later qualified for a Special Allowance under legislation which provided payments for disability, illness or infirmity, but her financial circumstances were the subject of repeated assessment over the course of twenty years. Hanna died in her ninety-third year at a Tralee nursing home in February 1993. Her solicitor, Thomas O'Halloran, advised the Department of Defence of her passing and asked that the £300 grant towards her funeral expenses – to which pension recipients were entitled – be paid. Following lengthy correspondence over the following two years, the department advised that O'Connor's funeral grant could not be paid because of an overpayment in her allowance two years before she died. 'The Department', wrote a civil servant, 'has an accounting responsibility to recover the loss to public funds', and a request was made for a refund of £445.05 before the funeral expenses could be paid.[39] Having recouped the funds, the department finally considered the matter closed in 1996, three years after Hanna O'Connor died. Even in death, the veterans of the Civil War were often hounded by and entangled in the bureaucracy that typified the meagre supports to which they were entitled.

CHAPTER 19

'What in God's Holy name am I to do?'

Not many citizens of the Irish Free State were writing to their Taoiseach in the 1930s. In an age of greater deference to those in high office, and when residents of the newly independent state would rarely approach senior political figures with their problems and concerns, letters from ordinary men and women arriving on the desk of Éamon de Valera would have been a rarity. De Valera, the leader of the campaign against the Anglo-Irish Treaty during the Civil War, had been in office as president of the Executive Council (later Taoiseach) for two years when he received a typed letter from Kathleen Horan. De Valera's party, Fianna Fáil, had swept to power in 1932, bringing an end to W.T. Cosgrave's Cumann na nGaedheal government, which had, for a decade, presided over the establishment and administration of the Free State. Notwithstanding the fact that Kathleen Horan and her family had been supporters of the Cumann na nGaedheal regime, and her husband a member of the Free State Army, she felt driven to write an emotional and emotive letter to de Valera in the summer of 1934.

Kathleen's husband, John Joe Horan, who grew up at Francis Street in Tralee, had fought the Crown Forces at the GPO during

Easter Week and served time in an internment camp in Frongoch in Wales with several of his fellow Kerry men and the Volunteers across the country who had mobilised for revolution. During the War of Independence, he took the fight to the Black and Tans in his native Tralee, including during the so-called Siege of Tralee in November 1920. When that war came to an end, John Joe Horan went pro-Treaty. Politics might not have been his only reason for joining the Free State Army in August 1922 – the prospect of secure employment and an income to help him to bring up his six children with Kathleen was also a likely enticement. After being demobilised from the overmanned army along with thousands of others in 1924, John Joe fell on hard times and was out of work. Like many of his former colleagues, he applied, and waited patiently for, the pension payment for which he qualified under the Army Pensions Act of 1923.

The process of application was tedious and slow, but given his circumstances, securing a payment was an urgent concern for Horan, who was twenty-seven when the Civil War came to an end.[1] He pleaded with the Department of Defence in 1926 to deal with his application. He was, he told them:

> [A] married man with five children whose ages are from 7 years to 5 days. I have also an aged father dependant, my mother having died whilst I was operating with the National Army Column in Kerry in 1923 … I am able to just feed them but as for clothing including myself and wife who is at present ill, we are absolutely in the rags.[2]

Horan finally qualified for a pension in recognition of his eleven years of service during the Rising, the War of Independence and the Civil War. In subsequent years, when the family moved to Dublin, where Horan had acquired a job after a period of unemployment, his wife, Kathleen, appealed to President Cosgrave for an advance on her husband's pension so they could afford a house in which to live. She wanted to 'save my children from going into decline' and was 'almost distracted at the change which had taken place' in her young children since their arrival in Dublin in 1927.[3] Mrs Horan's request was politely declined by President Cosgrave's office, citing ineligibility under the pensions legislation.

But Mrs Horan's hardship did not end there. John Joe Horan died, intestate, on 29 July 1934, leaving Kathleen alone to raise six young children at her home at Donnycarney on Dublin's northside. Kathleen was bereft, financially as well as emotionally. Her husband's death prompted her to put pen to paper to contact President de Valera:

> Dear Sir,
> Would you please help me in my very sad plight?
>
> My husband died on the 29th July, 1934 and I am left with six young children. He had a Military Service pension which I received on the 1st August[.] I returned same to Pension Office, Parkgate Street on 2nd August because it was in my husband's name. I have heard nothing about it since although it was due to me up to the time of his death.
>
> I would also like if you could help me to get my three little boys into O'Brien's Orphanage, Malahide Road, Marino.
>
> It is an Orphanage for respectable boys, as I have heard some ladies left sums of money to be used for respectable boys like mine whose father dies.
>
> Their father has died at the early age of 35 years as the result of his fight for Irish freedom. He took part in the 1916 Rising and continued his service up to 1924.

Up to the time of his death, he was employed in the Office of Public Works, 51 St. Stephen's Green.

I have no pension or means of support whatever to rear my six little children. Their ages are from 14 years to 2 years, and what in God's Holy name am I to do?

So I make this appeal to you, Dear Sir, to help me if possible and may God's blessing pour down on you and yours is the sincere prayer of a poor widow and her six little orphans.

Yours faithfully,
(Mrs.) Kathleen Horan.[4]

Kathleen Horan received a reply from de Valera's private secretary four days later. He conveyed the sincere sorrow of the president on learning of her plight. The payment of the balance of her husband's pension would be raised with the Department of Defence, but any acceptance of her three sons by the O'Brien Orphanage would be a matter for 'Brother Geoghegan, Superior, who will no doubt, be glad to assist you with information if you will make application to him.'[5] A month later, the balance of Horan's pension, totalling six pounds, eighteen shillings and eight pence was transferred to Kathleen.

Even forty years later, Kathleen Horan's lot had improved little, despite qualifying for a pension as John Joe's widow. Living in Glasnevin in 1975, she told the Department of Defence that the pension was so small that she was 'living on bread and tea from one end of the year to another. My pension is £6 weekly, it is dreadful in these hard times.'[6] In April 1975 Kathleen finally received some good news: the department agreed to increase the amount of her monthly widow's allowance. But it was too little, too late. When Kathleen failed to cash some of her payments, the Department of Defence asked An Garda Síochána to ascertain her whereabouts and circumstances. Sergeant Denis Hurley of Mountjoy Garda Station was able to discover that Kathleen had been admitted to the Geriatric Unit of the Richmond Hospital 'some time ago'. A social worker envisaged that she would be 'a patient in the hospital for the foreseeable future'.[7] Even when she returned to her home, she continued to plead her case with the authorities until her death on 6 December 1978, ironically the anniversary of the signing of the Treaty which her husband had fought against his fellow Irishmen to defend.

+++

There was no monopoly of suffering, hardship and misery in post-Civil War Kerry and the pension application files of Free State Army officers who served in Kerry and the applications of the relatives of those killed point to a litany of poor health, financial difficulties and other challenges in the years after the Civil War. The new army offered the prospect of employment and a stable income for many men who were out of work in the years after the War of Independence. For example, John Brosnan of Fahavane, Kilflynn, a neighbour of Stephen Fuller, had 'abandoned his education many years before he intended' in order to join the army, which is suggestive of how attractive a career in the army was.[8] But for many of those who survived the conflict in Kerry, discharge from the army followed in 1924 as the government moved to demobilise tens of thousands of officers from the overmanned force. This left many men out of work and they fell on hard times, financially and psychologically.

John Egan from Laccamore, Abbeydorney, had spent years in the IRA before joining the Free State Army. He 'became an active supporter of the Government and when recruiting started for the new army, he was one of the first that went to army headquarters in Dublin to enlist'.[9] He served for a time as an officer in Waterville before demobilisation. Many of the former officers of the Free State Army could afford to stay in Ireland, but many emigrated too. Egan and his wife, Bridget, moved to South Shiels in Devon and fell on hard times. He was eventually awarded a pension of £25 in 1926, but there was no evident improvement in his financial position. Egan, then a general labourer, died of tuberculosis in a workhouse hospital in 1927 and there was no money to pay for his burial. All his family could manage towards the cost of interment was £4 and the undertaker in South Shiels was forced to write to the Department of Defence to secure the balance of the funeral bill.[10] 'There is no insurance or anything to fall back on and we have been entirely dependent on strangers,' wrote Bridget.[11] She did not want her husband buried in a pauper's grave in 'a strange country'.

For the relatives of many deceased Free State officers, the challenge of daily living was immense. 'Sometimes, I don't have anything to eat' wrote Teresa Quinn on the third day of January 1950.[12] Her husband and the father of their three children, Private Patrick Quinn of Meath Street in Dublin, had been killed in action at The Spa on the day the Free State Army landed by sea at Fenit. One of their children died of cardiac failure at the age of seventeen.[13] Teresa was facing eviction from her home because she could not afford to pay the rent. Another widow, Christina Noone, whose husband, Sgt Edward Noone, died at Rathmore in September 1922, found it impossible to 'keep the children in bootwear' when going to school.[14] Meanwhile, the mother of Private James O'Neill, who died during the siege at Clashmealcon caves in April 1923, was 'very badly off' a year after his death and was 'solely dependent' on the government for assistance.[15]

Like the members of the IRA and Cumann na mBan, the families of Free State Army soldiers who had died in active service were required to prove the level of their financial dependence on the deceased in order to determine the level of applicable gratuity or pension payment. The Army Pensions Acts of 1923 and 1927 stipulated that 'no allowance shall be payable to any person unless such person was at the date of the death of the soldier in respect of whom the allowance is claimed, wholly dependent on such soldier'.[16] In special circumstances, gratuity payments could be made. The threshold of evidence was high for the families of Free State Army soldiers whose loved ones were killed in the conflict. In most cases, applicants were reliant on what would be contained within a report by the local sergeant with An Garda Síochána, who would testify as to the level of dependency. It also often necessitated appeals to local TDs and government ministers if and when dependency could not be verified or proved. The application files therefore contain countless letters and appeals from relatives of soldiers killed outlining various levels of reliance on those who had died. For example, the mother of Private Michael Rock, who had 'rendered distinguished service during the Great War' and was 'shot through the heart' near Cahersiveen in January 1923, was left in 'very great poverty' after he died, her solicitor told the department.[17] The fact that Mrs Rock was partially supported by another son, John, also an army officer, meant she only received a gratuity of £50.

The family of Sgt Jeremiah Quane from Ardfert was 'wholly dependent' on him at the time of his death near Caherciveen in March 1923. Quane had left a job in the post office to enlist in the new army. His elderly father, Michael, a former RIC officer, as well as a sister, described in a garda report as 'an imbicile [*sic*] for life', relied on Jeremiah as the 'main support of the household' that lived in a 'labourer's cottage with no land attached'.[18] When twenty-two-year-old Sgt John Donoghue from Knockrower, Scartaglin, died from a 'bullet through the brain' at Ohermong in September 1922, his widowed father, James, was left to raise his remaining children, the homeplace 'had to be neglected' and the 'three next eldest' to John 'had to emigrate to America'.[19] Both the Quane and Donoghue families eventually received gratuities.

The family of Private Timothy Murphy from Banard, Gneeveguilla, who died in Kilmallock, County Limerick in July 1922, was deemed only partially dependent on the deceased, despite his father being unemployed and his mother and family of seven remaining boys living 'in very poor circumstances'.[20] Four of the boys were still in school. Mrs Mary Murphy's application for compensation was initially turned down by the Pensions Board, but this decision had 'given rise to some feeling locally' and she eventually received a payment of £50 under the Army Pensions Act of 1923.[21]

+++

What value was placed by the new State on the life of those who died in defending it? Many applicants were appalled at the paucity of what they received. Killarney tailor Patrick Nagle, a father of twelve, one of whom, Private Daniel Nagle, died in an engagement with anti-Treatyites near Tralee, was disillusioned and angered at the decision to award a gratuity of £50 in 1924. In an appeal to President Cosgrave, Patrick explained that his wife was ill, he had 'no prospect of work' and another son had 'lost his eye at the hands of the anti-national party for which I never made a claim'.[22] He told his local TD, Fionán Lynch, that Daniel was worth £160 a year to him: 'Surely the Saorstát [Free State] is capable of granting a sum in appraisement of my loss ... I hope that it will not be spoken of abroad as the value set on the life of a soldier in the cause of the defence of the Country.'[23] Five years later, Patrick Nagle told the Department of Defence his business was being boycotted by many customers because he was 'a Free State Sympathiser' and that his son had responded to the call of Motherland, and enflinchingly [*sic*] gave all – even his life – to save his country from the destruction, which at the time seemed most inevitable ... Can it be said that the country's representatives, who now reap the fruits of the untiring efforts of 'the rank and file' fail in endeavouring to compensate – even in a small way – those who suffered for their country? – I will readily answer 'No', as I cannot believe that they would allow their minds to concentrate on such a great wrong.[24]

Not long after troops arrived in Killarney in August 1922, Cornelius Hayes left his job as a postman to enlist.[25] When Private Hayes of Clovers Lane, Killarney, was accidentally shot at Newtownsandes in March 1923, his sister, Norah Hayes (23), implored the army leadership for assistance. Their parents were deceased and Norah was looking after three younger sisters. Norah had worked in the laundry in the military barracks in the town but was out of work after the Civil War:

We are orphans alone in the world with nobody to work for us and our only support killed while fighting for the Free State Army, and we were left to the kind consideration of the Government. My brother deceased Cornelius Hayes was accidentally shot at Newtownsandes on March 25th, 1923, chief support to us, but nobody misses him but his heartbroken sisters who are not able to work and are sometimes hungry. I am in debt everywhere in Killarney and we are threatened of being in the streets, with rent and rates calling in on us, also shopkeepers which were kind enough to give us credit are calling on us.[26]

Michael O'Donoghue from Quay Street in Cahersiveen was just seventeen years old when he joined the 9th Infantry Battalion of the new army. The Civil War was over when he met his death, but the wounds opened by the conflict were still raw.[27] Private O'Donoghue had received 'a severe beating by Irregulars' in June 1923 near Mountain Stage.[28] He was struck on the head with rifle butts and, on returning to his post in Cahersiveen, 'took to his bed and became unconscious'. He was treated at Tralee Fever Hospital but later succumbed to his injuries, which were compounded by typhoid fever. It was claimed that he did not receive sufficient medical attention immediately after the incident.[29] O'Donoghue died as voters went to the polls in the first general election after the conflict, which was held on 23 August. Before he died, he 'confessed to the Nun in charge, Sister Xavier that he was dying from the beating [he had received]'.[30] Michael was the eldest of six children; his youngest sibling was just a year old when he lost his brother. The family, dependent on their father's income from carpentry, were 'in rather poor circumstances' a year after his passing.[31] His mother described the depth of her loss in a letter to the Department of Defence in June 1924:

> He was a very intelligent boy having obtained passes in the Junior and Middle Grade Intermediate Examinations and in 1920 he obtained an appointment in the Engineering Departments of the Cable Office at Valentia at a salary of £5 per month to be doubled after an apprenticeship of three years, but his appointment was not ratified by the then Manager, Mr Scaiff [sic], owing to his connection with the Boy Scouts of the Volunteers. You will readily observe that he suffered something for endeavouring to free his country from the chains of a stranger. He was the eldest of six children and my principal help.[32]

Anger and frustration permeate the application files. James Reilly from Cromane was unable to find a job after leaving the army and by 1925 realised he could 'stick this country no longer' as he awaited a decision on his application by the department.[33] Reilly emigrated and lived at six different addresses in England until his death in 1973. James McCarthy, whose son, Patrick McCarthy, from Lixnaw, was killed in an accident in January 1923, told the Department of Defence that a gratuity payment of £60 was 'miserable' and insisted that 'if this man was killed by the Black and Tans, I would get at least £1,000 from your Government'.[34] Caherdaniel native Michael McGillycuddy, who had contracted rheumatic fever because of several 'wettings' during the War of Independence, and who was based with the Free State Army in Waterville, spent his final years trying to secure a pension and told Fionán Lynch TD that 'to have our opponents be laughing at us now at the way we were treated' was adding insult to injury.[35] When he died in 1926, it was left to his widow, Nora, to pursue an allowance, which was finally received in 1953. Sometimes, no matter which side they fought on or which party happened to be in power, those left still standing after the Civil War had to continue to fight for their survival, if on a different battleground.

CHAPTER 20

'We never took Free State literature in this house'

Listowel solicitor Robert Pierse approached the house at Lixnaw with some trepidation. A candidate for Fine Gael in Kerry North in the February 1982 general election, Pierse was canvassing a rural part of the constituency in the quest for votes. The election was taking place at a tempestuous and feverish time in Irish politics. A trio of elections of 1981–82 saw a series of titanic battles between Charles Haughey's Fianna Fáil and Garret FitzGerald's Fine Gael, the two Civil War parties. In June 1981, after the first of the trio, a coalition government of Fine Gael and Michael O'Leary's Labour Party was formed, but it collapsed in January 1982 over a controversial attempt by the Minister for Finance, John Bruton, to introduce VAT on children's shoes. In Kerry North, Fine Gael had been without a TD in the three-seat constituency since Listowel TD Gerard Lynch, the son of a Free State Army captain, had been unseated in 1977, and Robert Pierse had been nominated as the sole Fine Gael standard-bearer for the February 1982 election. Though it was his first election contest, Pierse was no political novice. A dyed-in-the-wool activist, he could trace his political lineage back to none other than Michael Collins, his mother's uncle. The Pierses were also able to trace their family history in the locality 'back 700 years'.[1] As he suggested knocking on the door of a particular house near Lixnaw, his canvassing partner suggested:

> 'There's no point going down that road, they're all inoculated with Fianna Fáil.' I said I would do every road ... I did my little bit ... 'You won't forget me' sort of thing. And as I was going out, I put my leaflet on the table and the man of the house came over and picked up the leaflet by the corner ... and said, 'Sorry Mr Pierse, we never took Free State literature in this house.'[2]

The comment may have been made in jest, but it illustrated clearly that sixty years after the Civil War had ended, its legacy in local politics endured. For the century after the conflict, politics and the party system locally continued to be infused with the venom and bitterness of the war.

+++

The first electoral test of voter sentiment after the end of the Civil War came when Kerry voters went to the polls on 27 August 1923. Voting to fill the seven available seats took place at 260 polling stations with just over 90,000 electors eligible to vote.[3] There were fifteen nominees for the seven available Dáil seats: Cumann na nGaedheal – James Crowley TD, Fionán Lynch TD, Thomas Dennehy and John Marcus O'Sullivan; Sinn Féin – Austin Stack TD, Patrick Cahill TD, Thomas O'Donoghue TD and Thomas McEllistrim; Independents – Thomas O'Donnell, Edward J. Gleeson and Jeremiah McSweeney; Labour – Cormac Walsh and Patrick Casey; and Farmers' Party – Denis Brosnan and John O'Neill. The final result saw all of the republican candidates – Austin Stack, Thomas McEllistrim, Thomas O'Donoghue and Patrick Cahill – elected. Stack headed the poll with 10,333 votes and almost 19 per cent of the poll. The remaining seats were filled by Cumann na nGaedheal candidates Fionán Lynch, James Crowley and UCD professor John Marcus O'Sullivan. Nationally, the republicans polled 27 per cent of first preferences, but in Kerry the result very much bucked the trend: 45 per cent of voters backed republican candidates, proving that there was 'a huge reservoir of political support for the anti-Treaty wing of Sinn Féin in the county'.[4] The republican vote in Kerry was second only to that in Clare, where republicans polled 47 per cent.[5]

Although the campaign in Kerry passed off largely peacefully, there were several outbreaks of disorder and violence. During a Cumann na nGaedheal rally in Cahersiveen, the *Irish Independent* reported, 'there were hand-to-hand encounters between opposing crowds. Fists and sticks were freely used, and there were numerous cut heads and black eyes, and Civic Guards had great difficulty in restoring order. A military picket paraded the streets.'[6] Girls carrying black flags and dummy coffins – representing the republican dead – marched past the government supporters, and the Civic Guards used the flag staffs 'on the heads of the volunteers. The coffins were seized and smashed.' A local man, Eugene O'Neill, was shot through the thigh.[7] Shots were also fired during a melee involving the rival parties near Lixnaw, and a young man named Costello was wounded in the shoulder. Sinn Féin's director of elections claimed the man was fatally wounded.[8] Elsewhere, the 'most disorderly meeting ever held in Dingle' was how a pro-Treaty meeting at the local Temperance Hall just two days before the election was described by the *Liberator*'s reporter. 'Boohs, political catch-cries such as "Up Stack" and "Up De Valera" came from different sections of the crowd. The interrupters came in for rough handling, and they stoutly defended themselves with sticks. At times terrible confusion and excitement prevailed. There were many free fights, and sometimes it looked as if there would be a general stampede.'[9]

Despite the tensions, allegations of voter intimidation or efforts to subvert the casting of ballots were rare. 'All IRA men were prevented from voting, as the polling places were patrolled by soldiers and civic guards,' claimed Jeremiah Murphy, but he offered no particular evidence.[10] Meanwhile, a report from the Kerry Command to army headquarters claimed that

> systematic intimidation of Electors was resorted to by Irregulars, and that their Organisation for this purpose was perfect ... a Miss Coffey, Beaufort, Killorglin had reported that she was 'turned away' from the Polling Booths, because the 'Republican' agents noted that she and her Father had been speaking with the P.P. (Rev Father Fitzmaurice) who is a well-known supporter of ours; it is reported also, that amongst others, the well-known Irregulars Jeremiah Moriarty and __ Landers were engaged in intimidating voters in Listellick district (N.E. of Tralee) on Election Day.[11]

Such incidents were the exception rather than the rule but may have had some effect on the turnout, which was low: approximately 35,000 eligible Kerry voters chose not to cast their ballots. Though turnout at elections would rise as the decades went on, for the first contested general election in Kerry since 1910 this was low and suggested that many were less than enamoured with the political parties after a bitter and divisive Civil War, and a campaign which was dominated by the Treaty rather than the bread-and-butter problems which ordinary citizens were facing.

+++

The political situation remained volatile throughout the 1920s. There was a major outbreak of violence at a Fianna Fáil meeting in Knocknagoshel in September 1927, just a few days before polling.[12] It was perhaps no coincidence that the party was holding its election rally just a short distance from where the Knocknagoshel trip-mine incident had claimed the lives of five Free State soldiers in March 1923. Among the speakers was Eamon Horan, a former brigadier general in the Free State Army and a candidate for the Clann Éireann party in the June 1927 election.[13] Ahead of the meeting on 12 September, Garda Superintendent J.J. McNulty had allegedly dispatched detectives to Knocknagoshel, and McNulty had held up and searched a Fianna Fáil supporter. The car owned by the local Catholic curate (who was due to speak at the meeting) was seized and 'driven through the crowd of people'. From the moment the meeting opened, McNulty, who brandished his gun, 'kept up a running stream of interruptions and heckling directed towards the speakers' calculated to provoke a breach of the peace.[14] In response, Eamon Horan launched a verbal attack on Garda Commissioner Eoin O'Duffy and said that the gardaí, as 'renegades of the State', deserved 'the same fate as the Black and Tans and the Auxiliaries'. Horan and two others were arrested, but, after a lengthy hearing, the judge declined to send Horan forward for trial: Horan, he suggested, had been blowing off 'hot air'.[15]

Perhaps the most extreme example of politically motivated violence in Kerry in the decades after the Civil War occurred during a highly charged meeting of the Blueshirts in Tralee at the beginning of October 1933. In January 1933 Eoin O'Duffy, who was no stranger to Kerry, was sacked as Garda Commissioner and established the Army Comrades' Association (which morphed into the Blueshirts), a controversial organisation set up to protect Cumann na nGaedheal from an increasingly active IRA, many of whose members had been released from jail by Éamon de Valera after Fianna Fáil swept to power in 1932. The Blueshirts had many activists in Kerry, among them Kerry North TD James Crowley and his wife, Clementine Burson, who was a member of the women's wing of the group, the so-called Blueblouses. On 6 October 1933, O'Duffy arrived in Tralee to address the County Convention of the newly established Fine Gael, the successor to Cumann na nGaedheal.[16] The meeting was to be held in the Foresters' Hall and as the main speakers walked through Bridge Street, O'Duffy was struck on the head with a hammer. Several people with hurleys jostled the party and a man was set upon and beaten with the weapons. The windows in the Foresters' Hall were broken and stones were thrown at cars bringing delegates to the convention. That evening, O'Duffy's car was set alight and burned out in Denny Street. A fully armed military unit was needed to escort the principals back to the Grand Hotel. Windows in the hotel were smashed and, at around 1 a.m., a machine gun discharged around twenty rounds into the local garda station. The following morning, an undetonated bomb was found in the Foresters' Hall. 'I was left completely at the mercy of the mob,' O'Duffy complained in an interview in Killarney.[17]

By the general election of January 1933, nine of every ten electors in Kerry were voting for the Civil War parties, Fianna Fáil and Cumann na nGaedheal (Fine Gael from September 1933). For most of the remainder of the twentieth century, Kerry politics was dominated by the two parties, but Fianna Fáil, the inheritors of the anti-Treaty republican vote, remained by far the more dominant of the two. At the 1932 and 1933 elections, the party won five of the seven seats in Kerry, prompting the *Kerry Champion* newspaper – which was run by former TD and IRA leader Paddy Cahill – to declare that 'Kerry is now more republican than ever.'[18] Fianna Fáil held three of the six seats in the county for most of the 1960s, 1970s and 1980s, winning four out of six at the 1977 election. This success was partly a consequence of internal rivalries between, for example, the McEllistrims and Foleys in Kerry North, and the O'Connor, O'Donoghue and O'Leary families in Kerry South. Those internecine battles actually contributed, paradoxically, to the party's electoral success. It was only in 1997, when Jackie Healy-Rae won a seat as an Independent TD in Kerry South, that that supremacy of Fianna Fáil was undermined, beginning a period of significant local decline. In parallel with its nationwide collapse, in 2011 the party was left without a Dáil seat in Kerry for the first time in its eighty-five-year history.[19] At the election of 2020, Fianna Fáil and Fine Gael returned just one seat each, illustrating how much less the divisions of the Civil War were a factor in Kerry politics a century later.

In the decades after the conflict, barbs about the causes of the Civil War and who was to blame were part and parcel of election campaigns, but the specific incidents of conflict themselves hardly ever surfaced as an issue during elections. Perhaps the voters of the Kerry didn't need to be reminded of the horrors of the Civil War. At times, it wasn't even referred to by name by politicians and in newspapers. In 1925 anti-Treaty TD Paddy Cahill described it as the 'late inhuman war'.[20] Even the editorial columns sometimes avoided referring to the conflict by name, labelling it 'the later trouble', as if it was an unfortunate and tragic addendum to the Tan War.[21] Kerry's TDs generally didn't talk about the Civil War. A notable exception was a comment from Kerry Fianna Fáil TD Timothy 'Chub' O'Connor, who reminded the Dáil in 1970 that the government of the day had 'condoned' the murder of the men at Ballyseedy.[22] The tragedy at Knocknagoshel was never raised on the floor of the Dáil by Kerry deputies. Critically, it was the generation of Kerry TDs most closely involved in the Civil War who decided not to invoke its horrors during election campaigns.

At no point, either immediately after the war or in subsequent decades, did the spectre of the Civil War threaten to derail or disrupt the democratic process. It is truly remarkable that democratic politics endured despite the trauma and tragedy of the early 1920s. Combatants on both sides of the divide went head-to-head with each other for decades. In 1961 Patrick O'Connor-Scarteen of Fine Gael, a brother of John and Tom O'Connor-Scarteen, who were murdered at their home in Kenmare in September 1922, contested the general election in Kerry South. Among the other candidates was John Joe Rice, also from Kenmare, O/C of the IRA in south Kerry when the Scarteens were killed. Rice had already won a Dáil seat for Sinn Féin in 1957 but did not take his seat in keeping with the party's policy of abstentionism at the time. Not once during either election campaign was anything said publicly about the events of 1922–23.

Almost a century after the Civil War, a symbolic handshake in the arena of local government suggested that the divisions of the conflict were no longer a discernible feature of politics in the county. It was just a few weeks after the votes were cast in the local government elections of 2014, a poll which denied both of the two major parties in Kerry politics a working majority on Kerry County Council. In a portent of what would follow in a national Fine Gael–Fianna Fáil coalition a few years later, the two political behemoths of Kerry politics had been forced to agree a voting pact to secure control of the local authority in Kerry, which had traditionally been the preserve of their predecessors since the Civil War nine decades before. The results of the election and the voting agreement between the old Civil War parties also meant that the descendants of some of the main protagonists in that conflict were taking their seats together in the council chamber. Thomas McEllistrim, whose grandfather Tom was one of the most notorious adversaries of the Free State Army in 1922 and 1923, and Patrick Connor-Scarteen, whose granduncles Tom and John had been killed for being part of that army, sat side by side at the new council's inaugural meeting.[23] McEllistrim, who, like his father and grandfather had served in the Dáil, and Connor-Scarteen, a third-generation county councillor, shook hands before taking their seats. 'It's a historic day but the numbers dictated the two main parties had to come together for the first time,' said Connor-Scarteen. 'It's a unique experience for us all but we have to be realistic and move forward.'[24]

The handshake between the descendants of some of the most high-profile combatants in Kerry's Civil War was as significant for the relatively little commentary it provoked as it was for the fact that it happened at all, even if it did prompt newspaper editors to hail the end of Civil War politics in the county. But there was also plenty of evidence that, despite the passage of ninety years, there were still some uncomfortable reminders of the Civil War in Kerry and evidence that some people were not yet minded to forgive or forget. The handshake between Councillors McEllistrim and Connor-Scarteen came just a few weeks after the monument to the five Free State soldiers murdered at Knocknagoshel on 6 March 1923 was vandalised and smashed in what was described as an 'act of thuggery'.[25] For decades, there had been no such monument. As Anne Dolan wrote, maybe it was 'foolish to expect otherwise' in a county which had 'run too red with republican blood'.[26] Dan Nolan of *The Kerryman* had written to Richard Mulcahy in 1965, lamenting the absence of a memorial, but as Anne Dolan suggests, 'the outpost of the republic had no place on its roads for simple crosses to the soldier dead'.[27]

In November 2013 the Knocknagoshel Fine Gael branch erected the marble tablet, which listed the names of Laurence O'Connor, Edward Joseph Stapleton, Michael Dunne, Paddy 'Pats' O'Connor and Michael Galvin. In a historical symmetry, the unveiling ceremony was attended by Paudie Fuller, a son of Stephen Fuller, the only man to survive the Ballyseedy Massacre in the hours following the Knocknagoshel mine explosion. Fine Gael TD Jimmy Deenihan told those gathered that Paudie had 'done more than any other man in North Kerry to bring us all together', and his attendance at the unveiling of the monument was widely appreciated by the 200 people present.[28] Within three years, however, the granite slab to the five men who were killed was vandalised again, with nobody ever apprehended.[29] The vandalism was condemned by the Sinn Féin TD for Kerry North, Martin Ferris, who insisted that it was 'disgraceful'.[30]

These two incidents were not the only attacks on the memory of the men who died at Knocknagoshel. On 17 October 1925 the grave of Paddy 'Pats' O'Connor was defaced and damaged by 'at least 50 marks' and nine wreaths were 'broken to pieces'. The Celtic cross standing on his grave had been placed in the new cemetery in Castleisland the previous July by the family at a cost of £120. At Tralee Circuit Court in January 1926, the O'Connor family sued Kerry County Council, which was responsible for the cemetery. Judge J.E. McElligott granted an order for £71 15s to Patrick O'Connor Senior in compensation. The judge described the incident as 'a horrible outrage' and levied the charge on the people of the electoral division of Castleisland.[31] Nobody was ever charged with the act, nor was any clear motive established, but it was proof, if it were needed, that the visceral hatreds which the Civil War provoked ran deep and endured long after the war itself had ended.

POSTSCRIPT

'Maybe it could have been avoided'

Despite forty-six years as a TD – the longest Dáil career in the history of Kerry – Tom McEllistrim never mentioned the Civil War, or what led to it, in parliament. That was not unique among Dáil deputies, but McEllistrim had plenty of experience to reference on the Dáil floor if he had been so inclined: he had seen more combat than many of his contemporaries in Kerry, from the moment he ushered Robert Monteith to safety after he landed at Banna Strand with Roger Casement in 1916 to an attack on Gortatlea RIC barracks in 1918 (considered by some to be the first engagement of the War of Independence), to the final days of fighting on the republican side in the Civil War. In a very rare interview on his life and times conducted by journalist Nollaig Ó Gadhra in 1970, McEllistrim spoke briefly about the paroxysms of 1922–23, even if he was conscientiously conciliatory, magnanimous and diplomatic.[1] 'Old Tom Mac' as he was usually known, was often described as being less military-minded than some of his contemporaries and he recognised the need to move on from the bitterness of the early 1920s.[2] During the war itself, he had been party to peace talks on a few occasions. In his remarks to Ó Gadhra, however, he went even further, suggesting that enemies had reconciled almost immediately and that the conflict might not have been necessary at all. McEllistrim perceived a benefit from the war, however:

> The Civil War served a purpose though it was unfortunate that we had to have it at all ... Maybe it could have been avoided ... The Civil War was a godsend to us in this country, because we weren't trained, we weren't disciplined, we hadn't a proper civil spirit – the fellows that went through the Tan War, with that kind of freedom they had during that period, it spoilt them, with the result that the Civil War chastised us on both sides and we were better citizens afterwards.

'Do you talk to those who opposed you, for example?' probed Ó Gadhra.

'Always. We were never unfriendly with anyone over the Civil War. Sure, I met soldiers, we captured them, we shook hands and embraced each other during the Civil War.'

McEllistrim's mollifying comments decades after the conflict were noble and well-intentioned. But he, more than many, knew the true toll that the war had taken on families and the civilian population in the county he represented in the Dáil. For decades, from his office in Leinster House, he wrote copious letters to ministers and officials imploring them to support the pension claims of combatants and demanding better treatment for the men and women who took part in the War of Independence and the Civil War. Much of his correspondence – which his son, Thomas, also a TD, continued to generate through to the 1990s – reflects a wider theme of the pension archives from this period. Many of those who joined either the republican forces or the Free State Army felt for many years that they were never adequately compensated or recognised by successive governments. Letters to Leinster House were replete with stories of poverty, hardship and ill-health among combatants and their families, but also a salient anger and disgust at perceived political biases and discrimination against applicants, depending on which side they had taken during the conflict. The pensions were deeply political, and party political at that, with relatives of those on both sides of the conflict decrying their treatment at the hands of those whom they believed were their own political representatives in Leinster House.

Dan Mulvihill of Castlemaine, who spent much of the conflict in jail, was one of those who spent many years writing to fellow IRA veteran and his local Fianna Fáil TD, Timothy 'Chub' O'Connor, decrying the treatment of the Old IRA by the party who represented the anti-Treaty tradition. He observed, for example, that while ministers were getting pay rises in the 1970s, his comrades were being taxed too heavily:

> I was looking at the Paper today and I saw about the Ministerial [pay] Rises. I got a Dead Fit of laughing. Out of a thousand they took three hundred and fifty off me. I want you to the do the following for me. Go to Bobby Molloy [Minister for Defence] and say to him is it a fact that you are taxing what's left of the old I.R.A. They are all over eighty ... They are the fellows that put us here. I think the people of the country will be interested to hear about it.[3]

Mulvihill's friend and neighbour Annie Cronin, who was a member of the anti-Treaty Cumann na mBan, was furious when her military service pension was cut in 1971: 'I got a bit of a shock ... if that's the treatment I deserve in my old age ... We never gave this [Fianna Fáil] government a bad turn, always looked after them.'[4] Bridget Coakley-Kennedy, president of Castlegregory Cumann na mBan, insisted in

1939 that 'if Austin Stack lived, I'd get my pension', adding that Humphrey Murphy 'took my papers up and he promised me I'd be one of the first' to be paid.[5] In 1934 Edward Hartnett, whose brother, Patrick, was blown up at Ballyseedy Cross in March 1923, pleaded with Fianna Fáil headquarters to intercede when he was turned down for an allowance by the Department of Defence. Writing in his capacity as secretary of the Killocrim Cumann of Fianna Fáil to the local party TD, Eamonn Kissane, he said that this was 'the biggest slur that could be cast on any Government who claim to be national and patriotic'.[6]

Richard Bunyan of the anti-Treaty IRA, who was injured by the fragments of the skull of Seán Linnane when he was killed near Duagh, decried what he perceived to be inequalities in the administration of payments to those on both sides of the Civil War conflict. Writing just days after Fianna Fáil was returned to government in the January 1933 general election, Bunyan expressed his frustrations:

> I am entitled to get a pension as much as any other man. Is it fair that Free State Soldiers should be drawing pensions for the past ten months under a FIANNA FÁIL Government, whilst men, who have suffered for the cause from the very beginning and who proved true when the test came in 1921, should still be left living without any recompense for their faithfulness. I hope that FIANNA FÁIL will see justice done to these men.[7]

Those who had fought to defend the new State, and their survivors, were equally angered by how they were treated by successive governments. Mary O'Shea from Mary Street, Tralee, felt compelled to write directly to Richard Mulcahy in anger and frustration at the delay in receiving compensation following the death of her son,

Private Cornelius O'Shea. She accused Mulcahy and his government of 'callous treatment':

> The relatives of people who were killed subsequent to my son are provided for and why should my case be singled out for inattention while I have to beg to maintain my young orphans. It is not, to say the least, human to treat me in this way, as I was willing to give my son to save the Free State at the time of its peril.[8]

At the 1932 general election, the eleven votes in O'Shea's family were given 'to Mr De Valera's Party for the purpose of forming a government to get our rights'. It was, the family protested, 'a shame to see William Cosgrave getting 25 hundred pounds a year' while the mother of a dead army private was 'begging for a way of living'.[9] For decades after the war, politicians in Kerry and beyond continued to be bombarded with the anger and frustration of Civil War combatants and their families.

If the Civil War and the tragedies and massacres in Kerry were notable by their absence from electioneering rhetoric and Dáil speeches in the decades after the conflict, the politics of compensating and supporting the surviving combatants and the relatives of those who died screamed loudly from the archives of the Department of Defence and the filing cabinets of constituency TDs. And if the TDs shied away from publicly confronting the barbarities of 1922–23 and their legacy, there were continual reminders of the traumas borne by the people of Kerry for many decades afterwards. Was there a collective political shame or regret about the ten months of murder and mayhem in Kerry? And was this shame and regret compounded by an unspoken acknowledgement that an independent Ireland and the Irish Free State did not, in so many instances, provide sufficient support and succour for the men and women who had fought to defend that Free State or those who had continued to pursue the goal of an Irish Republic? One Kerry republican is said to have remarked, as he left his native county for foreign shores, 'If I knew seven years ago what I know now, and if I was given a loaded revolver and told to fire one round in the air to free Ireland, I would not do it.'[10]

+++

'There was no middle path in the Civil War' in Kerry: the handwritten note of Dan Mulvihill of Castlemaine appears in the files of the Military Archives and encapsulates the bitter cleavages caused by the Civil War in politics and society in County Kerry.[11] His comments were echoed by the Civil War historian Calton Younger, who, in 1979, wrote that 'in Kerry, little quarter was given on either side'.[12] There is practically no dispute among historians that in Kerry the divisions were more – if not the most – bitter, violent and atavistic in the country. Because of its notorious experience, historian Gavin Foster rightly asserts that Kerry has come to symbolise Ireland's short but deeply traumatising Civil War: it demands 'sustained attention' in our efforts to understand the descent into fratricide and its legacy in 'politics, social life and collective memory'.[13]

There is also much agreement about the veil of silence which prevailed in the decades that followed.[14] The wall of quietude about what Eoin Neeson called the 'unspeakable war' was not unique in Ireland: civil wars are considered far more embittering and devastating than conflicts with a common foreign enemy.[15] Bill Kissane notes that silence has been the preferred way in many countries, including Finland and Ireland.[16] As Anne Dolan surmises: 'Although there could be no forgetting, there was a will to forget, a retreat to the type of silence that erased all but the victory. The end had been reached; there was no need to reminisce about the means ... Silence was better than hypocrisy. Silence was also better than disgust.'[17]

That silence was often actively encouraged by newspapers and publishers in the years after the conflict. The editorial of the *Kerry People* in the days after the war finally ended urged a collective sweeping under the carpet: 'The nine months have been very tragic ones for Ireland. It would be well if their memory could be blotted out altogether. The people should try at any rate to forget what has happened and to look forward to the future with confidence and with hope.'[18] When, in 1947, *The Kerryman* newspaper published *Kerry's Fighting Story*, a series of anonymised first-hand recollections from participants in the revolution, the collection of anecdotal essays did not address events after 1921. The vast majority of the statements collected by the Bureau of Military History in the 1940s and 1950s do not deal with the Civil War. The 'four glorious years' of 1918–21 were to be celebrated, the two years which followed stifled and unspoken because they were so visceral and painful.[19] Some combatants and survivors, Joe Lee observes, 'suppressed their feelings in the interest of the national good while others – a minority – would miss no opportunity to lacerate the wounds'.[20] In Kerry, however, with the exception of the occasional provocative catchcry and rare incidences of politically motivated violence during election campaigns, the wall of silence stood tall.

Kerry combatants, their relatives and civilians rarely spoke publicly about the tragic and traumatic events of 1922–23. Even when some combatants were summoned before committees of assessors when they applied for various pensions and allowances, and when there was a legal imperative to provide information to ensure a pension application could be considered, there was a reticence to engage with the gory detail. Donal O'Donoghue, a teacher from Glenflesk and a Fianna Fáil TD for Kerry South between 1944 and 1948, took part in several ambushes of the Free State Army, usually armed with his machine gun. When asked by the department's advisory committee in 1937 to elaborate on specific incidents of the Civil War, he responded: 'I would rather not mention them ... These things are rather gruesome to talk of.'[21] There were, after all, 'anomalously high levels of violence in Kerry' during the period, as well as the massacres of March and April 1923, which were too appalling and too painful to recall.[22]

While the deep cleavages and torment of 1922–23 might not have been verbalised, they were eloquently and loudly expressed through the voluminous and hugely valuable records held in the Military Archives and the National Archives, many of which have only been published and digitised in recent years. Consisting of thousands of pension applications, letters and other documents, the files portray, sometimes in great detail, the enormous suffering and tragedy of this period in Kerry, which extended way beyond loss of life. They are accounts which have remained largely unexplored until now, but their contents are as enlightening as they are dreadfully saddening. As Fergal Keane wrote in his memoir of his family's involvement in the revolutionary period, these records allow us to 'glimpse the lived experience of the time rather than surmise the truth from the shreds of political rhetoric'.[23]

For too long, the totemic tragedies of the Civil War in Kerry, such as those near the railway line at Countess Bridge, on the rugged cliff face of Clashmealcon or in the dark woods of Knocknagoshel, have been used as political charges to argue over which side of the conflict was to blame for the barbarities of the war. The accounts of survivors and those who were bereaved invite us to look deeper into, but also beyond, the blood-soaked outrages, and to survey the wider contexts of personal, family and community traumas. The voices of combatants, which, as in any war, have dominated the narrative heretofore, can now be read and assessed alongside the accounts of their families, neighbours and friends, and the many thousands of civilians who played no active part in the conflict but who suffered deeply and bore the brunt of the hardship that the war created. Those voices tell of the manifold and complex multi-generational traumas which impacted the people of Kerry.

Writing in 1971, the historian F.S.L. Lyons claimed that the Irish Civil War was 'an episode which has burned so deep into the heart and mind of Ireland that it is not yet possible for the historian to approach it with the detailed knowledge or the objectivity which it deserves'.[24] His claim echoed that of T.M. Donovan, author of *A Popular History of East Kerry*. Donovan was criticised in *The Irish Press* for failing to address the Civil War in his book, but the author insisted that 'As to not writing a full account of the Civil War – well no one out of Paradise could do that, impartially, until the present generation has passed away.'[25]

Perhaps an unadulterated objectivity and impartiality will never be attainable. Who could not be moved, influenced or motivated by the almost unspeakable evil, tragedy and profound sadness of the events in Kerry in 1922–23? But now, on the centenary of these tumultuous events, the type of detailed knowledge to which F.S.L. Lyons referred has been greatly enhanced through the scribbled pleadings, typed interview transcripts and bureaucratic memoranda and reports in the accounts of the ordinary men and women who were deeply damaged and traumatised for decades afterwards. The centenary of these horrific events is the appropriate time to listen to their voices – and more importantly, to hear what they have to say – so that the great paroxysm that was the Civil War in Kerry might be considered, remembered and understood afresh. Perhaps, finally, the veil of silence can be lifted.

ENDNOTES

INTRODUCTION

1   *The Irish Times*, 11 April 1981.
2   *The Guardian*, 11 January 2013; Fergal Keane, *Wounds: A Memoir of War and Love* (William Collins, 2017), p. 17.
3   'Wanted: Irish eye-witnesses', newspaper cutting, undated, National Library of Ireland (NLI), Papers of Niall Harrington, MS 40,680/3.
4   Military Archives (MA), Military Service Pension Collection (MSPC) 34REF6759, pension application of Stephen Fuller.
5   Owen O'Shea and Gordon Revington, *A Century of Politics in the Kingdom: A County Kerry Compendium* (Merrion Press, 2018), pp. 234–5; Charles Townshend, *The Republic: The Fight for Irish Independence* (Allen Lane, 2013), p. 450.
6   *The Kerryman*, 26 December 1980.
7   Ibid.
8   Speaking to *Ireland: A Television History* by Robert Kee in 1980; 'Ireland – A Television History – Part 10 of 13 – 'Civil War 1921–1923' – YouTube (accessed 26 October 2021).
9   *The Kerryman*, 30 January 1981.
10 Niall Harrington to Dan Nolan, 29 January 1981, NLI, Papers of Niall Harrington, MS 40,629/2.
11 Keane, *Wounds*, p. 17.
12 *The Kerryman*, 30 January 1981.
13 *The Kerryman*, 16 and 30 January 1981.
14 *The Kerryman*, 30 January 1981.
15 MA, MSPC 34REF6759, Stephen Fuller.
16 MA, MSPC 24SP4190, John Brosnan.

CHAPTER 1

1   For more on the Treaty debates, including the contributions of the Kerry TDs, see Gretchen Friemann, *The Treaty* (Merrion Press, 2021); Jason K. Knirck, *Imagining Ireland's Independence: The Debates over the Anglo-Irish Treaty of 1921* (Rowman & Littlefield, 2006); Mícheál Ó Fathartaigh and Liam Weeks, *Birth of a State: The Anglo-Irish Treaty* (Irish Academic Press, 2021).
2   Tim Dermot and Mary Lynch, 'Fionán Lynch: Revolutionary and Politician', in Bridget McAuliffe, Mary McAuliffe and Owen O'Shea (eds), *Kerry 1916: Histories and Legacies of the Easter Rising – A Centenary Record* (Irish Historical

Publication, 2016), pp. 151–62; O'Shea and Revington, *Century of Politics*, pp. 12–14.

3   Ó Fathartaigh and Weeks, *Birth of a State*, p. 33.
4   *Irish Independent*, 21 December 1921.
5   Dáil Debates, 20 December 1921.
6   Hilary Dully (ed.), *On Dangerous Ground: A Memoir of the Irish Revolution by Máire Comerford* (The Lilliput Press, 2021), p. 232.
7   O'Shea and Revington, *Century of Politics*, pp. 33–6; Padraig Ó Loingsigh agus Padraig Mac Fhearghusa, *Gobnait Ní Bhruadair: the Hon. Albinia Lucy Brodrick* (Coiscéim, 1997), passim.
8   *The Kerryman*, 2 January 1965.
9   *Kerry People*, 25 March 1922.
10 Dáil Debates, 20 December 1921.
11 O'Shea and Revington, *Century of Politics*, pp. 7–10. Ó Fathartaigh and Weeks categorise Béaslaí as one of seven TDs in the Second Dáil who had been born to the Irish Diaspora in Britain, *Birth of a State*, p. 66.
12 O'Shea and Revington, *Century of Politics*, p. 10.
13 Dáil Debates, 3 January 1922.
14 O'Shea and Revington, *Century of Politics,* pp. 14–18; J. Anthony Gaughan, 'Austin Stack: Portrait of a Kerry Separatist', in McAuliffe et al., *Kerry 1916*, pp. 89–97.
15 Michael Harrington, *The Munster Republic: The Civil War in North Cork* (Mercier Press, 2009), p. 163.
16 Gaughan, 'Austin Stack', p. 96.
17 Ó Fathartaigh and Weeks, *Birth of a State*, p. 53.
18 Ibid., p. 115.
19 Dáil Debates, 19 December 1921.
20 T. Ryle Dwyer, *Tans, Terror and Troubles: Kerry's Real Fighting Story* (Mercier Press, 2001), p. 29.
21 Diary of Markham Richard Leeson Marshall, 1 January 1922, Muckross House Library, transcription kindly provided by Dr John Knightly.
22 NLI, Papers of Piaras Béaslaí, MS 33,914(4).
23 *Evening Herald*, 2 January 1922.
24 Ibid.
25 *Evening Echo*, 27 December 1921.
26 *Irish Independent*, 31 December 1921.
27 *Kerry People*, 12 January 1922.
28 *Kerry People*, 7 January 1922.
29 *The Cork Examiner*, 6 January 1922.
30 Dáil Debates, 9 January 1922.
31 Gavin Foster, 'The Civil War in Kerry in history and memory', in Maurice Bric (ed.), *Kerry: History and Society* (Geography Publications, 2020), p. 474.
32 John Joe Rice in Cormac K.H. O'Malley and Tim Horgan (eds), *The Men Will Talk to Me: Kerry Interviews by Ernie O'Malley* (Mercier Press, 2012), p. 282.
33 Testimony of Dan Mulvihill, unpublished, author's collection, p. 17.
34 John Borgonovo, 'IRA Conventions', in John Crowley, Donal Ó Drisceoil, Mike Murphy and John Borgonovo (eds), *Atlas of the Irish Revolution* (Cork University Press, 2017), p. 671.
35 MA, Bureau of Military History (BMH) Witness Statement (WS) 1413, Tadhg Kennedy.

36   Jeremiah Murphy, *When Youth Was Mine: A Memoir of Kerry 1902–1925* (Mentor Books, 1998), pp. 181–2.
37   Sinead Joy, *The IRA in Kerry* (Collins Press, 2005), p. 120.
38   Tim Horgan, *Dying for the Cause: Kerry's Republican Dead* (Mercier Press, 2015), p. 85.
39   J. Anthony Gaughan, *Listowel and its Vicinity* (Currach Press, 2004), pp. 433–5.
40   Tom O'Connor, in O'Malley and Horgan (eds), *The Men Will Talk to Me*, p. 138.
41   Martin Moore, *The Call to Arms: Tom McEllistrim and the Fight for Freedom in Kerry* (An Gabha Beag, 2016), p. 86.
42   Gregory Ashe, in O'Malley and Horgan (eds), *The Men Will Talk to Me*, p. 123.
43   John Joe Rice, in ibid., p. 285.
44   Joy, *IRA in Kerry*, pp. 115–20; Tom Doyle, *The Civil War in Kerry* (Mercier Press, 2008), pp. 68–70; Owen O'Shea, *Ballymacandy: The Story of a Kerry Ambush* (Merrion Press, 2021), pp. 76–80.
45   Doyle, *Civil War in Kerry*, p. 69.
46   Joy, *IRA in Kerry*, p. 121.
47   Doyle, *Civil War in Kerry*, p. 70.
48   *Kerry People*, 21 January 1922.
49   *The Cork Examiner*, 13 January 1922.
50   *Kerry People*, 4 February 1922.
51   *The Cork Examiner*, 31 January 1922.
52   *Kerry People*, 11 February 1922.
53   Doyle, *Civil War in Kerry*, p. 73.
54   Dominic Price, *We Bled Together: Michael Collins, The Squad and the Dublin Brigade* (Collins Press, 2017), p. 245.
55   Often referred to as 'Daly' but referred to throughout this book as 'O'Daly'.
56   Niall C. Harrington, *Kerry Landing: An Episode of the Civil War* (Anvil Books, 1992), p. 7.

CHAPTER 2

1   *The Cork Examiner*, 20 March 1922.
2   MA, BMH WS 952, Maurice Horgan; O'Shea and Revington, *Century of Politics*, pp. 83–4; Department of Housing, Planning and Local Government, *Democracy and Change: The 1920 Local Elections in Ireland* (Local Government Archivists and Records Managers, 2020), p. 56.
3   MA, BMH WS 485, Brighid Mullane.
4   *Kerry People*, 25 March 1922.
5   *Irish Independent*, 20 March 1922.
6   *The Cork Examiner*, 20 March 1922.
7   David McCullagh, *De Valera: Volume 1, Rise 1882–1932* (Gill, 2017), p. 408.
8   *Irish Independent*, 20 March 1922; Dwyer, *Tans, Terror and Troubles*, pp. 346–7.
9   Diary of Markham Richard Leeson Marshall, 20 March 1922.
10   Keane, *Wounds*, p. 222; Dwyer, *Tans, Terror and Troubles*, p. 346.
11   Dwyer, *Tans, Terror and Troubles,* p. 347; Harrington, *Kerry Landing*, p. 20.
12   *The Cork Examiner*, 25 April 1922.
13   'Answer to Question 26' by Hannah Mary Moynihan, MA, MSPC W5D47, Patrick Moynihan.
14   Dwyer, *Tans, Terror and Troubles*, p. 348; Doyle, *Civil War in Kerry*, p. 90.

15 Harrington, *Kerry Landing*, p. 20.
16 *The Cork Examiner*, 25 April 1922; *The Freeman's Journal*, 25 April 1922.
17 Dwyer, *Tans, Terror and Troubles,* p. 350.
18 *Kerry People*, 6 May 1922. One of the committee members, P.W. Palmer, was later a Fine Gael TD for Kerry South.
19 Michael Gallagher, 'The Pact General Election of 1922', *Irish Historical Studies*, Vol. 22, No. 84 (September 1979), pp. 405–6.
20 Tadhg Kennedy, in O'Malley and Horgan (eds), *The Men Will Talk to Me*, p. 94.
21 *The Cork Examiner*, 5 June and 7 June 1922.
22 Lady Edith Gordon, *The Winds of Time* (J. Murray, 1934), p. 199.
23 Murphy, *When Youth Was Mine*, p. 187.
24 See Ronan McGreevy, *Great Hatred: The Assassination of Field Marshal Sir Henry Wilson* (Faber & Faber, 2022).
25 McAuliffe et al., *Kerry 1916*, p. 234; MA, MSPC 24SP3908, James Dempsey.
26 *Kerry People*, 1 July 1922.
27 Mulvihill, *Testimony*, p. 18.
28 Harrington, *Kerry Landing*, p. 31.
29 Harrington, *Munster Republic*, p. 53; Noel Ó Murchú, *The War in the West 1918–1923* (Mountain Range Press, 2020), p. 259.
30 Tom Doyle, *The Summer Campaign in Kerry* (Mercier Press, 2010), p. 24.
31 Johnny O'Connor, in O'Malley and Horgan (eds), *The Men Will Talk to Me*, p. 241.
32 *Kerry People*, 6 May 1922.
33 *Kerry People*, 8 July 1922.
34 MA, MSPC W2D147, Edward Michael Sheehy; *Kerry People*, 8 July 1922.
35 Harrington, *Kerry Landing*, p. 35.
36 *Kerry People*, 8 July 1922.
37 *The Cork Examiner*, 5 July 1922; *Kerry People*, 8 July 1922.
38 *The Cork Examiner*, 5 July 1922.
39 Keane, *Wounds*, p. 226.
40 *Kerry People*, 29 July 1922.
41 *Irish Independent*, 3 January 1922.
42 *Kerry People*, 29 July 1922.
43 Dwyer, *Tans, Terror and Troubles*, p. 353.

CHAPTER 3

1   Harrington, *Kerry Landing*, p. 77.
2   Dan King to Niall Harrington, NLI, Papers of Niall Harrington, MS 40,629/1.
3   Harrington, *Kerry Landing*, p. 91.
4   *Ballyseedy*, RTÉ Television, 12 November 1997.
5   Harrington, *Kerry Landing*, p. 48.
6   Ibid., p. 72.
7   Johnny O'Connor, in O'Malley and Horgan (eds), *The Men Will Talk to Me*, p. 250; Doyle, *Summer Campaign*, pp. 40–1.
8   Harrington, *Kerry Landing*, p. 80.
9   Dwyer, *Tans, Terror and Troubles*, p. 355.
10 Dan King to Niall Harrington, NLI, Papers of Niall Harrington, MS 40,629/1.
11 Hanna O'Connor to Dan Nolan, Christmas 1980, NLI, Papers of Niall Harrington, MS 40,685/2.

12 Ibid.
13 Harrington, *Kerry Landing*, pp. 98–9.
14 Ibid., p. 114.
15 NA, Department of Finance: Post-Truce (Damage to Property (Compensation) Act 1923), Compensation Files, FIN/COMP/2/8 (Kerry).
16 Secretary of the Department of Justice to Niall Harrington, 11 August 1977, NLI, Papers of Niall Harrington, MS 40,680/1; List of Free State Army casualties from monument in Glasnevin Cemetery, theirishstory.com.
17 MA, MSPC 2D332, Patrick Harding.
18 *Free State*, 19 August 1922.
19 Harrington, *Kerry Landing*, p. 120.
20 Dwyer, *Tans, Terror and Troubles*, p. 354.
21 Harrington, *Kerry Landing*, p. 125.
22 Doyle, *Summer Campaign*, p. 47.
23 Ibid., p. 16; Tim Horgan, *Fighting for the Cause: Kerry's Republican Fighters* (Mercier Press, 2018), p. 110.
24 Harrington, *Munster Republic*, p. 69.
25 Tom McEllistrim, in O'Malley and Horgan (eds), *The Men Will Talk to Me*, p. 209.
26 Harrington, *Kerry Landing*, p. 134.
27 Foster, 'Civil War in Kerry', p. 475.
28 Doyle, *Summer Campaign*, p. 110.
29 Dwyer, *Civil War in Kerry*, p. 362.
30 MA, MSPC 24SP3755, Matthew Daly.
31 *Black Sheep? The Sons of O'Connor-Scarteen*, RTÉ Television, 21 May 1996.
32 Ibid.
33 Doyle, *Summer Campaign*, p. 100.
34 John Marcus O'Sullivan TD to Department of Defence, 2 July 1924, MA, MSPC 2D160, Thomas O'Connor.
35 Harrington, *Kerry Landing*, p. 140.
36 *Black Sheep?* (RTÉ).
37 O'Malley and Horgan (eds), *The Men Will Talk to Me*, p. 139, n. 139.
38 *The Cork Examiner*, 24 August 1923.
39 NA, FIN/COMP/2/8/311.
40 Johnny O'Connor, in O'Malley and Horgan (eds), *The Men Will Talk to Me*, p. 233. O'Connor was more commonly known as Connor, which has been used throughout the text.
41 Ibid.
42 Ibid., p. 259.
43 John Joe Rice, in O'Malley and Horgan (eds), *The Men Will Talk to Me*, p. 300.

CHAPTER 4

1 *Evening (Saturday) Herald*, 19 August 1922.
2 NA, FIN/COMP/2/8/733.
3 *Evening (Saturday) Herald*, 19 August 1922.
4 *Free State*, 2 September 1922.
5 Mary A. Fitzgerald to President de Valera, 17 May 1932, MA, MSPC Cecil Fitzgerald, W2D286.
6 *The Cork Examiner*, 16 August 1923.

7   MA, MSPC W2D242, William David Carson.
8   MA, MSPC W2D270, John Joseph Young.
9   MA, MSPC W2D22, James Byrne.
10 MA, MSPC DP24836, Michael J. Ryle.
11 Horgan, *Dying for the Cause*, pp. 76–7.
12 Ibid., pp. 69–70.
13 MA, MSPC DP6534, Michael Sinnott; Horgan, *Dying for the Cause*, p. 79, 363.
14 MA, MSPC DP1303, Eugene Fitzgerald.
15 Murphy, *When Youth Was Mine*, p. 248.
16 Horgan, *Dying for the Cause*, p. 208.
17 Dorothy Macardle, *Tragedies of Kerry* (Irish Freedom Press), p. 15.
18 MA, BMH WS 938, Dan Mulvihill; Horgan, *Dying for the Cause*, p. 208.
19 *Irish Independent*, 29 September 1922.
20 Leeann Lane, *Dorothy Macardle* (UCD Press, 2019), p. 131.
21 *Irish Independent*, 5 October 1922.
22 For a detailed account of the battle for Killorglin, see Doyle, *Summer Campaign*, pp. 123–32 and Doyle, *Civil War in Kerry*, pp. 181–6.
23 Diary of Markham Richard Leeson Marshall, various entries in August and September 1922.
24 NA, FIN/COMP/2/8/325.
25 NA, FIN/COMP/2/8/109.
26 NA, Department of Justice, 2017/46/665.
27 Markham Richard Leeson Marshall to his daughter, May, 1 October 1922, Muckross House Library, transcription kindly provided by Dr John Knightly.
28 NA, FIN/COMP/2/8.
29 The *Irish Times* report on the 'Killorglin Battle', UCD Archives (UCDA), Richard Mulcahy Papers, P7-B-210.
30 Diary of Markham Richard Leeson Marshall, 29 and 30 June 1922.
31 Doyle, *Summer Campaign*, p. 130.
32 Price, *We Bled Together*, p. 246; Doyle, *Summer Campaign*, p. 17.
33 Dwyer, *Tans, Terror and Troubles*, p. 362; Doyle, *Civil War in Kerry*, p. 191.
34 Macardle, *Tragedies of Kerry*, p. 15.
35 Johnny O'Connor, in O'Malley and Horgan (eds), *The Men Will Talk to Me*, p. 233.
36 *Poblachta na h-Éireann*, 4 December 1922.
37 MA, MSPC 34REF6000, Annie Mary O'Connor.
38 Price, *We Bled Together*, p. 247; MA, MSPC 2RBSD157, John Galvin.
39 Doyle, *Summer Campaign*, p. 140.
40 Doyle, *Civil War in Kerry*, p. 219.
41 Macardle, *Tragedies of Kerry*, p. 38; Horgan, *Dying for the Cause*, p. 365.
42 MA, MSPC DP8427, William Myles; MA, MSPC 2D177 Daniel Nagle.
43 MA, MSPC W24SP3908, James Dempsey; Doyle, *Civil War in Kerry*, p. 228; McAuliffe at el., *Kerry 1916*, p. 234; Macardle, *Tragedies of Kerry*, p. 49.
44 Macardle, *Tragedies of Kerry*, p. 52.
45 NA, FIN/COMP/2/8/218 and 375.
46 NA, FIN/COMP/2/8/379.
47 NA, FIN/COMP/2/8/512.
48 Diary of Markham Richard Leeson Marshall, 2 April 1922.
49 Letter from William West, Ahane, Ballymacelligott, *Kerry People*, 15 April 1922.
50 Ibid.

51 Thomas Earls FitzGerald, *Combatants and Civilians in Revolutionary Ireland, 1918–1923* (Routledge, 2021), p. 218.
52 *The Cork Examiner*, 20 June 1922 and 17 June 1922.
53 Report from Kerry Command to Army Headquarters, UCDA, Papers of Richard Mulcahy, P7/B/117.
54 Letter from Fr Alexander O'Sullivan to Minister for Home Affairs, 31 May 1922, NA, Department of Justice Files, H5/324.
55 Letter from Fr Alexander O'Sullivan to Minister for Home Affairs, 10 June 1922, NA, Department of Justice Files, H5/324.
56 Diary of Markham Richard Leeson Marshall, 9 June 1922.
57 Doyle, *Civil War in Kerry*, p. 237.
58 Diary of Markham Richard Leeson Marshall, 7 March 1922.
59 Ibid., 3 August 1922.
60 FitzGerald, *Combatants and Civilians*, p. 219.
61 Terence Dooley, *The Decline of the Big Houses in Ireland* (Wolfhound Press, 2001), p. 287.
62 John Knightly, 'The destruction of the country house in Kerry, 1920–1923', unpublished article provided with the kind permission of the author.
63 Dooley, *Big Houses*, p. 192.
64 Report on destruction of Derreen, cited by Dooley, *Big Houses*, p. 196.
65 NA, FIN/COMP/2/8/784.
66 Doyle, *Civil War in Kerry*, pp. 198–9; Valerie Bary, *Houses of Kerry* (Ballinakella Press, 1994), pp. 3–4; Knightly, 'Destruction of the country house'.
67 Doyle, *Civil War in Kerry*, p. 203.
68 Knightly, 'Destruction of the country house'.
69 Ibid.

CHAPTER 5

1 NA, FIN/COMP/2/8/377.
2 Ibid.
3 Ibid.
4 Gordon, *Winds of Time*, p. 210.
5 Diary of Markham Richard Leeson Marshall, 2 June 1922.
6 Doyle, *Summer Campaign*, p. 74.
7 *Irish Independent*, 1 August 1923.
8 *The Liberator*, 18 August 1923.
9 Dáil Debates, 14 December 1923.
10 Letters from William Long, Ballyferriter, to Minister Kevin O'Higgins and James Crowley TD, 27 November 1923, NA, Department of Justice Files, H5/1095.
11 NA, FIN/COMP/2/8/646.
12 *The Irish Times*, 3 March 1923.
13 *The Irish Times*, 13 March 1923.
14 T.J. Liston to Ministry of Home Affairs, 25 August 1923, NA, Department of Justice Files, Kerry Quarter Sessions File, H85/18.
15 NA, FIN/COMP/2.
16 Some addresses have been abbreviated.
17 *The Cork Examiner*, 23 November 1923.
18 Doyle, *Civil War in Kerry*, p. 203.

19 Murphy, *When Youth Was Mine*, p. 215.
20 NA, FIN/COMP/2/8/491 and 714.
21 NA, FIN/COMP/2/8/881.
22 NA, FIN/COMP/2/8/217.
23 NA, FIN/COMP/2/8/411.
24 *The Cork Examiner*, 22 November 1922, cited by Doyle, *Civil War in Kerry*, p. 214.
25 *The Freeman's Journal*, 26 June 1923.
26 Gordon, *Winds of Time*, p. 205.
27 NA, FIN/COMP/2/8/185.
28 NA, FIN/COMP/2/8/1035.
29 Murphy, *When Youth Was Mine*, p. 236.
30 NA, FIN/COMP/2/8/340.
31 NA, FIN/COMP/2/8/910.
32 NA, FIN/COMP/2/8/1018.
33 Diary of Markham Richard Leeson Marshall, 12 June 1922.
34 *The Cork Examiner*, 1 May 1923.
35 *Kerry News*, 8 September 1924.
36 NA, FIN/COMP/2/8/200.
37 NA, FIN/COMP/2/8/682.
38 NA, FIN/COMP/2/8/285 and 268.
39 NA, FIN/COMP/2/8/291.
40 NA, FIN/COMP/2/8/775.
41 NA, FIN/COMP/2/8/264.
42 NA, FIN/COMP/2/8/441.
43 NA, FIN/COMP/2/8/491.
44 NA, FIN/COMP/2/8/796 and 970.
45 NA, FIN/COMP/2/8/286.
46 NA, FIN/COMP/2/8/955.
47 John Joe Rice, in O'Malley and Horgan (eds), *The Men Will Talk to Me*, p. 287.
48 NA, FIN/COMP/2/8/399.
49 Report from Kerry Command to Army Headquarters, 2 February 1922, UCDA, Papers of Richard Mulcahy, P7/B/72.
50 Letter from Timothy Devane, Rathanny, Tralee, to Fionán Lynch TD, 27 January 1924, NA, H5/1226.
51 Ibid.
52 Staff Officer Dublin District South to Department of Defence, 13 December 1928, MA, MSPC W5D47, Patrick Moynihan.
53 Adjutant General's office to Army Pensions Board, 29 October 1928, MA, MSPC W5D47, Patrick Moynihan.
54 'Answer to Question 26', note written by Hannah Mary Moynihan, MA, MSPC W5D47, Patrick Moynihan.
55 Report of Garda Sergeant D. Dennehy, 22 January 1926, MA, MSPC 24SP9795, Patrick O'Sullivan.
56 MA, MSPC 24SP3726, William Horan.

CHAPTER 6

1 Field General Headquarters, Kerry Command, 7 December 1922, to Commander in Chief, UCDA, Papers of Richard Mulcahy, P7/B/72.

2   Kerry Command to GOC, 2 January 1923, UCDA, Papers of Richard Mulcahy, P7/B/72.
3   John Joe Rice, in O'Malley and Horgan (eds), *The Men Will Talk to Me*, p. 307.
4   Kerry Command Intelligence Office, 30 April 1923, MA, Civil War Operations and Intelligence Reports Collection, CW/OPS/08/07.
5   Kerry Command, General Weekly Return, 25 April 1923, MA, CW/OPS/08/07.
6   John Joe Rice, in O'Malley and Horgan (eds), *The Men Will Talk to Me*, p. 307.
7   Dwyer, *Tans, Terror and Troubles*, p. 367.
8   Murphy, *When Youth Was Mine*, p. 219; O'Connor, *Tomorrow Was Another Day*, p. 80.
9   Gregory Ashe, in O'Malley and Horgan (eds), *The Men Will Talk to Me*, p. 124.
10   Evidence of Jeremiah Kennedy to Pensions Board, 5 October 1945, MA, MSPC 60354, Jeremiah Kennedy.
11   Sworn statement of Jeremiah O'Sullivan, 15 October 1946, MA, MSPC 34REF7106, Jeremiah Sullivan.
12   Moore, *Call to Arms*, p. 90.
13   Doyle, *Civil War in Kerry*, p. 196.
14   Sworn statement of William O'Leary to Advisory Committee, 16 March 1937, MA, MSPC 34REF31576, William O'Leary.
15   MA, MSPC 56706, Sarah (Sally) Sheehy.
16   MA, MSPC 57640, Mary Coffey (*née* Cremin).
17   Capt. J.E. Penrose, General Weekly Return, 25 April 1923, MA, CW/OPS/08/07.
18   Sworn statement of Thomas Rohan to Advisory Committee, 27 April 1937, MA, MSPC 34REF 13932, Thomas Rohan.
19   O'Connor, *Tomorrow Was Another Day*, p. 80.
20   Gregory Ashe, in O'Malley and Horgan (eds), *The Men Will Talk to Me*, p. 124.
21   Doyle, *Civil War in Kerry*, p. 194.
22   MA, MSPC W2D290, Matthew Ferguson.
23   Department of Military Statistics, 25 January 1923, UCDA, Papers of Richard Mulcahy, P7/B/72; Tom McEllistrim, in O'Malley and Horgan (eds), *The Men Will Talk to Me*, p. 209.
24   NA, FIN/COMP/2/8/339.
25   Austin Stack to Winifred Gordon, 5 August 1922, NLI, Austin Stack Papers, MS 22,398.
26   Price, *We Bled Together*, p. 251.
27   Foster, 'Civil War in Kerry,' p. 476; Karl Murphy, 'An Irish General: William Richard English Murphy, 1890–1975', *History Ireland*, Vol. 13, No. 6 (2005), pp. 10–11.
28   Doyle, *Civil War in Kerry*, p. 250.
29   Field General Headquarters, Kerry Command, 7 December 1922, to Commander in Chief, UCDA, Papers of Richard Mulcahy, P7/B/72.
30   Seán Enright, *The Irish Civil War: Law, Execution and Atrocity* (Merrion Press, 2019), p. 65.
31   Bill Bailey, in O'Malley and Horgan (eds), *The Men Will Talk to Me*, p. 106.
32   Courtesy of Jim Cunningham.
33   *The Irish Times*, 6 February 1923.
34   Price, *We Bled Together*, p. 251.
35   Bill Bailey, in O'Malley and Horgan (eds), *The Men Will Talk to Me*, p. 104.
36   John Joe Rice, in ibid., p. 286.

37   Johnny O'Connor, in ibid., p. 235.
38   May Daly, in ibid., p. 96.
39   Ibid.
40   Keane, *Wounds*, p. 234.
41   Gregory Ashe, in O'Malley and Horgan (eds), *The Men Will Talk to Me*, p. 124; Macardle, *Tragedies of Kerry*, pp. 67–8.
42   Macardle, *Tragedies of Kerry*, p. 68.
43   Gregory Ashe, in O'Malley and Horgan (eds), *The Men Will Talk to Me*, pp. 124–5.
44   Ibid., p. 125.
45   Doyle, *Civil War in Kerry*, p. 277.
46   Denis Daly, in O'Malley and Horgan (eds), *The Men Will Talk to Me*, p. 328.
47   Billy Mullins, in ibid., pp. 75–6.
48   Memorandum for Minister, MA, MSPC W2D22, James Byrne.
49   Fr Harrington to Miss Keane, 12 December 1922, MA, MSPC W2D22, James Byrne.
50   Michael Laffan, *Judging W.T. Cosgrave* (Royal Irish Academy, 2014), p. 124.
51   *The Irish Times*, 24 February 1923.
52   Dwyer, *Tans, Terror and Troubles*, p. 359.
53   Foster, 'Civil War in Kerry', p. 476.

CHAPTER 7

1   Fr M. O'Connor to Office of the Adjutant General, 30 April 1923, MA, MSPC WCL1059, Patrick O'Connor.
2   Fr M. O'Connor to Office of the Adjutant General, 19 May 1923, MA, MSPC WCL1059, Patrick O'Connor.
3   Doyle, *Civil War in Kerry*, p. 270.
4   Keane, *Wounds*, p. 241.
5   Horgan, *Dying for the Cause*, pp. 197–8.
6   Ibid., p. 200.
7   *Ballyseedy* (RTÉ); Price, *We Bled Together*, p. 253.
8   Peig O'Mahony, *Ballyseedy* (RTÉ).
9   Army Report, 16 June 1924, MA, MSPC W3D58, Patrick O'Connor; O'Connor, *Tomorrow Was Another Day*, p. 88.
10   Army Report, 16 June 1924, MA, MSPC W3D58, Patrick O'Connor.
11   *Ballyseedy* (RTÉ).
12   Copy of Report re Ballyseedy by Humphrey Murphy, O/C, Kerry No. 1 Brigade to Liam Lynch, Chief of Staff, NLI, Papers of Niall Harrington, MS 40,629/1; Enright, *Irish Civil War*, p. 90.
13   O'Connor, *Tomorrow Was Another Day*, p. 88.
14   Enright, *Irish Civil War*, p. 90.
15   O'Connor, *Tomorrow Was Another Day*, p. 89.
16   Bill Bailey, in O'Malley and Horgan (eds), *The Men Will Talk to Me*, p. 101; Horgan, *Dying for the Cause*, p. 201.
17   Evidence of Sgt Matthews, Proceedings of Court of Enquiry into deaths at Knocknagoshel, 19 June 1923, MA, MSPC WCL1059, Patrick O'Connor.
18   *The Cork Examiner*, 8 March 1923.
19   *Ballyseedy* (RTÉ).
20   *Irish Independent*, 8 March 1923.

21   Enright, *Irish Civil War*, p. 90.
22   Bill Bailey, in O'Malley and Horgan (eds), *The Men Will Talk to Me*, p. 101.
23   *Irish Independent*, 8 March 1923.
24   O'Connor, *Tomorrow Was Another Day*, p. 89.
25   Diarmaid Ferriter, *Between Two Hells: The Irish Civil War* (Profile Books, 2021), p. 107.
26   *Evening Herald*, 9 March 1923.
27   *Ballyseedy* (RTÉ).
28   Ferriter, *Between Two Hells*, p. 107.
29   *Ballyseedy: 75th Commemoration of Ballyseedy Massacre*, p. 6.
30   Eoin Neeson, *The Civil War in Ireland, 1921–23* (Mercier Press, 1966), p. 172.
31   Dwyer, *Tans, Terror and Troubles*, p. 369.
32   Macardle, *Tragedies of Kerry*, p. 24; *Ballyseedy* (RTÉ).
33   Speaking to *Ireland: A Television History* by Robert Kee in 1980 and featured in *Ballyseedy* (RTÉ).
34   Kerry Command Report, 20 March 1923, MA, CW/OPS/08/03. Breslin's pension application makes no reference to his role at Ballyseedy or any injury sustained during the explosion, MA, MSPC 24SP1301, Edmund Joseph Breslin.
35   J.J. Barrett, *In the Name of the Game* (Dub Press, 1997), p. 91.
36   Report to General Headquarters, 26 September 1924, UCDA, Moss Twomey Papers, P69/137 (47).
37   Moore, *Call to Arms*, p. 101.
38   Ibid.
39   Medical report of Dr Edmond R. Shanahan, 18 February 1933, WDP6809, Stephen Fuller.
40   *Ballyseedy* (RTÉ).
41   *The Cork Examiner*, 9 March 1923.
42   'Murder of Republican Prisoners in Kerry', UCDA, Moss Twomey Papers, P69/26 (7).
43   Bill Bailey, in O'Malley and Horgan (eds), *The Men Will Talk to Me*, p. 102. The 'Sheik of Araby' was performed by the American musician and performer Spike Jones and his outlandish and irreverent band in the early 1940s.
44   'Murder of Republican Prisoners in Kerry', UCDA, Moss Twomey Papers, P69/26 (7).
45   *Ballyseedy: 75th Commemoration of Ballyseedy Massacre*, p. 7, n. 6.
46   *Ballyseedy* (RTÉ).
47   Receipts from Patrick Daly's application for a gratuity, MA, MSPC WDP51, John Daly.
48   UCDA, Moss Twomey Papers, P69/252 (5).
49   Dorothy Macardle, *The Irish Republic* (Wolfhound Press, 1995), p. 340.
50   *Éire*, 14 April 1923.
51   Letter from Superintendent Seamus Ua Hannagáin to Commissioner Eoin O'Duffy, 26 April 1923, NA, Department of Justice Files, H197/7.
52   *Ballyseedy* (RTÉ); information from Dr Conor Brosnan.
53   Horgan, *Dying for the Cause*, pp. 210–2.
54   *Ballyseedy* (RTÉ).
55   Ibid.
56   Barrett, *In the Name of the Game*, p. 86.
57   Dan Nolan to Niall Harrington, 10 June 1978, NLI, MS 40,680/2.
58   Ibid.
59   Undated, NLI, Papers of Niall Harrington, MS 40,629/1.

CHAPTER 8

1   Return of Officers, Warrant Officers, N.C.O.s and Men serving at Tralee, 12 November 1922–13 November 1922, MA, Irish Army Census Collection.
2   MA, MSPC W3D248, Daniel Sugrue.
3   Mary Sugrue to Department of Defence, 24 July 1924, MA, MSPC W3D248, Daniel Sugrue.
4   Macardle, *Tragedies of Kerry*, p. 29.
5   Horgan, *Dying for the Cause*, p. 304; Macardle, *Tragedies of Kerry*, p. 31.
6   Macardle, *Tragedies of Kerry*, p. 29; Doyle, *Civil War in Kerry*, p. 275; Horgan, *Dying for the Cause*, p. 301.
7   Command Adjutant, Southern Command to Adjutant General, GHQ, MA, MSPC W3D248, Daniel Sugrue.
8   Mary Sugrue to Army Pensions Board, 12 June 1924, MA, MSPC W3D248, Daniel Sugrue.
9   Orson McMahon, 'Civil War Violence in Kerry: A Necessary First Principle', MA thesis, Leiden University (2020), p. 60; Horgan, *Dying for the Cause*, p. 305.
10 McMahon, 'Civil War Violence in Kerry', p. 60.
11 'Murder of Republican Prisoners in Kerry', UCDA, Papers of Moss Twomey, P69/26 (9); McMahon, 'Civil War Violence in Kerry', p. 60.
12 Macardle, *Tragedies of Kerry*, p. 34.
13 Fionán Lynch TD to Department of Defence, 15 April 1943, MA, MSPC DP3621, Jeremiah O'Donoghue.
14 In the Dáil, General Mulcahy indicated the time the incident took place was 3 a.m., Dáil Debates, 17 April 1923.
15 'Murder of Republican Prisoners in Kerry', UCD Archives, Moss Twomey Papers, P69/26 (8).
16 Macardle, *Tragedies of Kerry*, pp. 32–3.
17 Doyle, *Civil War in Kerry*, p. 275; Dwyer, *Tans, Terror and Troubles*, p. 371; Macardle, *Tragedies of Kerry*, p. 33.
18 Unpublished account of the 'Battle of Gurrane' by Paddy O'Connor, courtesy of Noreen O'Connor; *The Irish Times*, 7 March 1923.
19 Doyle, *Civil War in Kerry*, p. 269.
20 Horgan, *Dying for the Cause*, p. 352.
21 Horgan, *Fighting for the Cause*, p. 104.
22 Report of Hugh O'Friel, Secretary General, 8 January 1924, NA, Department of Justice, H/197/52.
23 Riordan is sometimes spelled Reardon in official documents and other sources. Riordan is used here based on the correspondence with family members that is contained in the Military Archives.
24 Horgan, *Dying for the Cause*, pp. 372, 374.
25 Secretary of Department of Defence to Compensation (Personal Injuries) Committee, November 1923, MA, MSPC DP 3816, Eugene Dwyer.
26 Macardle, *Tragedies of Kerry*, pp. 57, 60.
27 NA, H/197/52; *The Irish Times*, 31 December 2008.
28 Macardle, *Tragedies of Kerry* p. 59; Ó Murchú, *War in the West*, p. 276.
29 Macardle, *Tragedies of Kerry*, p. 60.
30 Court of Enquiry, 19 April 1923, NA, H/197/52.
31 Macardle, *Tragedies of Kerry*, p. 56.
32 *The Irish Times*, 31 December 2008.

33 Ferriter, *Between Two Hells*, p. 109.
34 Details of the confidential report which was published by the National Archives in December 2008 were first reported in *The Irish Times* on 31 December 2008.
35 Court of Enquiry, 19 April 1923, NA, H/197/52.
36 Dáil Debates, 17 April 1923.
37 Court of Enquiry, 19 April 1923, NA, H/197/52.
38 Ryle Dwyer, 'Two weeks of bloody massacres', in Simon Brouder (ed.), *Rebel Kerry: From the Pages of The Kerryman* (Mercier Press, 2017), p. 185.
39 *The Irish Times*, 31 December 2008.
40 Report of Hugh O'Friel, Secretary, Department of Justice, 8 January 1924, NA, H/197/52.
41 Meeting of Executive Council, 22 January 1924; O'Friel to Compensation (Personal Injuries) Committee, 6 May 1924, NA, JUS/2008/152/27.
42 Minute of Department of Defence, 12 November 1923, MA, MSPC DP3844, William Reardon.
43 Report from 1933 cited in Memorandum, Department of Defence, 18 September 1957, MA, MSPC DP3844, William Reardon.
44 Colonel M. Costello to Minister for Defence, 24 October 1923, MA, MSPC DP3816, Eugene Dwyer.
45 Doyle, *Civil War in Kerry*, p. 279.
46 Macardle, *Tragedies of Kerry*, p. 59.
47 Harrington, *A Kerry Landing*, p. 149.
48 Dwyer, *Tans, Terror and Troubles*, p. 372.
49 MA, MSPC 24SP9573, Timothy Jones.
50 MA, MSPC 34REF60315, Peg Cahill.
51 Horgan, *Fighting for the Cause*, p. 362, n. 35.
52 'Murder of Republican Prisoners in Kerry', UCDA, Moss Twomey Papers, P69/26 (8).
53 Doyle, *Civil War in Kerry*, p. 290; Dwyer, *Tans, Terror and Troubles*, pp. 372–3.
54 Doyle, *Civil War in Kerry*, p. 290.
55 Findings of Court of Enquiry, NA, JUS/152/27.
56 Dáil Debates, 17 April 1923.
57 Ibid.
58 Ibid.
59 Note to Department Secretary, undated, NA, H/197/7.
60 Report of Kerry Command, 14 March 1923, MA, CW/OPS/08/11.
61 Doyle, *Civil War in Kerry*, p. 285; Townshend puts the figure at thirty-two, *The Republic*, p. 443.
62 Diary of Markham Richard Leeson Marshall, 9 March 1923.
63 'Murder of Republican Prisoners in Kerry', UCDA, Moss Twomey Papers, P69/26 (8).

CHAPTER 9

1 *An t-Óglach*, 21 April 1923.
2 Ibid.
3 Bill Kissane, *Explaining Irish Democracy* (UCD Press, 2002), p. 182.
4 *The Irish Times*, 24 July 1999.
5 Ibid.
6 Foster, 'Civil War in Kerry', p. 477; UCDA, Monthly Report from Kerry Command, 24 April 1923, Papers of Todd Andrews, P91/84.

7   Ferriter, *Between Two Hells*, p. 136; MA, MSPC 24SP424, Patrick O'Daly.
8   Price, *We Bled Together*, p. 286.
9   Ibid.
10 Ibid., pp. 262–3.
11 Summary Report of Kerry Command, 19 April 1923, MA, CW/OPS/08/03; Gaughan, *Listowel and its Vicinity*, p. 414; Doyle, *Civil War in Kerry*, pp. 297–8; Dwyer, *Tans, Terror and Troubles*, p. 377.
12 Cecelia Lynch, *From the GPO to Clashmealcon* (North Kerry Republican Memorial Committee, 2003), pp. 16–17.
13 Ibid, p. 17.
14 MA, MSPC 3D233, James O'Neill.
15 *The Irish Times*, 17 April 1923.
16 Application of Timothy Lyons (Senior), MA, MSPC 2RB481, Timothy Lyons.
17 Report to IRA Headquarters, 26 September 1924, UCDA, Moss Twomey Papers, P69/167 (47).
18 Summary Report of Kerry Command, 19 April 1923, MA, CW/OPS/08/03; Ferriter, *Between Two Hells*, p. 109; Horgan, *Dying for the Cause*, p. 106.
19 Lynch, *GPO to Clashmealcon*, p. 21.
20 Macardle, *Tragedies of Kerry*, p. 86.
21 Lynch, *GPO to Clashmealcon*, p. 24.
22 Application of Elizabeth Quinlan, MA, MSPC, DP3323 Edward Greaney.
23 Foster, 'Civil War in Kerry', p. 476.
24 Dwyer, *Tans, Terror and Troubles*, p. 377.
25 *The Cork Examiner*, 28 April 1923; Report of Southern Command, 3 June 1924, MA, MSPC 3D224, Michael Behan.
26 Doyle, *Civil War in Kerry*, p. 302. In his dissertation, Orson McMahon places the number at seventy: 'Civil War Violence in Kerry', p. 31.
27 Doyle, *Civil War in Kerry*, pp. 323–31.
28 Ibid.
29 McMahon, 'Civil War Violence in Kerry', p. 64.
30 Foster, 'Civil War in Kerry', p. 478.
31 Estimates for the total national death toll during the Civil War range from 1,500 to 2,000: Andy Bielenberg, 'Fatalities in the Irish Revolution', in Crowley et al., *Atlas of the Irish Revolution*, pp. 759–61.
32 Doyle, *Civil War in Kerry*, p. 331.
33 Tom Doyle lists all the known civilians killed during the conflict, *Civil War in Kerry*, p. 331.
34 Markham Richard Leeson Marshall to his daughter, May, 1 October 1922.
35 NA, Department of Justice, 2017/46/656.
36 *The Freeman's Journal*, 11 November 1922; *The Cork Examiner*, 13 November 1922; NA Department of Justice, 2017/46/2001; Diary of Markham Richard Leeson Marshall, 8 November 1922.
37 *The Times*, 12 April 1923.
38 Townshend, *The Republic*, p. 447.
39 Dwyer, *Tans, Terror and Troubles*, p. 375.
40 James O'Leary to the Taoiseach, date unclear, MA, MSPC DP2715, Jeremiah O'Leary; *Ballyseedy* (RTÉ).
41 Harrington, *Kerry Landing*, p. 149.
42 James O'Leary to the Taoiseach, date unclear, MA, MSPC DP2715, Jeremiah O'Leary.

43 MA, MSPC DP2715, Jeremiah O'Leary.
44 James O'Leary to the Taoiseach, 14 July 1938, MA, MSPC DP2715, Jeremiah O'Leary.

CHAPTER 10

1   The correct spelling of the family name is MacCarthy, which has been used throughout this chapter. See Mary Coleman Schwab and John Randal Coleman, 'Bound to Speak', *Kenmare Chronicle* (Kenmare, 2021), p. 175.
2   Report prepared by Attorney General, Hugh Kennedy for President W.T. Cosgrave, 27 September 1923, NA, TSCH/3/S3341; Coleman Schwab and Coleman, 'Bound to Speak,' pp. 173–5.
3   Report prepared by Attorney General.
4   Price, *We Bled Together*, p. 259.
5   'Raid on MacCarthy's House, Kenmare, Co. Kerry', 17 June 1924, NLI, MS 49,612; *Cogadh ar Mhná*, TG4, 2021.
6   *Cogadh ar Mhná*, TG4, 2021.
7   'Raid on MacCarthy's House, Kenmare, Co. Kerry', 17 June 1924, NLI, MS 49,612; Report prepared by Attorney General; MA, BMH WS 1751, Cahir Davitt.
8   Connolly, 'Sexual Violence', p. 136.
9   Price, *We Bled Together*, p. 259.
10 Connolly, 'Sexual Violence', p. 138.
11 Report prepared by Attorney General.
12 *Cogadh ar Mhná*, TG4, 2021.
13 Ibid.
14 Bill Bailey, in O'Malley and Horgan (eds), *The Men Will Talk to Me*, p. 105.
15 Price, *We Bled Together*, p. 259.
16 Report prepared by Attorney General; MA, BMH WS 1751, Cahir Davitt.
17 Bill Bailey, in O'Malley and Horgan (eds), *The Men Will Talk to Me*, p. 105.
18 Ó Caoimh, *Richard Mulcahy*, p. 307, n. 92.
19 Price, *We Bled Together*, p. 259.
20 John M. Regan, presentation to Irish National Civil War Conference at University College Cork, 17 June 2022, https://www.ucc.ie/en/theirishrevolution/irish-civil-war-national-conference-june-2022/full-conference-proceedings/ (accessed 29 June 2022).
21 Ibid.; Ó Caoimh, *Richard Mulcahy*, p. 307, n. 92.
22 Ibid.
23 Randal MacCarthy to Kevin O'Higgins, 27 January 1927, NA, TSCH/3/S3341; Dáil Debates, 23 July 1924.
24 Price, *We Bled Together*, p. 259.
25 Bill Bailey, in O'Malley and Horgan (eds), *The Men Will Talk to Me*, p. 105.
26 Ó Caoimh, *Richard Mulcahy*, p. 185.
27 NLI, Papers of Niall C. Harrington, MS 40,629 (1).
28 Randal MacCarthy to Kevin O'Higgins, 27 January 1927, NA, TSCH/3/S3341.
29 Randal MacCarthy to Secretary of Executive Council, 28 October 1923, NA, TSCH/3/S3341.
30 Ibid.
31 Ibid.

32   Dáil Debates, 23 July 1924.
33   Ó Caoimh, *Richard Mulcahy*, p. 184.
34   MA, BMH WS 1751, Cahir Davitt.
35   Ibid.
36   Ibid.
37   Mulcahy's statement to the Army Enquiry Committee, 7 May 1924, UCDA P7a/133, cited in Knirck, *Afterimage of the Revolution*, p. 85; Ó Caoimh, *Richard Mulcahy*, p. 185.
38   MA, BMH WS 939, Ernest Blythe.
39   Regan, *Counter Revolution*, p. 173.
40   Kevin O'Higgins to W.T. Cosgrave, 17 August 1923, UCDA, Mulcahy Papers, P7a/133.
41   Knirck, *Afterimage of the Revolution*, p. 86.
42   Report prepared by Attorney General.
43   Ó Caoimh, *Richard Mulcahy*, p. 186.
44   Report prepared by Attorney General.
45   Ibid.
46   *Cogadh ar Mhná*, TG4, 2020.
47   Report prepared by Attorney General.
48   Ibid.
49   Ibid.
50   Ferriter, *Between Two Hells*, p. 106.
51   MA, BMH WS 939, Ernest Blythe; Ferriter, *Between Two Hells*, p. 106; Fearghal McGarry, *Eoin O'Duffy: A Self-Made Hero* (Oxford University Press, 2005), p. 132.
52   Meeting of Executive Council, 28 September 1923, Extract from Minutes C.2/5, 'Alleged Ill Treatment of Misses MacCarthy, Kenmare', NA, TSCH/3/S3341; Knirck, *Afterimage of the Revolution*, p. 87.
53   Randal MacCarthy to Secretary of Executive Council, 28 October 1923, NA, TSCH/3/S3341.
54   Ibid.
55   Randal MacCarthy to Kevin O'Higgins, 27 January 1927, NA, TSCH/3/S3341.
56   Ibid.
57   *Irish Independent*, 14 September 1922.
58   Barrett, *In the Name of the Game*, p. 87.
59   MA, MSPC 34REF9055, Bridget O'Sullivan.
60   MA, MSPC 34REF60954, Ellie Cotter.
61   MA, MSPC 34REF5737, Mary Barron.
62   MA, MSPC 34REF45929, Kate Mannix.
63   MA, MSPC 34REF6000, Annie Mary O'Connor.
64   MA, MSPC 34REF14043, Elizabeth O'Donnell.
65   Tom Garvin, *Nationalist Revolutionaries in Ireland, 1858–1928* (Gill & Macmillan, 1987), p. 168.
66   Free State Army Monthly Report from Kerry Command, 24 April 1923, cited by Foster, 'Civil War in Kerry', p. 488.

CHAPTER 11

1   *The Liberator*, 16 February 1924.

2   *The Cork Examiner*, 5 September 1923; *The Freeman's Journal*, 5 September 1923; *The Liberator*, 16 February 1924.

3   *The Liberator*, 16 February 1924.

4   Radio Report, Kerry Command, 4 September 1923, MA, CW/OPS/08/12.

5   *The Liberator*, 6 and 13 September 1923 and 16 February 1924.

6   Conor Brady, *Guardians of the Peace* (Gill & Macmillan, 1974), p. 225.

7   *The Liberator*, 11 September 1923.

8   Letter from Seamus Ua Hannagóin, Chief Superintendent's Office, Tralee, to the Commissioner, 19 October 1923, NA, H21/29.

9   Proclamation of Kerry No. 1 Brigade, undated, Papers of Niall Harrington, MS 40,644/3.

10   While Woods was the first sergeant to die after the establishment of An Garda Síochána, he was the second officer to be killed: Garda Henry Phelan was murdered in Mullinahone, Co. Tipperary, on 14 November 1922. Interview with retired Garda Chief Superintendent Donal O'Sullivan, Radio Kerry, 17 July 2015; An Garda Síochána Roll of Honour information on Garda James Woods: www.garda.ie/en/About-Us/Our-History/Roll-of-Honour/Roll-of-Honour-description/Woods-James.html (accessed 14 July 2020).

11   Report of Justice Richard Johnson, State Solicitor Terence Liston and Supt Hannigan to Minister for Home Affairs, 21 December 1923, 2007/56/9.

12   Garda Commissioner to Minister for Home Affairs, 8 December 1923, NA, 2007/56/9.

13   *The Cork Examiner*, 9 July 1927; *Kerry News*, 9 July 1924.

14   Garda Commissioner to Minister for Home Affairs, 8 December 1923, NA, 2007/56/9.

15   *The Liberator*, 4 December 1923.

16   Report to Garda Commissioner on enquiry into allegations made against Lt Gaffney, NA, 2007/56/9.

17   Report of Justice Richard Johnson, State Solicitor Terence Liston and Supt Hannigan to Minister for Home Affairs, 21 December 1923, NA, 2007/56/9.

18   Supt J.J. Hannigan to Garda Commissioner, 1 December 1923, NA, 2007/56/9.

19   *The Cork Examiner*, 15 December 1923.

20   *The Liberator*, 8 December 1923.

21   *The Freeman's Journal*, 6 December 1923; *The Liberator*, 8 December 1923.

22   *The Liberator*, 8 December 1923.

23   Ibid.; Report on the Scartaglin Murders, NA, 2007/56/9.

24   MA, MSPC DP836, Cornelius Brosnan.

25   Supt J.G. Kelly to Garda Commissioner, 9 December 1923, NA, 2007/56/9.

26   *The Cork Examiner*, 17 December 1923.

27   MA, Military Service Pension Collection blog, 14 November 2019.

28   MA, MSPC DP836, Thomas Brosnan.

29   McMahon, 'Civil War Violence in Kerry', p. 83.

30   Garda Commissioner to Ministry of Home Affairs, 5 January 1924, Report on the Scartaglin Murders, NA, 2007/56/9.

31   MA, MSPC 24SP10196, Robert McNeill.

32   Ibid.

33   *The Cork Examiner*, 15 December 1923; *The Liberator*, 10 January 1924.

34   Garda Commissioner to Ministry of Home Affairs, 5 January 1924; Report on the Scartaglin Murders, NA 2007/56/9.

35 *The Liberator*, 13 March 1924.
36 *The Kerryman*, 15 March 1924.
37 Report of Justice Richard Johnson, State Solicitor Terence Liston and Supt J.J. Hannigan to Minister for Home Affairs, 21 December 1923, NA, 2007/56/9.
38 Supt J.J. McNulty to Chief Supt, 13 August 1924 and Supt J.J. Hannigan to Commissioner, 9 May 1924, NA, 2007/56/9.
39 Supt Hannigan, Confidential Note, 9 May 1934, NA, 2007/56/9.
40 Petition of Daniel Casey to Minister for Justice, 4 August 1924, NA, 2007/56/9.
41 Correspondence with Fionán Lynch TD, 26 November 1924 and Ellen Lyne to Minister for Justice, 10 November 1924, NA, 2007/56/9.
42 Extract from letter of Deputy Professor J.M. O'Sullivan, NA, 2007/56/9.
43 S.J. Murphy, Peace Commissioner to Minister for Home Affairs, 16 June 1924, NA, 2007/56/9.
43 Dáil Debates, 14 December 1923.
44 Supt J.J. McNulty to Chief Supt, 4 July 1924, NA, 2007/56/9.
45 Thomas Johnson TD to Minister for Home Affairs, 31 March 1924, NA, 2007/56/9.
46 Secretary of Department of Justice to Commissioner, 24 April 1924, NA, 2007/56/9.
47 Supt J.J. McNulty to Garda Commissioner, 2 July 1924, NA, 2007/56/9.
48 *The Liberator*, 24 January 1925.

CHAPTER 12

1 Dorothy Macardle to Army Pensions Board, 6 January 1936, MA, MSPC 34REF23009, Tadg [Tadhg] Coffey.
2 Lane, *Dorothy Macardle*, pp. 107, 125.
3 Ibid., p. 107; Anne Dolan, *Commemorating the Irish Civil War: History and Memory* (Cambridge University Press, 2003), p. 167.
4 Lane, *Dorothy Macardle*, p. 132.
5 Macardle, *Tragedies of Kerry*, p. 26.
6 Ibid.
7 Ernie O'Malley, *The Singing Flame* (Mercier Press, 2012), p. 240.
8 Dermot Keogh, 'The Catholic Church and the Irish Free State', *History Ireland*, Vol. 2, No. 1 (Spring, 1994), p. 47.
9 *Kerry People*, 11 March 1922.
10 Patrick Murray, *Oracles of God: The Roman Catholic Church and Irish Politics 1922–1937* (UCD Press, 2000), p. 100.
11 *The Cork Examiner*, 2 January 1922.
12 *Kerry People*, 25 March 1922.
13 *Irish Independent*, 3 January 1922.
14 Letter from Charles O'Sullivan, Bishop of Kerry, to Piaras Béaslaí, 5 January 1922, NLI, Papers of Piaras Béaslaí, MS 33,917(12).
15 Murray, *Oracles of God*, p. 71.
16 Gordon, *Winds of Time*, p. 220.
17 *The Freeman's Journal*, 8 September 1922.
18 Doyle, *Civil War in Kerry*, p. 238.
19 *The Freeman's Journal*, 8 September 1922.
20 Murphy, *When Youth Was Mine*, p. 200.
21 Horgan, *Fighting for the Cause*, pp. 169–70.
22 Horgan, *Dying for the Cause*, p. 212.

23 Thomas Rohan to Army Pension Board, undated, MA, MSPC 34REF13932, Thomas Rohan.
24 Horgan, *Dying for the Cause*, p. 44.
25 Ibid., p. 231.
26 O'Connor, *Tomorrow Was Another Day*, p. 108.
27 Doyle, *Civil War in Kerry*, p. 275; Murray, *Oracles of God*, p. 89.
28 Sworn statement of Patrick (Poppy) Healy to Advisory Committee, 23 May 1939, MA, MSPC 34REF31736, Patrick Healy.
29 Hanna O'Connor to Dan Nolan, Christmas 1980, NLI, Papers of Niall Harrington, MS 40,685/1.
30 John Joe Rice, in O'Malley and Horgan (eds), *The Men Will Talk to Me*, p. 306.
31 John Bowman (ed.), *Ireland: The Autobiography* (Penguin Ireland, 2016), pp. 92–3.
32 Ibid., p. 92; Murray, *Oracles of God*, pp. 225–6.
33 Murray, *Oracles of God*, p. 235.
34 NA, FIN/COMP/2/8/459.
35 NA, FIN/COMP/2/8/539.
36 *The Irish Times*, 14 November 1922.
37 O'Shea, *Ballymacandy*, pp. 117–19.
38 *The Freeman's Journal*, 8 September 1922.
39 *The Kerryman*, 5 January 1924.
40 Letter from Acting Command Adjutant to GHQ, 26 May 1924, MA, MSPC 1D270, William Scully.
41 *The Kerryman*, 5 January 1924.
42 Letter from Acting Command Adjutant to GHQ, 26 May 1924, MA, MSPC 1D270, William Scully.
43 RIC County Inspector Report cited by J. Anthony Gaughan, *Austin Stack: Portrait of a Separatist* (Kingdom Books, 1977), p. 38.
44 Murray, *Oracles of God*, p. 151; O'Shea and Revington, *Century of Politics in the Kingdom*, pp. 83–4; Horgan, *Fighting for the Cause*, pp. 157–74.
45 Horgan, *Fighting for the Cause*, p. 170.
46 Murray, *Oracles of God*, p. 152.
47 Kerry Diocesan Archives, cited in Murray, *Oracles of God*, p. 152.
48 Murray, *Oracles of God*, p. 284; Fianna Fáil Archives, UCDA, P176/396.
49 *The Freeman's Journal*, 14 August 1923.
50 *The Cork Examiner*, 27 August 1923.
51 *Irish Independent*, 1 September 1923.
52 *The Cork Examiner*, 14 August 1923.

CHAPTER 13

1 MA, MSPC 34REF14043, Elizabeth O'Donnell.
2 O'Connor, *Tomorrow Was Another Day*, p. 66.
3 S.J. Murphy, Peace Commissioner for Cork regarding prisoners from Kerry, to Minister for Home Affairs, 16 June 1924, NA, 2007/56/9.
4 Denis Daly, in O'Malley and Horgan (eds), *The Men Will Talk to Me*, p. 328.
5 MA, MSPC 34REF4488, Timothy Herlihy.
6 MA, MSPC W2D22, James Byrne.
7 Statement of Denis Quille, MA, MSPC 34REF12059, Denis Quille.
8 Johnny O'Connor, in O'Malley and Horgan (eds), *The Men Will Talk to Me*, p. 231.

9   Denis Daly, in ibid., p. 328.
10 Ibid.
11 Johnny O'Connor, in O'Malley and Horgan (eds), *The Men Will Talk to Me*, p. 235.
12 Ibid., p. 269.
13 Medical report, 15 Oct. 1937, MA, MSPC 34REF3998, Sheila O'Connell.
14 Ellen Hurley to Department of Defence, 5 October 1937, MA, MSPC DP4592, Nora Hurley.
15 Mulvihill, *Testimony*, p. 21.
16 Moore, *Call to Arms*, p. 107.
17 Ferriter, *Between Two Hells*, p. 115.
18 Billy Mullins, *Memoirs of Billy Mullins* (Kenno, 1983), p. 163.
19 *The Freeman's Journal*, 22 October 1923.
20 *Irish Independent*, 26 October 1923.
21 Mulvihill, *Testimony*, p. 23.
22 Sworn statement to the Advisory Committee, 13 December 1935, MA, MSPC 34REF15842, Denis Daly.
23 Bridget Coakley-Kennedy to Department, 22 September 1938, MA, MSPC 34REF14043, Elizabeth O'Donnell.
24 Austin Stack to Winifred Gordon, 24 October 1923, NLI, Papers of Austin Stack, MS 22,398/14.
25 *The Freeman's Journal*, 7 November 1923.
26 *The Cork Examiner*, 14 November 1923.
27 Intercepted letter from Éamon de Valera to prisoners in Tralee Gaol, 17 August 1923, Papers of Desmond and Mabel Fitzgerald, UCDA, P80/800.
28 General Weekly Return, Kerry Command, 18 Oct. 1923, MA, IE/MA/CW/OPS.
29 General Weekly Return, Kerry Command, 18 Oct. 1923, Department of Defence, Military Archives, Civil War Operations and Intelligence Reports Collections, IE/MA/CW/OPS; Peter Pyne, 'The New Irish State and the Decline of the Republican Sinn Féin Party', *Éire/Ireland*, xi (1979), p. 40.
30 *The Liberator*, 20 September 1923.
31 *The Liberator*, 29 November 1923. Brodrick, a sister of the Earl of Middleton and a convert to republicanism, had been shot in the leg by a patrol while cycling near her home in May 1923 and went on hunger strike when she was jailed in Dublin; Breda Joy, *Hidden Kerry: The Keys to the Kingdom* (Merrion Press, 2014), pp. 157–61.
32 *The Liberator*, 22 November 1923.
33 *Irish Independent*, 26 September and 30 October 1923.
34 *Irish Independent*, 26 September 1923.
35 *The Kerryman*, 10 January 1924.
36 Ferriter, *Between Two Hells*, p. 117.
37 Austin Stack to Winifred Gordon, 5 February 1924, NLI, Papers of Austin Stack, MS 22,398/24.
38 Horgan, *Fighting for the Cause*, p. 283.

CHAPTER 14

1   *The Cork Examiner*, 23 October 1922. Thanks to Síobhra Aiken for the reference.
2   Kieran McNulty, 'The Social and Economic Background of Kerry in the Early

Twentieth Century,' *Saothar: Journal of the Irish Labour History Society*, No. 46 (2021), pp. 123–4.
3   McNulty, 'Social and Economic Background of Kerry', p. 134.
4   Mick McQuaid to *The Liberator*, 31 January 1924.
5   Gavin Foster found that Kerry No. 1 and No. 2 Brigade feature strongly in a cross-section of emigrants to Britain and the United States. See Foster, 'Locating the "Lost Legion": IRA emigration and settlement after the Civil War', in Crowley et al., *Atlas of the Irish Revolution*, pp. 741–7.
6   Murphy, *When Youth Was Mine*, pp. 281–2. The reference to republicans emigrating in droves is from John Joe Sheehy and is cited in Gavin M. Foster, *The Irish Civil War and Society: Politics, Class and Conflict* (Palgrave Macmillan, 2015), p. 282. See also O'Shea, *Ballymacandy*, pp. 176–7 and Macardle, *Irish Republic*, p. 883.
7   *Kerry News*, 29 September 1924.
8   Handwritten notes of Investigating Officer, 2 December 1928, MA, MSPC DP5402, John Linnane.
9   Report of Investigating Officer, 24 June 1938, MA, MSPC DP5402, John Linnane.
10 Handwritten notes of Investigating Officer, 2 December 1928, MA, MSPC DP5402, John Linnane.
11 Margaret Linnane, 24 September 1935 to Department of Defence, MA, MSPC DP5402, John Linnane.
12 *The Kerryman*, 7 May 1927.
13 Ó Murchú, *War in the West*, p. 283.
14 Report to Adjutant General, 19 March 1924, UCDA, Papers of Moss Twomey, P69/81/19.
15 Ibid.
16 Report from Captain Tomás Ó Dálaigh, Kerry Command to IRA headquarters, January 1925, UCDA, Papers of Moss Twomey, P69/99/12-13.
17 NLI, Papers of Niall Harrington, MS 40,685/3.
18 NLI, Papers of Ted O'Sullivan, MS 49,668/5.
19 MA, Brigade Activity Reports, A7 2 Kerry Brigade.
20 List of members of Keel Cumann na mBan, 7 July 1936, MA, Cumann na mBan Nominal Roles, CMB/116.
21 Letter from members of Keel Cumann na mBan to the Department of Defence, 24 March 1938, MA, MSPC 34REF6698, Nora Corcoran.
22 Síobhra Aiken, 'Sinn Féin permits in the heels of their shoes': Cumann na mBan emigrants and transatlantic revolutionary exchange', *Irish Historical Studies*, Vol. 44 (2020), p. 112.
23 Pension file of Edward Langford, MA, MSPC 16492.
24 Foster, 'Locating the "Lost Legion": IRA emigration and settlement after the Civil War', p. 747.
25 *Voice of Labour*, 27 January 1923.
26 Letter from Patrick Callaghan, Hon. Sec. Inch Sinn Féin Club, to Minister for Home Affairs, 2 June 1922, NA, Department of Justice, H88/5.
27 Mary Sullivan to Department of Defence, 13 January 1926, W2D152, Con Sullivan.
28 MA, MSPC 34REF1907, Madge O'Connor.
29 *The Irish Times*, 15 February 1923.
30 *Irish Independent*, 14 May 1923.
31 Petition from Ardfert Tenants Group, cited by Diarmaid Ferriter, *A Nation and not a Rabble: The Irish Revolution 1913–23* (Profile Books, 2015), p. 235.

32 Peter Rigney, 'Railways: Campaign of Destruction', in Crowley et al., *Atlas of the Irish Revolution*, pp. 688–9; Diary of Markham Richard Leeson Marshall, various dates in 1922 and 1923.
33 Doyle, *Summer Campaign*, p. 66.
34 Sworn Statement before Advisory Committee on 25 June 1936, MA, MSPC 34REF23009, Tadg [Tadhg] Coffey.
35 *The Cork Examiner*, 15 August 1922.
36 Doyle, *Summer Campaign*, p. 68; Harrington, *Kerry Landing*, pp. 145–6.
37 Quoted in the *Workers' Republic* newspaper, 28 October 1922.
38 Gordon, *Winds of Time*, p. 192.
39 *The Irish Times*, 29 January 1923.
40 *The Freeman's Journal*, 20 January 1933.
41 Ibid.
42 NA/FIN/COMP/2/8/850.
43 *The Cork Examiner*, 27 January 1923.
44 Horgan, *Dying for the Cause*, p. 34.
45 *Poblacht na h-Éireann*, 3 March 1923.
46 Harrington, *Kerry Landing*, p. 147; Barrett, *In the Name of the Game*, p. 83.
47 NA/FIN/COMP/2/8.
48 MA, MSPC 24SP9573, Timothy Jones.
49 Diary of Markham Richard Leeson Marshall, 18 July 1922 and 11 August 1922.
50 NA/FIN/COMP/2/8/437.
51 Ibid.
52 *The Cork Examiner*, 21 September 1922, cited in Doyle, *Civil War in Kerry*, p. 164.
53 Doyle, *Civil War in Kerry*, p. 203.
54 Murphy, *When Youth Was Mine*, p. 197.
55 O'Connor, *Tomorrow Was Another Day*, p. 100.
56 Diary of Markham Richard Leeson Marshall, 24 January 1923.
57 O'Connor, *Tomorrow Was Another Day*, p. 100.
58 *The Irish Times*, 25 November 1922.
59 Doyle, *Summer Campaign*, pp. 76–7.
60 NA, FIN/COMP/2/8.
61 NA, FIN/COMP/2/8/1123 and information in the possession of the author.
62 Diary of Markham Richard Leeson Marshall, 18 July 1921.
63 Report of Kerry Command, 20 March 1923, MA, CW/OPS/08/03.
64 Kerry Command Intelligence Office, 30 April 1923, MA, CW/OPS/08/07/07.
65 NA, FIN/COMP/2/8/671.
66 Diary of Markham Richard Leeson Marshall, 23 February 1923.
67 Report of Kerry Command, 20 March 1923, MA, CW/OPS/08/03.
68 Letter from Commissioner Eoin O'Duffy to the Minister for Home Affairs, 19 March 1923, NA Department of Justice Files, H65/135.
69 Letter from the Secretary of the General Post Office, Dublin to the Minister of Home Affairs, 14 March 1923, NA, H65/135.
70 Secretary to General Secretary, Department of Education, 10 November 1922, NA, TAOIS/S1867.
71 NA, FIN/COMP/2/8/459.
72 NA, FIN/COMP/2/8/330; *Irish Independent*, 26 January 1923.
73 *Irish Independent*, 26 January 1923.

74 O'Shea, *Ballymacandy*, p. 62.
75 NA, FIN/COMP/2/8/225.
76 NA, FIN/COMP/2/8/, numbers 208, 212, 408, 437, 777.
77 NA, FIN/COMP/2/8/10.
78 Ibid.
79 Jeremiah Kennedy to Department of Defence, 2 November 1945, MA, MSPC 60354, Jeremiah Kennedy.
80 Dan Flavin, in O'Malley and Horgan (eds), *The Men Will Talk to Me*, p. 26.
81 Report on the military situation, 31 March 1923, cited by Kissane, *Explaining Irish Democracy*, p. 154.
82 Kerry Community Intelligence Office, report of 30 April 1923, MA, CW/OPS/08/09.
83 Tom Garvin, 'Unenthusiastic Democrats: the Emergence of Irish Democracy', in Ronald J. Hill and Michael Marsh, *Modern Irish Democracy: Essays in Honour of Basil Chubb* (Irish Academic Press, 1993), pp. 22–3.
84 Diary of Markham Richard Leeson Marshall, 15 August 1922.
85 Report on the military situation, 31 March 1923, cited by Kissane, *Explaining Irish Democracy*, p. 154.

CHAPTER 15

1   Medical report, 21 March 1924, MA, MSPC W4P66, Joseph O'Brien.
2   Undated telegram from Adjutant General to Margaret O'Brien, MA, MSPC W4P66, Joseph O'Brien.
3   Dáil Debates, 8 July 1924.
4   Margaret O'Brien to Army Pensions Board, 11 March 1925, MA, MSPC W4P66, Joseph O'Brien.
5   Ibid.; John O'Brien to Army Pensions Board, 18 December 1925, MA, MSPC W4P66, Joseph O'Brien; Ferriter, *Between Two Hells*, p. 107; Ferriter, *Nation and not a Rabble*, p. 288.
6   Joseph O'Brien to Army Pensions Board, 12 May 1926 and 9 January 1929, MA, MSPC W4P66, Joseph O'Brien.
7   Joseph O'Brien to Army Pensions Board, 18 October 1927, MA, MSPC W4P66, Joseph O'Brien.
8   Housing Welfare Officer to Assistant Officer in Charge, 16 April 1955, MA, MSPC W4P66, Joseph O'Brien.
9   Alan Shatter TD, Minister for Defence, *Guide to the Military Service (1916–1923) Pensions Collection* (Department of Defence, 2012), p. 9; Marie Coleman, 'The Military Service Pensions Collection', in Crowley et al., *Atlas of the Irish Revolution*, pp. 881–5; *Guide to the Military Service (1916–1923) Pensions Collection* (Department of Defence, 2012); Ferriter, *Nation and not a Rabble*, p. 21.
10 *Guide to Military Service Pension Collection*, pp. 84–104; *The Kerryman*, 16 December 1935.
11 Coleman, 'The Military Service Pensions Collection,' p. 885; Ferriter, *Nation and not a Rabble*, pp. 22, 333.
12 Sgt Denis Carroll, Lad Lane Station, Dublin Metropolitan Police, MA, MSPC W3D164, Michael Dunne.
13 Catherine Dunne to Army Pensions Board, 16 January 1924, MA, MSPC W3D164, Michael Dunne.

14 Minute of Army Pensions Board meeting of 12 January 1925, MA, MSPC W3D164, Michael Dunne.

15 Application of Julia Stapleton, MA, MSPC W3D70, Edward Stapleton.

16 Julia Stapleton to Department of Defence, 7 November 1923, MA, MSPC W3D70, Edward Stapleton.

17 Department of Finance to Army Pensions Board, 17 April 1924, MA, MSPC W3D70, Edward Stapleton.

18 Pension application of Patrick O'Connor (Snr), MA, MSPC W3D58, Patrick O'Connor.

19 Proceedings of Court of Inquiry on Patrick O'Connor claim for compensation, 14 June 1923, MA, MSPC WCL1059, Patrick O'Connor.

20 Acting Command-Adjutant, Southern Command to Adjutant General, GHQ, 16 June 1924, MA, MSPC W3D58, Patrick O'Connor.

21 *Kerry News*, 13 January 1926.

22 Fr M. O'Connor to Officer of the Adjutant General, 19 May 1923, MA, MSPC WCL1059, Patrick O'Connor.

23 John O'Connor to Department of Defence, February 1933, MA, MSPC W3D57, Laurence O'Connor.

24 Particulars of claim of Margaret O'Connor, MA, MSPC WF30, Laurence O'Connor.

25 Margaret O'Connor to Army Finance Officer, 19 July 1924, MA, MSPC W3D57, Laurence O'Connor.

26 Margaret O'Connor to Army Finance Officer, 5 May 1925, MA, MSPC W3D57, Laurence O'Connor.

27 Report of Sgt James Crehan, Killarney Garda Station, 10 June 1924, MA, MSPC W3D137, Michael Gallivan [Galvin].

28 Minute on application file of Ellen O'Shea, 15 November 1954, DP6572, George O'Shea.

29 Summary of applicant's activities completed by her brother, Daniel, MA, MSPC 34REF57057, Mollie O'Shea.

30 Ibid.

31 Report of Julia Hassett, Brigade Secretary, Cumann na mBan, undated, MA, MSPC 34REF57057, Mollie O'Shea.

32 High Court documents regarding Ward of Court, 16 July 1943, MA, MSPC 34REF57057, Mollie O'Shea.

33 Summary of applicant's activities completed by her brother, Daniel, MA, MSPC 34REF57057, Mollie O'Shea.

34 Letter from Superintendent to Department of Defence, 23 February 1943, MSP34REF57057, Mollie O'Shea.

35 MA, MSPC 34REF30595, Mary Dunne.

36 Medical report, 17 September 1956, MA, MSPC 34REF30595, Mary Dunne.

37 Report from St Finan's Hospital, 21 February 1967, MA, MSPC DP4728, James Walsh.

38 Kathleen Hartnett speaking to *Ballyseedy* (RTÉ); Summary report regarding application of Edward Hartnett, 4 April 1933, WDP4224, Patrick Hartnett.

39 Summary report regarding application of Edward Hartnett, 4 April 1933, and Edward Hartnett to Eamonn Kissane TD, 8 November 1934, WDP4224, Patrick Hartnett.

40 Note from Stephen Fuller on letter from Edward Hartnett to Department of Defence, 28 February 1938, MA, MSPC WD9533, Patrick Hartnett.

41 Deputy Commissioner, An Garda Síochána to Ministry of Home Affairs, 21 May 1924, NA, JUS/2008/152/27.

42   Tom McEllistrim TD to Minister for Defence, 6 January 1935, MA, MSPC WDP51, John Daly.
43   Horgan, *Dying for the Cause*, pp. 436–9.
44   *Léargas*, (RTÉ), 12 January 1998.
45   Horgan, *Dying for the Cause*, p. 438.
46   *Éire*, 21 April 1923.
47   Application form and correspondence of Áine Ceannt with Department of Defence, MA, MSPC WDP4098, John O'Connor.
48   Report of Sgt J. Cornes, Liverpool CID Branch, 2 January 1935, MA, MSPC WDP4098, John O'Connor.
49   *The Kerryman*, 19 March 2014. The original model for the baby on the monument was a neighbour of the sculptor, Yann Renard-Goulet of Bray, Co. Wicklow, NA, Papers of Niall Harrington, undated newspaper cutting, MS 40,680/1.
50   *The Cork Examiner*, 4 March 1998.
51   *The Cork Examiner*, 4 March 1998 and 10 March 2003.

CHAPTER 16

1   Medical report of Frank Murray, Medical Officer, New York, November 1934, MA, MSPC 34REF23009, Tadg [Tadhg] Coffey.
2   Medical report for Army Pensions Board, November 1939, MA, MSPC 34REF23009, Tadg Coffey.
3   Medical report dated 1 December 1942, MA, MSPC 34REF23009, Tadg Coffey.
4   Note from St Bricin's Hospital, 12 November 1941, MA, MSPC 34REF23009, Tadg Coffey.
5   Edward Pat Carey to Department of Defence, 27 August 1934, MA, MSPC 34REF23009, Tadg Coffey.
6   Sworn statement of Edmond Sullivan on behalf of Tadg Coffey, 25 June 1936, MA, MSPC 34REF23009, Tadg Coffey.
7   Service Certificate of Tadg Coffey, 668 Eagle Avenue, Bronx, New York, MA, MSPC 34REF23009, Tadg Coffey.
8   Dáil Debates, 2 November 1927; MA, MSPC 34REF23009, Tadg Coffey.
9   Dorothy Macardle to Army Pensions Board, 6 January 1936, MA, MSPC 34REF23009, Tadg Coffey.
10   Murphy, *When Youth Was Mine*, p. 247.
11   Tadg Coffey to Éamon de Valera, 24 February 1943, MA, MSPC DP3743, Tadg Coffey.
12   John O'Leary TD from Department of Defence, 26 November 1969, MA, MSPC 34REF23009, Tadg Coffey.
13   Hannah Buckley to Army Pensions Board, November 1932, MA, MSPC DP878, Stephen Buckley.
14   Report on file of Hannah Buckley, MA, MSPC DP878, Stephen Buckley.
15   Department of Defence to Mary Sullivan, August 1955, MA, MSPC DP878, Stephen Buckley.
16   Report of Social Welfare Officer, 15 July 1954, MA, MSPC DP739, Daniel Donoghue.
17   Cornelius Healy, Solicitor to Army Pensions Board, 14 March 1933, MA, MSPC DP739, Daniel Donoghue.
18   Report of Army Pensions Boards, 15 November 1933, MA, MSPC DP739, Daniel Donoghue.

19 Cornelius Healy, Solicitor, to Army Pensions Board, 16 October 1933, MA, MSPC DP8168, Timothy Murphy.
20 Report, December 1933, MA, MSPC DP8168, Timothy Murphy.
21 Julia O'Donoghue to Éamon de Valera, 1 November 1942, MA, MSPC DP3621, Jeremiah O'Donoghue.
22 Margaret O'Donoghue to Department of Defence, undated, MA, MSPC DP3621, Jeremiah O'Donoghue.
23 Julia O'Donoghue to Éamon de Valera, 1 November 1942, MA, MSPC DP3621, Jeremiah O'Donoghue.
24 Fionán Lynch TD to Department of Defence, 15 April 1943, MA, MSPC DP3621, Jeremiah O'Donoghue.
25 Insp. C. Reynolds to Chief Superintendent, Tralee, 7 February 1924, NA, JUS/2008/152/27.
26 Michael Dwyer to Department of Defence, 13 October 1942, MA, MSPC DP3816, Eugene Dwyer.
27 Report of Garda Supt J. McCarron, April 1955, MA, MSPC DP7845, John Sugrue.
28 Reply of Department of Finance, 16 November 1923, MA, MSPC DP2588, Daniel Shea.
29 John B. Healy TD, Solicitor to Department of Defence, 9 June 1943, MA, MSPC DP2588, Daniel Shea.
30 Summary report, 22 June 1933, MA, MSPC DP3844, William Reardon.
31 William Evans, Medical Officer, 3rd Kerry Brigade, 1 March 1933, MA, MSPC DP3844, William Reardon.
32 Dorothy Macardle to Frank Aiken TD, 27 March 1934, MA, MSPC DP3844, William Reardon.
33 J.B. Hurley, DMO Derrynane, certificate dated 10 August 1957, MA, MSPC DP3844, William Reardon.
34 John O'Shea to Department of Defence, 8 August 1955, MA, MSPC DP6892, Patrick O'Shea.
35 Mary McGrath to Department of Defence, undated, MA, MSPC DP3164, Thomas McGrath.
36 Horgan, *Dying for the Cause*, p. 93.
37 Application of Elizabeth Quinlan, MA, MSPC DP3323, Edward Greaney.
38 Application of Walter and Edith Stenning, MA, MSPC DP7023, Reginald Walter Stenning.
39 Application of Hannah McEnery and related report, and minutes of details of application of Hannah O'Halloran [James's sister], 13 October 1954, MA, MSPC DP5905, James McEnery.
40 Hannah O'Halloran to Department of Defence, 3 August 1954, MA, MSPC DP5905, James McEnery.

CHAPTER 17

1 *The Freeman's Journal*, 1 May 1923
2 Evidence of Richard Bunyan, MA, MSPC 5733, Richard Bunyan; Horgan, *Dying for the Cause*, p. 172.
3 Horgan, *Dying for the Cause*, p. 171; MA, MSPC 5733, Richard Bunyan.
4 *Irish Independent*, 14 April 1923; *The Freeman's Journal*, 14 April 1923; Macardle, *Tragedies of Kerry*, p. 71; O'Connor, *Tomorrow Was Another Day*, pp. 92–3.

5 *The Freeman's Journal*, 16 May 1923.
6 Ibid.; Medical Report and Assessment, MA, MSPC DP897, Richard Bunyan; Horgan *Dying for the Cause*, p. 172.
7 Medical Report and Assessment, 20 June 1934, MA, MSPC DP897, Richard Bunyan.
8 Medical Report and Assessment, 12 July 1940, MA, MSPC DP897, Richard Bunyan.
9 Moran & Clarke Solicitors to Army Pensions Branch, 15 August 1934, MA, MSPC DP897, Richard Bunyan.
10 Richard Bunyan to Department of Defence, 17 March 1962, MA, MSPC DP897, Richard Bunyan.
11 Medical report of Dr J.H. Gallagher, 5 June 1961, MA, MSPC DP897, Richard Bunyan.
12 John Linnane to Department of Defence, 30 October 1932, MA, MSPC DP5402, John Linnane.
13 Ibid.
14 Report of Investigating Officer, 6 January 1939, MA, MSPC DP5402, John Linnane.
15 Allowance applications of John Linnane (Senior), MA, MSPC W313/DP5402, John Linnane.
16 Thomas Linnane to Department of Defence, 31 August 1944, MA, MSPC DP5402, John Linnane.
17 Thomas Linnane to Department of Defence, 2 October 1953, MA, MSPC DP5402, John Linnane.
18 MA, MSPC 34REF7106, Jeremiah Sullivan.
19 Summary of activities of Michael O'Connor, MA, MSPC 34REF5874, Michael O'Connor.
20 Statement of Michael O'Connor, 13 April 1943, MA, MSPC 34REF5874, Michael O'Connor.
21 MA, MSPC 34REF63767, Lena Brosnan and 34REF32222, Hannah Walsh.
22 Summary of evidence of John McEllistrim, 4 March 1938, MA, MSPC 34REF55913, John McEllistrim.
23 Sworn statement of John McEllistrim, 4 March 1938, MA, MSPC 34REF55913, John McEllistrim.
24 John McEllistrim to Department of Defence, 19 July 1938, MA, MSPC 34REF55913, John McEllistrim.
25 Sworn statement of William O'Leary to Advisory Committee, 16 March 1937, MA, MSPC 34REF31576, William O'Leary.
26 Tom McEllistrim TD to Minister for Defence, 3 June 1967, MA, MSPC DP30950, Michael Enright.
27 Memoirs of Con Casey, unpublished, courtesy of Kerry County Museum; Horgan, *Dying for the Cause*, p. 263.
28 Horgan, *Fighting for the Cause*, pp. 114–5.
29 Billy Mullins, *Memoirs of Billy Mullins: Veteran of the War of Independence* (Kenno, 1983), p. 165.
30 Medical report, 1 November 1935, MA, MSPC 11308, David Fitzgerald.
31 Reference from Jerry Myles, undated, and reference from Eamon O'Connor, 22 October 1935, MA, MSPC 11308, David Fitzgerald.
32 David Fitzgerald on 'Active Service Rendered', 27 October 1935, MA, MSPC DP3439, David Fitzgerald.
33 Kerry Command report, 12 February 1924, MA, MSPC 1P98, Michael O'Connell.

34 Application of Michael O'Connell, MA, MSPC 1P98, Michael O'Connell.
35 Michael O'Connell to Department of Defence, 29 March 1933, MA, MSPC 1P98, Michael O'Connell.
36 John Francis O'Shea to Army Pensions Board, 25 March 1936, MA, MSPC 34REF17286, John Francis O'Shea; see also McAuliffe et al., *Kerry 1916*, p. 268.
37 William A. Crowley, solicitor, to Office of the Referee, 13 July 1942 and 14 October 1942, MA, MSPC 34REF44763, Cornelius Lucey.
38 Report of Social Welfare Officer, 9 December 1953, MA, MSPC 34REF4072, James Murphy.
39 Medical report on James Murphy, 1953, and note from Patrick Connolly, May 1953, MA, MSPC 34REF4072, James Murphy.
40 Bridget Murphy to Department of Defence, 17 April 1947, MA, MSPC 34REF4072, James Murphy.

CHAPTER 18

1 MA, MSPC 56706, Sally Sheehy.
2 Ibid.
3 MA, MSPC 34REF59953, Catherine MacKenna.
4 MA, MSPC 34REF51650, Mary Brosnan.
5 MA, MSPC 34REF13876, Mary Ann O'Dowd.
6 MA, MSPC 34REF22060, Jo Cashman.
7 MA, MSPC 34REF57903, Norah Keane.
8 MA, MSPC 34REF31510, Catherine (Katty) Quill.
9 Letter from Thomas O'Connor, 24 May 1940, MA, MSPC 34REF6698, Nora Corcoran; O'Shea, *Ballymacandy*, pp. 91–2.
10 MA, MSPC 34REF6698, Nora Corcoran.
11 MA, MSPC 34REF6698, Nora Corcoran and 34REF6638, Nellie Foley.
12 MA, MSPC 34REF14220, Hannah Carmody.
13 Michael Shanahan MD, 18 January 1939, MA, MSPC 34REF55152, Úna Frances Moriarty.
14 MA, MSPC 34REF59972, Joan Flynn.
15 MA, MSPC 34REF30634, Margaret Lyne O'Connell.
16 MA, MSPC 34REF9055, Bridie O'Sullivan.
17 MA, MSPC 34REF6615, Margaret Bedford.
18 MA, MSPC 34REF30491, Bridget O'Connor.
19 MA, MSPC 34REF33736, Ellen Griffin.
20 Minister for Defence, Frank Aiken, to Minister for Finance, Seán MacEntee, 23 Oct. 1937, MA, MSPC DP1681, Johanna Cleary.
21 Dr Cashman, Cork Mental Hospital, 15 July 1933, MA, MSPC DP1681, Johanna Cleary.
22 Ibid., note on file.
23 MA, MSPC 34REF19957, Joan Norton.
24 MA, MSPC 34REF6065, Lizanne O'Brien.
25 Letter from John Joe Sheehy to the Office of the Referee, 21 October 1940, MA, MSPC 34REF33736, Ellen Griffin.
26 Letter of 18 April 1950, MA, MSPC 34REF4667, Hannah Clifford.
27 MA, MSPC 34REF56609, Mary Moriarty.
28 MA, MSPC 34REF62871, Nora Lucey.

29   Ibid.
30   Ibid.
31   MA, MSPC 34REF14302, Mary O'Sullivan (*née* Moriarty)
32   MA, MSPC 34REF14140, Honoria (Norah) Casey.
33   MA, MSPC 34REF31796, Joan O'Brien.
34   MA, MSPC 34REF50431, Ellen (Nellie) Pierce.
35   MA, MSPC WDP2706, Nora O'Leary.
36   Cornelius Healy, Solicitor to Minister for Defence, 28 October 1937, MA, MSPC
      WDP2706 Daniel O'Leary.
37   MA, MSPC 34REF50888, Marguerite Sinnott.
38   Letter from Tom McEllistrim TD, 5 March 1954, MA, MSPC 34REF61926, Mary
      Slattery Breslin.
39   Department of Defence to Thomas O'Halloran, solicitor, 10 November 1995, MA,
      MSPC DP50621, Hanna Mary O'Connor.

CHAPTER 19

1   McAuliffe et al., *Kerry 1916*, p. 240.
2   Letter from J.J. Horan to the Army Finance Officer, MA, MSPC 24SP1267,
      J.J. Horan.
3   Letter from Mrs J. Horan to President Cosgrave, 9 October 1929, MA, MSPC
      24SP1267, J.J. Horan.
4   Letter from Mrs Kathleen Horan to President de Valera, 24 August 1934, MA,
      MSPC W24B282, J.J.Horan.
5   M. Ó Catháin to Mrs Kathleen Horan, 28 August 1934, MA, MSPC 24AP1267,
      J.J. Horan.
6   Kathleen Horan to Department of Defence, 17 February 1975, MA, MSPC
      24AP1267, J.J. Horan.
7   Report of Sgt Denis Hurley, An Garda Síochána, MA, MSPC 24AP1267, J.J. Horan.
8   Pat Byrne, Kerry No. 1 Brigade to Department of Defence, 2 January 1925, MA,
      MSPC 24SP490, John Brosnan.
9   John Scannell, Captain F Company, No. 2 Battalion, Kerry No. 1 Brigade, 7 Novem-
      ber 1924, MA, MSPC 24SP538, John Egan.
10   P. McManemy Undertakers to Department of Defence, 10 May 1927, MA, MSPC
      24SP538, John Egan.
11   Bridget Egan to Department of Defence, 22 April 1927, MA, MSPC 24SP538, John
      Egan.
12   Mrs T. Quinn to Department of Finance, 3 January 1950, MA, MSPC W2D342,
      Patrick Quinn.
13   Death certificate of Sheelah Quinn, MA, MSPC W2D342, Patrick Quinn.
14   Christina Noone to Army Pension Department, 26 January 1927, MA, MSPC
      W2D349, Edward Noone.
15   Jane O'Neill to Army Pensions Board, 7 July 1924, MA, MSPC W3D233, James
      O'Neill.
16   Note for Private Secretary to Minister for Education, 18 April 1929, MA, MSPC
      2D117, Daniel Nagle.
17   Patrick H. Rosney, solicitor to the Army Finance Officer, 26 August 1925, MA,
      MSPC W3D198, Michael Rock.
18   Report of Sgt John Allman, An Garda Síochána, MA, MSPC 3D65, Jeremiah Quane.

19 Acting Command Adjutant, Southern Command to Adjutant General, GHQ, 6 June 1924, and James Donoghue to Department of Defence, 17 December 1934, MA, MSPC 2D359, John Donoghue.
20 Report on application file of Mary Murphy, mother, MA, MSPC 2D113, Timothy Murphy.
21 MA, MSPC 2D113, Timothy Murphy.
22 Patrick Nagle to W.T. Cosgrave, 31 March 1925, MA, MSPC 2D117, Daniel Nagle.
23 Patrick Nagle to Fionán Lynch TD, 8 May 1924, MA, MSPC 2D117, Daniel Nagle.
24 Patrick Nagle to Minister for Defence, 30 April 1929, MA, MSPC 2D117, Daniel Nagle.
25 Adjutant's Department, Field General Headquarters, Kerry Command, 17 October 1923, MA, MSPC 3D136, Cornelius Hayes.
26 Norah Hayes letter to Army Headquarters, 23 May 1924, MA, MSPC 3D136, Cornelius Hayes.
27 MA, MSPC W3D60, Michael O'Donoghue.
28 Report of Adjutant General, 6 August 1924, MA, MSPC W3D20, Michael O'Donoghue.
29 Command Adjutant to Adjutant General, 30 July 1924, MA, MSPC W3D20, Michael O'Donoghue.
30 Mrs D. O'Donoghue to the Minister for Defence, 14 June 1924, MA, MSPC W3D20, Michael O'Donoghue.
31 Report of Garda Chief Superintendent, 23 August 1924, MA, MSPC W3D20, Michael O'Donoghue.
32 Mrs D. O'Donoghue to the Minister for Defence, 14 June 1924, MA, MSPC W3D20, Michael O'Donoghue.
33 James Reilly to Board of Assessors, 13 August 1925, MA, MSPC 24SP588, James Reilly.
34 James McCarthy to Army Pensions Board, 4 June 1924, MA, MSPC W3D40, Patrick McCarthy.
35 Michael McGillycuddy to Finian [Fionán] Lynch TD, 20 October 1925, MA, MSPC 24SP3745, Michael McGillycuddy.

CHAPTER 20

1   *The Kerryman*, 5 February 1982.
2   *The Saturday Supplement*, Radio Kerry, 26 February 2022.
3   Gallagher, *Irish Elections, 1922–1944*, p. 44.
4   Doyle, *Civil War in Kerry*, p. 312; J.J. Lee, 'The Irish Free State', in Crowley et al., *Atlas of the Irish Revolution*, p. 783.
5   Gallagher, *Irish Elections 1922–44*, p. 45; Basil Chubb, *The Government and Politics of Ireland* (Oxford University Press), p. 78.
6   *Irish Independent*, 20 August 1923.
7   *The Cork Examiner*, 17 and 20 August 1923; *Irish Independent*, 20 August 1923.
8   *The Cork Examiner*, 28 August 1923; Macardle, *Irish Republic*, p. 833.
9   *The Liberator*, 1 September 1923.
10 Murphy, *When Youth Was Mine*, pp. 271–3.
11 General Weekly Return, Kerry Command, 6 September 1923, MA, CW/OPS/08/07.
12 The author is grateful to Gordon Revington for drawing his attention to this episode.

13 Clann Éireann had just been disbanded and had declared its support for Fianna Fáil.
14 *Kerry Reporter*, 24 September 1927.
15 *Irish Independent*, 9 November 1927.
16 *Kerry Reporter*, 14 October 1933.
17 Ibid.
18 *Kerry Champion*, 4 February 1933.
19 Owen O'Shea, 'Party organisation, political engagement and electioneering in Kerry, 1927–1966' in Bric (ed.), *Kerry, History and Society*, p. 579.
20 *Kerry News*, 13 April 1925.
21 *Kerry Champion*, 7 January 1933.
22 Dáil Debates, 8 May 1970.
23 Connor-Scarteen dropped the O' to ensure a higher placement on the ballot paper which lists candidates alphabetically by surname.
24 *Irish Independent*, 6 June 2014; *Kerry's Eye*, 12 June 2014.
25 *The Kerryman*, 7 April 2014.
26 Dolan, *Commemorating the Irish Civil War*, p. 140.
27 Ibid, pp. 140–1.
28 *The Kerryman*, 7 April 2014.
29 *The Irish Times*, 21 August 2017.
30 Ibid.
31 *Kerry News*, 13 January 1926; *Kerry Reporter*, 16 January 1926. The author is grateful to Gordon Revington for the reference.

POSTSCRIPT

1 Interview with Thomas McEllistrim by Nollaig Ó Gadhra, courtesy of his grandson, Thomas; extracts from the interview contained in 'An Irishman's Diary' by Michael O'Regan, *The Irish Times*, 27 June 1998.
2 Doyle, *Civil War in Kerry*, p. 163.
3 Letter from Dan Mulvihill to Timothy 'Chub' O'Connor TD, 5 December 1979, MA, MSPC MSP34REF4800, Daniel Mulvihill.
4 O'Shea, *Ballymacandy*, p. 169.
5 Letter dated 4 September 1939, MA, MSPC 34REF7846, Bridget Coakley-Kennedy.
6 Edmond Hartnett to Eamonn Kissane TD, 8 November 1934, MA, MSPC WDP4224, Patrick Hartnett.
7 Richard Bunyan to Department of Defence, 30 January 1933, MA, MSPC DP897, Richard Bunyan.
8 Mary O'Shea to General Richard Mulcahy, 26 November 1923, MA, MSPC W2D132, Cornelius O'Shea.
9 Letter written on behalf of Mary O'Shea, 30 June 1932, MA, MSPC W2D132, Cornelius O'Shea.
10 Ó Murchú, *War in the West*, p. 283.
11 Handwritten note of Daniel Mulvihill on reports of the activities of the Kerry No. 2 Brigade, Military Service Pension Application, Brigade Activity Reports, A7 2 Kerry Brigade.
12 Calton Younger, *Ireland's Civil War* (Fontana Press, 1979), p. 501.
13 Foster, 'The Civil War in Kerry', p. 469.
14 Síobhra Aiken, *Spiritual Wounds: Trauma, Testimony and the Irish Civil War* (Irish Academic Press, 2022), 2022, p. 2.

15 Aiken, *Spiritual Wounds*, p. 1; Foster, 'Civil War in Kerry', p. 480.
16 Bill Kissane, *The Politics of the Irish Civil War* (Oxford University Press, 2005), p. 4.
17 Dolan, *Commemorating the Irish Civil War*, p. 200.
18 *Kerry People* editorial, reproduced in *The Freeman's Journal*, 1 June 1923.
19 Aiken, *Spiritual Wounds*, pp. 6–7.
20 J.J. Lee, *Ireland 1912–1985: Politics and Society* (Cambridge University Press, 1989), p. 68.
21 Interview with Advisory Committee, 2 September 1937, MA, MSPC Donal O'Donoghue, MSP34REF6153.
22 Gemma Clark, *Everyday Violence in the Irish Civil War* (Cork University Press), p. 8.
23 Keane, *Wounds*, p. 18.
24 Cited in Charles Townshend, *The Republic*, p. 450.
25 Letter to the Editor from T.M. Donovan, *The Liberator*, 16 January 1932.

ACKNOWLEDGEMENTS

This book would not have been published without the encouragement and professionalism of the team at Merrion Press including Conor Graham, Patrick O'Donoghue, Wendy Logue and Maeve Convery.

The staff of the National Archives, the Military Archives and UCD Archives provided advice and assistance throughout, as did Tommy O'Connor, Kerry County Librarian, and the staff of Kerry libraries. The availability of digitised records from the Military Service Pensions Collection at the Military Archives makes them not only an incredibly valuable resource but also makes research for a book like this so much easier.

I am grateful to Gordon Revington – with whom I wrote *A Century of Politics in the Kingdom* in 2018 – who read the manuscript and offered useful suggestions and information from his encyclopaedic archives. I would also like to thank Dr John Knightly for kindly providing the transcriptions of the diaries of Major Markham Richard Leeson Marshall.

The support and co-operation of many relatives of those mentioned in this book was always forthcoming and ensured key details and personal stories could be recounted.

Finally, I would like to express my gratitude to my wife Celia, and children, Peadar, Neasa and Aodhán, for their love, patience and support.

INDEX